Writing
HUMOR

Humor in Life and Letters Series

Writing
HUMOR

Creativity and the Comic Mind

Mary Ann Rishel

Wayne State University Press   Detroit

06   05   04   03   02   5   4   3   2   1

Library of Congress Cataloging-in-Publication Data
Rishel, Mary Ann.
   Writing humor : creativity and the comic mind / Mary Ann Rishel.
      p. cm.—(Humor in life and letters)
   Includes bibliographical references and index.
   ISBN 0-8143-2959-4 (alk. paper)—ISBN 0-8143-2960-8 (pbk. : alk.
paper)
   1. Wit and humor—Authorship.   2. Comedy—Authorship.   I. Title.
II. Series.
PN6149.A88 R57 2002
808.7—dc21   2001004776

I gratefully acknowledge permission to reprint the following:

"That Lean and Hungry Look" by Suzanne Britt from *Newsweek*, 1982.
Reprinted by permission of the author.

"Brother, Can You Spare a John" by Art Buchwald from *Newsweek*
(February 4, 1980): 15. Reprinted with permission of the author.

Excerpt from *Catch-22* by Joseph Heller reprinted with permission of
Simon and Schuster. Copyright © 1955. 1961 by Joseph Heller. Copyright
renewed c. 1989 by Joseph Heller.

"Hazel Tells LaVerne," c. 1977 by Katharyn Howd Machan. First published
in Rapscallion's Dream, vol 1. Reprinted by permission of the author.

"The Night the Bed Fell" from *My Life And Hard Times*. Copyright ©
1933, 1961 by James Thurber. Reprinted by arrangement with Rosemary A.
Thurber and the Barbara Hogenston Agency. All rights reserved.

Excerpt from *Getting Even* by Woody Allen, copyright © 1966, 1967, 1968,
1969, 1970, 1971 by Woody Allen. Used by permission of Random
House, Inc.

Excerpt from "Movie Tonight" from *M*A*S*H* reprinted by permission
from Twentieth Century Fox Television.

"Slow Talkers of America" reprinted with the permission of Scribner, a
division of Simon & Schuster from "From Approximately Coast to
Coast . . . It's the Bob and Ray Show" by Bob Elliott and Ray Goulding.
Copyright © 1983 Goulding-Elliott-Greybar Productions, Inc.

To the Three Bears
Dad, Bob, 'n' Nick

Contents

7

Chapter 6   Comedy 83

Chapter 7   Slapstick 112

Acknowledgments

Many thanks to my colleagues, students, friends, and family, who offered encouragement with laughs and supported my scholarly endeavors with faith. (Humor as *scholarship?* Only they believed.)

To my Ithaca College colleagues Cory Brown, Kathy Compagni, Antonio DiRenzo, Linda Godfrey, Lisa Harris, Frederica Kaven, Maggie Meyer, Frank Sharp, and Scott Smith, who sent me numerous references, many, many thanks. A very special thanks to colleagues Barbara Adams, LeMoyne Farrell, David Flanagan, and Katharyn Howd Machan, who far surpassed human librarianship by placing an untold number of articles about the most obscure—and valuable—humor in my mailbox almost daily for many years. Decades, really. Also thanks to writing department chairs Catherine Penner and Marian MacCurdy and to Dean Howard Erlich, who added both spirit and dollars. And to all my colleagues in the writing department who nudged me into theory and who validated Ithaca College's Humorous Writing course with nary a frown or inch of hesitation. Tip o' the hat to you.

Thanks to computer artist Fred Estabrook, who drew the charts, and to computer whizzes Michael Morley at Cornell and June Hannah at Ithaca College, who taught me how to transfer files and hang paragraphs. And thanks to Dorothy Owens, who vigorously typed and edited the early drafts with perfection, rating everything I wrote from #1 to #10 so I'd know what was what.

And great thanks to my excellent colleagues in the International Society for Humor Studies, whose scholarship enriched my curiosity and love for humor and whose fine papers over the years lent validity to my own work: Wladyslaw Chlopicki, Jessica Milner Davis, Mel Helitzer, James R. Papp, George Pocheptsov, Joyce Saltman, and especially Don L. F. Nilsen and Alleen Pace Nilsen for their exuberant support for humor studies and their lifelong commitment to the field. I am also grateful to the following scholars, whose ideas invaluably informed my research: Salvatore Attardo, Maurice Charney, Robert W. Corrigan, Patricia Keith-Spiegel, Arthur Koestler, Gerald Mast, Paul E. McGhee, William Miller, John Morreall, Victor Raskin, and Milton Wright. Of course, all errors and folly in this manuscript are mine alone.

More thanks: to Doug Alfors, whose world-famous puns cheered me forward, and to Howard and Florence Aderhold, who lent me a small part of their home so I could write in solitude and quiet; to my brother-in-law Gerry Rishel, who had a million of 'em; to my family from hometowns Port Vue and Monessen, PA, from whom I inherited a genial love of life; to my students who so graciously and enthusiastically supported my teaching over the years and who generously and patiently wrote their hearts out so that all humanity could laugh. I'm especially grateful to the following Ithaca College students who have given permission to reprint their work: Daniel E. Amrich, Richard W. Anderson, Susan Aronson, Kenneth M. Ayoub, Julie Switzer Caplan, Christopher A. Capozzi, Philip P. Cormier, Christine Decker, Anne Marie Di-Nardo, Steven DiPietro, Peter Dranoff, John C. Duff, Paul Dunscomb, Scott Giessler, Lisel M. Gorell, Michael Greenzeig, Alan Haft, Steven Hartman, David Hearne, Suzanne Smith Jablonski, Laura Klink, Adam Lantheaume, Kim S. Lazar, Scott Levy, Tom Longo, Richard Manfredi, Brett Matthews, Mark B. Matthews, Alan S. Miller, Jennifer Lynne Miller, Michael Alan Miller, Paul Nelson, Catherine E. Carchia Phillips, Vicky I. Puig, Christopher Regan, Brett W. Ross, Rudy Ruiz (pseudonym), John Sangimino, Jr., Jay Schneiderman, Michael Simonoff, Steven Simons, Gregory Tebbano, Todd Tibbetts, and David Vergano.

Thanks very much to my editors and the staff at WSU Press for their encouragement and support: Arthur Evans, Adela Garcia, Jennifer Backer, Alison Reeves, and Renee Tambeau, and to Sarah Blacher Cohen, series editor.

Of course, big hugs to my husband, Tom, whose incredible support and encouragement—and wit—kept me writing; and to Bob and Nick, who bring me great joy.

Introduction

In 1973, Ithaca College pioneered Humorous Writing 336, the first college in the nation (we think) to give recognition to the writing of humor as an academic discipline. LeMoyne Farrell and Joanne Travers were its founders. In 1976, our faculty agreed to raise the course's early one-credit designation to its current three, and Humorous Writing emerged as a full-fledged offering in our college catalogue, resting comfortably between Introduction to Beowulf and Shakespearean Tragedy. With good fortune blessing the virtuous, I was elected to teach it, a curriculum I thought to be a cinch. Having studied Jane Austen, Mark Twain, and Chaucer as a graduate student, I assumed that dozens of books about the *writing* of comic literature were lining the shelves of our college bookstore, and I could just pick up four or five at random for my syllabus. Alas, it was not so. And so ensued my quest to understand humor. After a long, futile search, lo and behold, I uncovered a single, lonely book from McGraw-Hill, Milton Wright's *What's Funny and Why*, a coffee-stained, thumb-printed, dog-eared tome dated 1939, long out of print—which made me realize, much to my horror, that the embryonic field of writing humor hadn't yet been born. To compound the problem, my course corkscrewed into a double helix, in that my students wanted to write *both* comedy and humor, and none of the philosophical texts I investigated explained the difference. I'd really gotten myself into it.

Since my course was soon to start, I intensified my search. I did find a few books on marketing humor, but they only offered general and inconclusive remarks about writing one-liners that I couldn't adapt to a course designed for substantive, literary writing like personal essays, short stories, and satiric arguments. I was stymied. So, with my heart in my hands, I went to my first class—September 1976—and in a trembling, humble

19

voice, quietly explained to my students that no textbook existed, and I had no background in theory to offer the class. At first my students jumped and cheered for joy but then, as the monumental seriousness of the dilemma dawned on them, they floated back to earth in snow-like silence and somberly pondered the situation. More silence. And more silence. And still more silence. We had arrived at an intellectual crisis of immense proportions. What to do? Change the curriculum? Cancel the course? An impossible thought. Then suddenly youth and inexperience erupted into courage and faith. Then a smile. Then a chuckle. Then a rumble and a roar that exploded through the class as they shouted, à la Mel Brooks's *Blazing Saddles*, "We'll do it ourselves!" and they rolled up their sleeves and sharpened pencils and flipped on computers and, matching wits with their favorite authors, they wrote and wrote, sometimes good and sometimes not so good, but they wrote. And thus, Ithaca College's course, Humorous Writing—and this book—came to be.

Organization and Design

Writing this book has been especially challenging because during its many drafts the paradigm for the teaching of writing shifted from traditional lecture to interactive instruction. New methodologies meant that writing was now taught as recursive process, and this led to new questions about how we create humor. This book revisits these methodologies within the context of humor.

Both process- and model-designed, each chapter begins with a definition and history of a humor genre, followed by examples from students and professionals. Writing exercises are included in each chapter. The writing process describes brainstorming, mapping, charting, memory searches, and other strategies that get a pen flowing. The book also offers the organizational patterns of description, narration, process analysis, contrast-comparison, analysis, argument, and—for you free spirits—the free form.

For folks who like humor spiced with theory—those of you who ask, "What exactly is humor?"—the introductory chapters examine its linguistic characteristics evolving from the latest research. Applying theory to your writing enables you to think cognitively about revision. Later chapters address audience reaction. I've also included tangential material about humor from the most frequently asked questions by my students. At the end of the book you'll find information on publishing, a glossary, and a bibliography. To appease the concerns of professors, this book generates practices for good writing in general—precise diction, vivid details, structure, voice and tone, thematic focus—and, therefore, students in any writing class, creative or expository, could benefit from the text, not just classes specific to humor.

Although each of us differs in what we find funny, I hope you'll like some of what you read here. But even if you don't, try to understand the intention of the writer. You'll want to educate yourself about the rich varieties of humor, since a serious writer needs to know what appeals to different audiences, young and old, naive and sophisticated. If you're open-minded, you can more easily decide what brand of humor is for you, and you'll write with more savvy.

I hope this book inspires you, and if you think it's OK to analyze the writing of humor, then this book is *really* for you.

The Sense of Humor Test

Sometimes we don't know ourselves very well, particularly when it comes to our sense of humor. Because humor is so integrated into our personalities and behavior, we don't think about it much. As a writer, you'll want to know your sense of humor, since you need to see where you're coming from when you write. One way to study yourself is to take a sense of humor test. You can find them in the library, usually in the psychology section, but if you only want an informal, anecdotal assessment, it's easy to make one up yourself.

Find two dozen jokes or cartoons in books or magazines, either general ones that include pockets of humor or ones specifically published for humor, making sure you select some from sources you don't usually read. If you're into fishing magazines or joke books on cars, select at random from there but then go to ones you never read—for example, magazines on cooking, fashion, or photography. Rummage through a couple dozen *to get a range* or the test won't work—from family and general magazines to age- and topic-specific ones; from *Reader's Digest* and *Family Circle* to the *New Yorker* and *MAD*.

Glance quickly at the cartoons or jokes. Record your response to them on a sheet of paper. Did you laugh a lot or not at all? Now study each one more closely. If you found one really funny, why? If not, why? The artwork? Subject matter? Because it was taboo? Corny? Intellectual? Absurd? Witty? Did it conjure up warm memories from your past? Remind you of someone you like? A satiric put-down of someone you dislike?

Now study yourself. What is it about you that made you laugh or not laugh? How does your background affect your laughter? Your religion? Your values and beliefs? Your education? Your interests? Your age? Your current mood? Physical well-being?

Gender? Maybe you didn't laugh because you didn't understand the joke? What does your self-study say about you? Are you more serious than foolish? Prefer philosophical jokes to people ones? Like taboo humor? Word play? Wit? Jokes about a specific topic? Do you limit your sense of humor to one kind or do you like a lot of different ones? Why? Do you sense "degrees" of humor, some types you like more than others? Some you're ho-hum about? If you find yourself restricting your appreciation of humor types, is that OK with you? How might that restrict your writing?

If you don't laugh very often, why? Shy? Pressures from childhood? Fear of being foolish? Status? Obligations to uphold the "right" behavior? Are you going through a sad time in your life? If so, you might want to forget humor for a while and first find your way through the sadness. That's OK.

Yes, You in the Back Row

Most Frequently Asked Questions

For starters, what exactly is a sense of humor?

A sense of humor is a person's ability to perceive, appreciate, enjoy, or create playful incongruity.

Why does it exist?

Our sense of humor fulfills many basic human needs: it allows us to confront fears and taboos in a socially acceptable way by giving us pleasure; it encourages other people to like us; and it's a means of creative, emotional, and intellectual expression. Laughter exercises the internal organs and, therefore, is good for us physically. Psychologically, humor allows us to cope with life's tragedies.

Can a person be born without a sense of humor?

Good news. Except in unusual circumstances, we're all born with the physical capacity to laugh—mouth, larynx, zygomatic muscles—and the intellectual capacity to perceive humorous incongruity. On the other hand, we don't at this time have any definite scientific evidence that a sense of humor is determined genetically.

Why do some people have a sense of humor and others don't?

The difference between people who display a terrific sense of humor and those who don't is determined by culture and learning. We develop a sense of humor by imitating and reacting to the people around us, which is why each person's sense of humor is unique. People with little or no sense of humor have been conditioned to live within the narrow confines of a strictly literal world; possibly they were repressed as children or they confronted some trauma that caused them to fear risks, so they take fewer imaginative leaps than a person with a well-developed sense of humor. One person walks down the street and sees a street; a person with a sense of humor sees a yellow brick road. People with a good sense of humor usually exhibit strong language skills, vivid fantasies, and animated imaging abilities. They're the ones who will squeeze two unlike things together to make something humorous: a teacup that dances; raisins that sing.

How does a sense of humor develop?

According to child psychologists, infants smile a few weeks after birth, possibly reflecting satisfaction when feeding, then laugh by the fourth month, usually in response to the voice or touch of the mother.[1] An infant might also laugh as she babbles or plays peekaboo games. Within two years or so, the child begins joking, doing such things as putting silly putty on her nose. This social-cognitive stage continues as the toddler begins to process behavior that's playfully unusual—imitating a father who growls like a bear or a mother who wrinkles her nose like a rabbit. By age seven, as preadolescents master language, riddles and puns become an important part of their sense of humor, and this cognitive development increases their ability to see humor in verbal and visual contexts. They love riddles like "What's the largest pencil in the world? Pennsylvania." As adolescents mature into adults, they develop an appreciation for highly sophisticated kinds of humor, from socially complex sexual and absurd joking to refined literary humor.

What's a warped sense of humor?

People can develop a warped sense of humor from childhood insecurities, fears, or anger, and therefore they laugh when most people wouldn't. Some psychologists would say that this isn't really a sense of humor at work but just the physiology of the body operating during bizarre cognition. People with a distorted sense of humor can have difficulty with a normal conversation; they constantly interrupt with excessive joking that distances them from the audience so that they don't have to form relationships they fear. Others will laugh at situations that would horrify most of us. A warped sense of humor can be a defense mechanism against reality.

Just exactly, what's laughter?

Laughter is a pleasurable physical response we experience as we respond to humor. Emotion builds in the body and then, because it can't be reabsorbed by the brain as quickly as cognition, it erupts as "excess energy." Once our intellect registers the humor, the zygomatic muscles in our faces contract, breathing intensifies, then spasms in the vocal folds interrupt the breathing. We bear our teeth and grimace as the corners of our mouth are drawn upward and our eyes squint and sometimes tear. As chest and stomach muscles contract, we gasp for air. We utter loud and guttural sounds, high and low, in various rhythms and tones. Spasms throughout our body reach a climax and then subside.[2] In heavy laughter, the spasms are wide; we might stretch our backs and then double over in fatigue or pain. The physiology of laughter is similar to that in an epileptic seizure or sexual orgasm. Physiologists have noted that it takes thirteen muscles to smile and fifty muscles to frown.

Why do we laugh?

Scholars hypothesize that laughter comes from humans' innate need to be intellectually challenged; without constant exercising, our brains atrophy. Although other kinds of "thinking," like serious thinking, could provide this catalyst, humor probably survives in our intellectual and physical makeup because it stimulates healthy intellectual and physical relief. An evolutionary defense reflex (the growling and bearing of teeth that animals effect to scare away attackers are similar to the laugh), laughter appears to be vital for our species' psychological, if not physical, survival.

What's tickling?

When we're tickled, our reflexes gyrate and withdraw in response to a surprise attacker's pincer on vulnerable areas of our bodies: the soles of the feet, the armpits, ribs, stomach. Generally, we can't tickle ourselves since tickling is a game that has to be perceived by its victims as a "mock attack" from a "mock" enemy. Some people find tickling wonderful fun, but if humorous clues aren't in place, we respond in fear or anger. A person can convulse from being repeatedly tickled, and in ancient China tickling was a method of torture. To be humorous, tickling must hide a caress inside its aggression.

Some researchers believe that the tickling response was orig-inally an instinctive defense of Homo sapiens to hostile attacks because it generates squirming and twisting body motions.[3] It may have evolved into a humorous game as that threat became more and more remote. Humorous tickling can simmer with erotic elements: young adolescents use it as fledgling flirtation and adults enjoy it as sexual foreplay.

What's giggling?

Giggling is a form of laughing characterized by a high pitch and staccato rhythm. Highly infectious, giggling often sets off a group reaction, especially among adolescents. Infectious giggling may derive from instinctive group behavior during the prehistoric hunt, where each person imitated the sounds of the next as the group prepared to attack an animal. It might also be interpreted as nervous sexual energy, thus the reason for its frequency in adolescents.

Have people everywhere—in all times, places, and cultures—laughed the same physical way we do today?

Although we don't have absolute proof, it appears that, like the development of language or walking on two feet, there's a genetic basis for laughter since it surfaces in all normal babies; the evi-dence, therefore, suggests that all people in all cultures at all times have experienced laughing in the same physiological way. Assum-ing that normal physiology and intellectual understanding of the humor are present, all people would correspondingly laugh un-der the same theoretical circumstances. When differences occur, most likely they stem not from physiology or intellect but from the third element, culture.

Please explain. If the way we laugh *physically* is the same, wouldn't that mean that people from other times, places, and cultures have laughed at the same things we do now?

No. Laughter physiology is the same, but what we laugh *at* dif-fers culturally. Public condoning of brutal humor surfaced more in previous centuries than ours, where people laughed at poverty, physical defects, and mental illness. In the seventeenth century, Elizabethans indulged themselves with a Sunday afternoon stroll to the local insane asylum to picnic and taunt the patients. And although we still laugh at the relevancy of ancient Greek come-dies to our present antics, we abhor the ancient Roman pastime of cheering on competitions between death-defying gladiators and lions. Differences between then and now center on sensibilities. This is not to say that people today are perfectly sensitive, since many people still laugh at brutality.

What are some ways non-western cultures use laughter that aren't found in traditional western culture?

Although many similar situations make people all over the world laugh—pratfalls, flatulence, sex—some cultural behavior diverges so widely that traditional Western culture finds it strange. The Nez Perce American Indian tribe from northeastern Oregon be-lieved the only punishment for misbehavior was derisive laugh-ter. The tribe member who misbehaved had to walk a gauntlet while the other members of the tribe laughed at him or her. In India, in the past, ritual burnings required individuals to laugh as they approached their fiery deaths. In the Japanese Shinto death ritual, mourners will gather at a table, clap their hands, and laugh to acknowledge life and death.

Are there other things besides "funny" things that make us laugh?

Sure. Marijuana, alcohol, and LSD can redirect nerve pathways of the central nervous system to signal laughter. Nitrous oxide (laughing gas) and ethyl alcohol also generate laughter, as do physical stimuli such as tickling or electric stimuli. Non-funny laughter also erupts from confusing emotions, such as nervous-ness, embarrassment, despair, stress, anxiety, and derision. When signals merge, we might simultaneously cry and laugh; when emotions numb to the extent they register opposite impulses, as in grief, we might laugh when we should cry instead.

Laughter makes up much of our social interaction. We laugh to be liked, to indicate approval, to desire approval, to attract attention, to flirt, to sign friendship, to be courteous, to smooth conversation, to show safety, to demonstrate confidence, and to celebrate triumph or joy.[4] Contagious laughter may have evolved from the verbal signaling necessary in the primitive hunt, and sometimes we'll laugh for no logical reason but just because every-one else is laughing.

Why is there abnormal laughter?

Since laughter is signaled by nerve impulses throughout the body, any illness triggering a similar pathway can cause laughter, even though the situation is nonhumorous. Diseases that could cause nonhumorous laughter include Kleine-Levine syndrome, Alzheimer's disease, Wilson's disease, Pick's brain atrophy, multi-infarct dementia, multiple sclerosis, epilepsy, hebephrenic schizo-phrenia, and any head trauma.[5] The reactions take different forms: hysterical laughter, like contagious laughter, has probably evolved from our primitive ancestors as one way of dealing with danger and usually results from shock or anger; the pseudobulbar palsy patient laughs uncontrollably and, once started, is unable to stop; and in another mental disorder, punning mania, the patient ex-hibits both excessive language and laughter. Laughing mania has been recorded as early as the twelfth century among the flagellants of northern Italy and in the witch-hunts of colonial America.

Has anyone ever died because someone laughed at them?

Yes. Some ancient Greeks found being laughed at so humiliating that they committed suicide. In this century, we've seen reports of suicides by children who had been mocked and laughed at so incessantly by classmates that it led them to utter despair.

What's this I hear about a laughing death?

Affecting a tribe of about 35,000 people in the Papua region of eastern New Guinea, the Kuru Syndrome, also known as the "laughing death," is so named because right before death the vic-tims burst out in a phase of loud, continuous laughter.[6] D. Car-leton Gajdusek received the Nobel Prize in Medicine in 1976 for his diagnosis of this illness. A degenerative disease of the cen-tral nervous system, the Kuru Syndrome causes victims to ex-perience tremors and spasmatic thrusts of the arms and legs, then difficulty swallowing, followed by the bursts of patholog-ical laughter. Some researchers say that "laughing death" is a misnomer for this complex disease. No known cases of the Kuru Syndrome have been found outside New Guinea, and its incidence has declined.

Could I laugh myself to death?

Sure. Intense laughing can cause a heart attack.[7]

Will smiling or laughing make me sexually attractive?

Definitely yes. In various research studies, when subjects were asked what they considered to be the most sexually attractive characteristic they wanted in a partner, the majority said a sense of humor, not appearance or money. However, the subjects distinguished between genial or witty sense of humor and an excessive or silly sense of humor. No one found silliness sexy because it suggested childishness.

Could I lose my virginity if I laughed too hard?

No information as yet, but it's highly unlikely. (It depends on what you're doing while you're laughing so hard, but the laughing itself won't cause you to lose your virginity.) Excessive laughter shouldn't cause a hymen to rupture or a first wet dream—as far as we know, that is.

Is smiling or laughing good for my sex life?

Sex therapists say yes. Since the sex act itself is so ridiculous, you'll enjoy yourself much more if you keep your sense of humor.

Two more questions, intellectual ones: what exactly is humor and how exactly do you write it?

Read on.

2

So What Exactly Is "Humor"?

W. C. Fields, with his bulbous nose, chomping on a cigar. Charlie Chaplin hitching up his pants. A piano lid slamming down on Oliver Hardy's fingers. Are those images funny? Is that what we mean by humor? What about Alvy, in Woody Allen's *Annie Hall*, accidentally tickling Annie between the legs with the handle of his tennis racket? Jackie Gleason's leg shake, like a dog peeing? The fans of these comics would say, yes, these images are humorous. But how do we know? What is humor? How do we define it? Is it anything that makes us laugh? Anything ludicrous or ridiculous? Anything joyous?

Humor's an extremely complex phenomenon that's not yet fully understood, and because many different things can cause us to laugh, not all of them humorous, not everyone agrees on what's funny. Unique among human behavior, humor creates the common physiological response of loud noises, a shaking body, increased respiration, and a facial grimace. If we watch a tragedy, we usually don't cry; if we watch a comedy, we expect to laugh, or at least smile, and the whole audience, filled with individual personalities, usually laughs at the same moment, often with the same intensity. Writers expect the laughter, pacing their lines accordingly, and so essential is laughter that it often flames a writer's rhythms and language.

Humor's uniqueness also comes about because we create it both unintentionally and intentionally. Unintentional humor includes slips of the tongue, the naive remarks of children, and awkward physical movements. Intentional humor centers on the arts: witty paintings or sculpture; songs, with eye-winking music and lyrics; jokes that we repeat; written texts like the short story, novel, or film script. We also use the word "humor" to refer to a person's emotions (he seems really jovial); a physiological state (look how she reddens and gasps for breath when she laughs); perception (Prof Berman thinks Johnny Carson and Picasso are both comic); language ("fizzle," "hiccup," and "burp" are tickle

32

words); or the object being laughed at (that puppy wagging its tail is so-o-o cute).

Humor scholars, after centuries of debate, still haven't agreed on a definition of the word, and its meaning is further complicated because little attention is given to it from the writer's point of view. What does a writer do to create humor? What does a writer do when the audience says, *make* your writing funnier, make it more humorous?

In the Beginning . . .

In ancient times medical practitioners believed that the body was composed of the same four elements that made up the natural world: black bile produced by the kidneys or spleen, which caused melancholy, depression, or gloom (earth); choler or yellow bile produced by the gall bladder, which caused irritability or anger (air); phlegm or mucus, which caused sluggishness or apathy (water); and blood, which caused cheerfulness (fire). The word used to describe these bodily fluids was "humours." If all four fluids balanced equally, the person was said to be in "good humour"; however, if any of the fluids appeared in excess, the personality was "lopsided" and the person was described as "out of humour." Because the ancient Greeks believed in moderation and propriety, anyone who exhibited an excess of any of the humours was ridiculed and laughed at; that person was then called a "humorist." Later the word "humorist" evolved to mean a state of mind in general, then one's ability to appreciate or create the ridiculous or comic.

In the seventeenth century, Ben Jonson developed comic plays that featured characters exhibiting excessive humours, and the term "comedy of humours" came to categorize this particular kind of drama. Thus the word "humor" became closely associated with comic characters in plays.

In the nineteenth and twentieth centuries, because many vaudeville performers bantered it about freely, the word "humor" wore many different hats, and since humor and comedy both result in laughter, those terms entangled. "Humor," "humorous," "comedy," and "comic" now loosely and interchangeably refer to the tone, technique, structure, genre, or subject matter of a text that results in laughter—or to the voice, mood, intention, language, or perception of the creator—or perceiver—of that text. Scratching your head? Confused? Join the rest of us.

At the beginning of the twenty-first century we basically have three working definitions of "humor." In the first, evolving from ancient sources, "humor" has come to mean anything funny or anything that anyone says is funny. The second meaning, more specific than the first, describes the soft, slow style of the American Old West narrative tale, as well as any person (a humorist) who narrates these tales. The humor in these Old West stories, usually gentle or whimsical, centers on quaint behaviors and somewhat fantastic events. By extension, this definition of humor refers to any literary work that does not contain the specifics of plot and theme, like anecdotes or simple narratives.

A third meaning of "humor," one that scholars are now honing, is particularly useful to writers, and this definition emerged from the work of philosophers who advocate incongruity theory. (See Appendix B for an historical summary of the major philosophies of humor.) In their search for the most precise definition, current humor scholars are seeking to isolate a humor "molecule" through the smallest common denominator that describes everything "humorous." This has singular importance, for if we reduce the meaning of the word "humor" to its purest form and understand that every time we apply this principle we'll create humor, writing humor should become easy (at least, reasonably easy).

Keep in mind that the definition is still evolving, and there's disagreement about it among scholars. My apologies, therefore, for not having the perfect answer to the question of "what is humor," but let me give it my best pitch.

Humor Is Playful Incongruity

Now your first response might be, "OK, fair enough." But then you do a double take. "Wait a minute," you say. "How about the word *incongruity*? What does that mean?"

Incongruity means anything that doesn't fit our logical expectations or our normal view of things: We expect a man in a winter storm to wear a heavy jacket and boots, but Charlie Chaplin in *Gold Rush* arrives in Alaska wearing his short, ill-fitting coat and bowler hat, naively unprepared for the freezing wind and snow. He's also followed by a bear.

Incongruity occurs when we expect something coherent and it veers off the track. When you make something humorous, you make it "not normal"; that is, you make it exaggerated, unusual, unexpected, understated, improbable, odd, strange, inverted, distorted, twisted, opposite, reversed, or switched. (Some of my students have said that they generate humor more easily if they think of "humor" not as "incongruity" but as "exaggeration." To create it, they say that they just *exaggerate* whatever they're writing. You'll be on the right track if you think this way, although the word "incongruity" is more inclusive and accurate than the word "exaggeration," which is why I use it in this definition.)

You produce humor through incongruity, and you can do this in hundreds of different ways. You can make any situation incongruous by changing what is normal, logical, or expected at the current time: Writers have Frank Burns, the most incompetent surgeon on the television show *M*A*S*H*, get the biggest promotion. In the film *Dr. Strangelove,* the president of the United States, learning that the military has accidentally set off a nuclear bomb, gets childishly flustered about how to call it back. In Monty Python's *Search for the Holy Grail,* King Arthur doesn't have a horse, so the writers have his squire clap two coconuts together, mimicking the sounds of trotting hoofs. This technique can work also with physical appearance: a little kid sports a top hat, as in *Our Gang;* in *Some Like It Hot,* Tony Curtis and Jack Lemmon dress as women musicians and wobble on high heels; in *Murphy Brown,* the sophisticated television newscaster Murphy becomes a raving madwoman as she gives birth to her first child. The appearances of these characters are inconsistent with what we or the other characters expect.

Incongruity can work in language, too. For example, a sign on a garbage truck:

> "It may be garbage to you but to us it's our bread and butter."

We don't expect garbage to be compared favorably to bread and butter, so we laugh.

We see the same principle in this Henny Youngman joke:

> "Now that I've turned fifty-five it takes me all night to do what I used to do all night."

We laugh at the twisted logic of the numerous times the younger Henny can have sex against his older body's long struggle for a single erection. We laugh at incongruity in anything we see, hear, smell, touch, or taste. In literary works, this incongruity can appear in *character* (actions, appearance, clothing, speech, gestures); *plot* (situation, structure, time sequences); *setting* (place, time, history, atmosphere, mood); *language* (diction, imagery, voice, tone, sounds, inflections, pacing, pauses, timing, organization, rhythms); and *theme* (subject, beliefs of characters or author, author's attitude toward the subject).

To visualize incongruity and normalcy, you can draw the concept of humor as shown in Figure 1.

For something to be funny it should rise above the normal or logical. This extension can increase by degrees, depending on what point of view you want to establish in the work. However, think twice about straying excessively far from normalcy, because that humor can dissolve into silliness or confusion. This is not to disparage silliness or pure nonsense, but that brand of humor, usually appreciated by young children, is only tangentially useful for writing adult humor. If your audience rejects your writing as too silly, it's probably because too many reference points stray too far from reality. In this case, touch base with the norm (reality) more often.

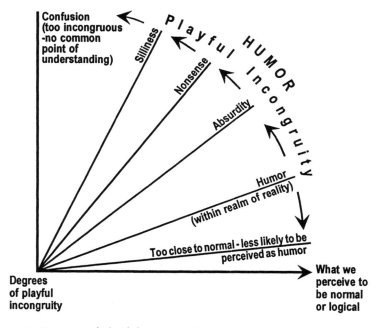

Figure 1. Degrees of playful incongruity

"So, is that all I need to know about the definition, that 'humor' is 'playful incongruity'?" you ask. Well, no, it's not that simple. The definition is, as I said earlier, a little complicated. Read on.

Tension

When you make something incongruous, be sure that you have *tension* between what's thought of as normal and what's incongruous, because mere differences by themselves won't be funny. Wearing a hat that's both red and blue doesn't make it inherently funny, just different. Juxtaposing a hairpin and a flower in a painting doesn't create humor. Something that's just different isn't incongruous. For incongruity to occur, there has to be a "pull" or a "contrast" or a "tension." Something that's unexpected merely surprises us; the incongruity has to contradict expectations:

A fourteen-year-old girl and a fifty-year-old man walking into a classroom are of different sexes and ages, but that by itself isn't funny. To make the scene humorous, you'd have to make her a precocious teenager with an IQ of 170 and have us discover that she's actually the professor, and he's the student.

It's the shock of what we expect the fourteen-year-old girl to be and what you've made her that makes this funny. Associated yet unrelated ideas have to bump against each other.

This "tension" or "pull" or "spring" has to stretch between two meanings (also called *scripts*), which sets up the *clash* that makes us laugh.[1] The tension must point to some absurdity or illogic, and when the audience processes then resolves cognitively the double meaning between the two, they understand or "get the joke." Some linguists believe that when we create humor, we envision two thoughts simultaneously, images diverging, each one in its own domain. At a certain point in our imagination, we cross those two scripts, forming the clash, and thus create humor.

"I think we need to go back a step," you say. "If incongruity with the appropriate tension defines humor, why do we need to add the word "playful" to the definition?"

Playful

Good question. "Incongruity" by itself isn't enough to make something humorous, because incongruity can also be nonhumorous. As humor scholar John Morreall points out, we can have all kinds of incongruity that wouldn't be funny. Some can be neutral, some embarrassing, some frightening, some puzzling. Some incongruities are so trivial we don't even notice them, and they produce little reaction in us, neither humorous nor nonhumorous: a pencil and a slice of bread next to each other on a table; a warm sun in winter; coffee dripping down the side of a cup; the hard seat we're sitting on.

Some incongruous situations create fear rather than laughter. An eerie noise in your kitchen during a dark and stormy night when you're alone in the house can scare you. Witnessing a shooting in the street would also frighten you. Incongruity can also require problem solving. You put on shorts and a t-shirt only to discover that the temperature outside has dropped and it's become very cold. The shorts and t-shirt are incongruous, but you wouldn't usually laugh in this situation, you would change your clothes. An unusually high telephone bill you can't account for is incongruous, but it would puzzle you rather than make you laugh.

So, to narrow the definition exclusively for humor, we have to add the word "playful" to the word "incongruity." You need incongruity in a playful or a nonthreatening context to create humor.

You blend playfulness with incongruity by signaling the audience that you're being nonserious through contextual or framework *clues.* These playful clues—like the incongruity clues—can appear in any of the elements of your writing: tone, plot, setting, actions, details, language, imagery, rhythms, or anything else that conveys a nonthreatening atmosphere to the audience. By a lighthearted attitude, you assure them that the work will not have inevitable tragic consequences.

You can also control the amount of humor in your writing by the number of playful clues you give. If you give a lot of them, the work becomes very light; if you mix and match playful with serious clues, you produce tragicomedy; if you give only a single playful clue within a very serious work, you'll create darker humor. The number and intensity of playful clues determine humor's place along a continuum of varying tones (see Figure 2).

Caution: Mixing humorous and serious clues randomly may confuse your audience. A coherent design of humorous clues very early in the work focuses your artistic intention.

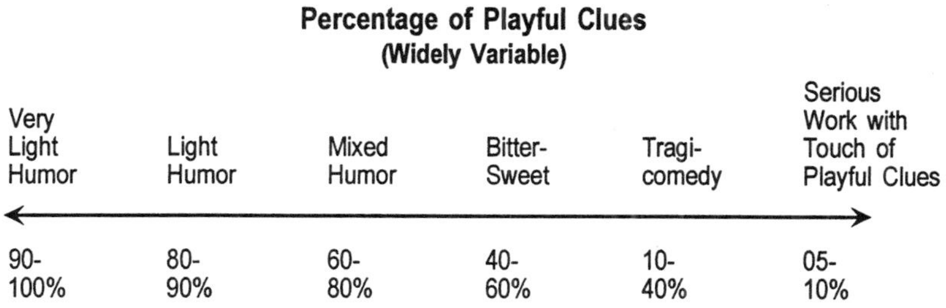

Percentage of Playful Clues
(Widely Variable)

Very Light Humor	Light Humor	Mixed Humor	Bitter-Sweet	Tragi-comedy	Serious Work with Touch of Playful Clues
90-100%	80-90%	60-80%	40-60%	10-40%	05-10%

Figure 2. Percentage of playful clues

Resolution

For something to be funny, the clash or spark has to be resolved in an original or clever way that surprises and delights your audience. If an image, for example, is clichéd or too obvious, the audience won't laugh because you haven't challenged their intelligence enough (not enough incongruity). Those images are dull, and dull writing—humorous or serious—always flops. A terrific *resolution* brings down the house.

The Humor Molecule

Now, take a joke, any joke:

> Henny Youngman: "Now that I know how to get the most out of life, most of it is over."

Look at the structure of the humor process in figure 3 and apply the joke to the diagram. Meaning #1 centers on the word play "most out of life," which we understand to mean the value of life, and which operates as a normal statement. Meaning #2 focuses on the amount of life left to live, "most of it is over." That becomes incongruous in comparison to meaning #1.

As we read the joke, we associate the two different meanings of the word "most" and sense the tension between them, which is the contrast between "joy" that's implied in meaning #1 and "limit" in meaning #2. Our realization of the joy in life and the brevity of life then clashes, but because we delight at the word

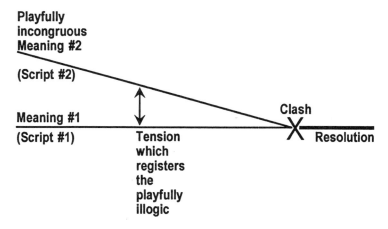

Figure 3. Diagram of the humor process

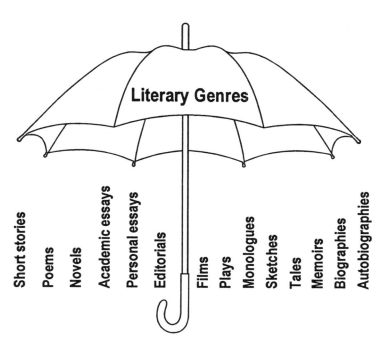

Figure 4. Literary genres

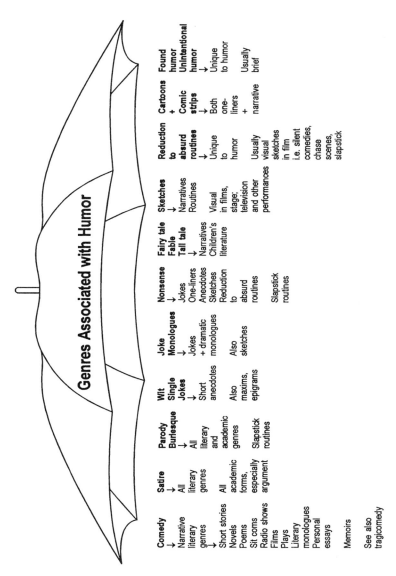

Figure 5. Humor genres (or genres associated with humor)

play—and at the human poignancy described in the joke—the resolution is humorous rather than serious.

This joke well illustrates our principle, but remember that humor isn't restricted to one-liners.

Genres

To further complicate the definition, sometimes writers confuse humor with literary genres. They're different things.

Humor embraces any literary form or genre. Poems, plays, novels, monologues, films, or essays can be either serious or comic, and they are humorous if and only if they contain humor (see Figure 4).

Some genres, however, are specific to humor because their structure tends toward playful incongruity. Some of these overlap the more traditional literary genres (see Figure 5).

Definition of Humor—Finally!

Humor is playful incongruity that contains a tension between two levels of meaning followed by a clash of sufficient complexity that surprises and delights and that leads to a resolution of that meaning. The playful incongruity must be understood and appreciated by the intellect, and it must be accepted by the social, cultural, psychological, individual, and momentary contexts.

Note: We use the word "joke" in this book synonymously with the word "humor" to mean any instance (pinprick) of playful incongruity. (See the other definition of "joke" in chapter 18.)

A complex definition, but don't let a heavy analysis of theory weigh you down and keep you from writing. Very few of us consciously realize that this process is racing through our minds as we write humor. You're not going to be thinking of this definition every time you write. *It comes in handy best when you're revising and you want to make what you've written funnier.* Theory is actually easier to apply to your writing than you might think, as you'll see in the discussion of simple techniques for writing humor in chapter 3.

Simple Techniques for Writing Humor

"OK," you say, "'nuff of this theory stuff. Get to the point."
"OK," says the Prof, stepping down from her lectern, sweat dripping from brow.

Exaggeration or Overstatement

In *Modern Times* a huge machine that Charlie is operating squashes his partner's pocket watch. The watch flattens to fifty times its normal size. In *The Gold Rush* Black Larsen spits at Charlie. Charlie falls back as though he's been punched. In *Safety Last*, Harold Lloyd climbs up the side of a building only to encounter tumbling obstacles—pigeons squat on him, a mouse runs up his leg, a ferocious dog drives him out to the end of a flagpole, his foot tangles in a rope and the pole inevitably breaks—but Lloyd saves himself, if only momentarily, by grabbing the minute hand of a huge clock that agonizingly slides down to the six. Lloyd's dangerous predicament has thrilled audiences for decades. And speaking of more danger and thrills, we all squeal in our seats during the signature car chases of the Keystone Kops.

What all these examples have in common is their *exaggeration*, one of the easiest ways to create humor.

The Silent Comedians were especially adept at this technique, since the absence of speech demanded broad visual gestures, and topping a joke (see next section), not the story line, usually drove the narrative. Comic team Stan Laurel and Oliver Hardy, who bridge the silent and talkie eras, use exaggeration in *Saps at Sea:*

> "Why are you looking like that?" asks Hardy.
> "I've got a nail in my shoe," says Laurel.
> Laurel tugs at a thread from his shoe, which stretches and

43

> stretches to at least ten feet of thread. When he yanks up his sock
> to adjust it, its foot is gone. He's completely unraveled the sock.

In this scene from the television series *Frank's Place,* exaggeration
is used to show a character's intelligence and wit, which both we
and the other characters have underestimated:

A bum, loitering in front of Frank Parrish's restaurant, is
asked to leave by Frank's lawyer, Si Weissburger. When Weissburger tries to persuade the bum that he should stop annoying
customers with his presence, the bum confronts the timid Weissburger with a lawyer's judicial logic. His intelligence woefully underestimated, the bum says that he'll take the case to the *state
court* and if necessary to the *Federal Court,* and if that doesn't
work he'll argue it as a *constitutional case,* and if that *still* doesn't
work, then he'll call the ACLU (American Civil Liberties Union)
and have the cream of this year's graduating law class down there
in New Orleans beating their breasts in his favor.

Weissburger is befuddled by the force of the bum's logic. By
expanding and intensifying his legal possibilities, the bum transforms into a larger-than-normal derelict; in fact, he metamorpho-
sizes into a real human being, with intelligence and inalienable
rights, the theme of the story. Shocked by the brilliance of the
bum's argument and utterly defeated, Weissburger retreats, like a
wounded puppy, back into the restaurant.

Exaggeration, of course, isn't limited to film since all kinds
of humorous works use it to get laughs.

Examples

Any element of a written text can be exaggerated for humorous
effect: description, characterization, dialogue, actions, thoughts,
plot, voice, tone, mood, setting, words, imagery, sounds, rhythms,
or the theme itself. Remember, though, that you don't want to
make all elements exaggerated at any one time because that jams
the work and it becomes too "busy" or confusing. In the following examples, how do these writers use exaggeration to develop
humor? Is it too much or just right?

> In my best childlike tone, I explained to my dog, Fleas, that going
> to the bathroom was a perfectly natural part of living and that
> when the occasion arose he should not be ashamed of such func-
> tions but could instead focus them in constructive and meaning-
> ful ways on newspaper. He seemed to understand, and I retired.

In the morning I discovered the *first fossils of a dietary geo-logic record enmeshed in newspaper that would stretch through the months to come; I added another layer. Fleas jumped up to show me how much his nails had grown overnight.*

Mark Matthews

Dr. Wiggle had numerous, extremely odd personality quirks. For instance, every morning he would *put his shoes on the wrong feet.* He claimed it was a precaution he took in order to avoid boredom. He believed that if he ever ran out of things to do, he could *always pass the time by switching his shoes to the correct feet.*

Once he completely unscrewed my neck bolts. At that point, as I turned to look at Natasha, *my head fell from my neck and dropped onto the table landing in my lentil soup.* A lady behind me screamed. A man called an ambulance. *Wires and diodes protruded from the hole in my shoulder like slimy insects shooting from a popcorn maker.*

"Now, that's impressive," said Natasha.

"I told ya," replied Dr. Wiggle.

I stood up and was able to *flail my arms above my head* because the circuits which controlled my bodily movements were located in my torso. *Someone called the police as I plunged into the chest of a waiter who, in turn, dropped a tray of twelve Caesar salads and a plate of escargot.*

Todd Tibbetts

In the following passage, how does Chris Capozzi's exaggerated narrative about his elementary school days advance the parochial culture he satirizes?

I served out my elementary school sentence at St. Stephen's School, a small Catholic school run by East German nuns. There I was subjected to harassment by old ladies who averaged four feet two inches in height, but could whip a pit bull. Each day started with morning prayers, which included an Act of Contrition, to ask God for "forgiveness in advance" for all the sins each of us were inevitably going to commit that day. This was deemed necessary by both the faculty and the administration, because after all, we were children and what living creature is more predisposed towards sin than a child? . . .

The teachers at St. Stephen's were inspirational, and they knew how to motivate students. I found a great source of motivation in my fifth grade teacher, Sister Gertrude, who threatened to "box my ears in" if I didn't do my homework. By no means did

I deem this an idle threat as I witnessed the "boxing in" of the ears of Michael Spizzano, and later heard of the excruciatingly painful operation of removing his ears from their embedded positions in the respective lobes of his brain.

CHRIS CAPOZZI

SUGGESTIONS FOR WRITING

Write on any topic you want, but if you're stuck for an idea, see the suggestions below. Brainstorm ideas or images first, listing at least ten, then write quickly until you have at least a full paragraph or a scene. Read your writing over and add exaggeration, using specific details wherever the humor falls flat.

1. Imagine a moment from your past when you first saw someone intriguing. Describe him/her. Physical appearance? Actions? Where were you? What did that person say to you? What did you say?
2. Imagine a conflict between a customer and a salesperson. If you can, take a scene from your own experience. Where did it take place? What did the salesperson look like? What did he or she say? What did the customer/you say? Give each of the characters some actions.

Topping the Joke

Remember that we're defining a "joke" in this book as any instance of playful incongruity, not just one-liners.

You can *top a joke* using exaggeration. Exaggeration lets you tumble joke on top of joke and leads naturally to a final joke topper. This works both visually and verbally. The idea is to gather the series of jokes in a unit so that one joke fires momentum for the next. You can tuck the topper in quietly within a larger scene for a more subtle structural play, and it works really well if you're creating a long work and you want to maintain comic interest in the middle, usually the sluggish part of any story. You'll especially want to do this when you're attempting a humorous crescendo as a grand finale for a scene.

To top a joke, you fool the audience into thinking that the previous joke is finished, but then you go for one more twist. The number of times you top a joke is up to you, but the method works best if the final joke caps the whole series in a logical or narrative flourish. Ending the joke crescendo is subjective, however, and you might end when you've completely run out of room for anything more to say.

For example, in *The Midnight Patrol*, Laurel and Hardy play two cops. They're on duty in a patrol car parked at a curb. Thieves crash a brick through their window. Hardy is struggling to open a soda. The brick pops Hardy on the head (joke #1), causing him to flick open his soda (joke #2), which squirts in his face (the *topper*).

An old vaudeville example of topping comes from the medieval Italian commedia dell'arte routine of confronting a series of obstacles within a small space. You've probably seen hundreds of variations of this routine where a large number of people emerge from a small container. Take, for example, an automobile, say an old Volkswagen bug. Ten or fifteen tall basketball players, one by one, crawl out of the VW. After a group of them has emerged, one last person comes out: a little kid holding a huge balloon. That tops the gag. Then when you think the balloon will break it doesn't; instead, the tires of the automobile collapse. That tops the topper.

You can take this as far as your audience will stand. Have the hood on the car pop up then steam explode from the car. Everyone runs for cover except the little kid. He watches objectively and challenges fate. Just when he thinks it's safe, the balloon breaks.

Examples

Study the written examples below for descriptive and action details. How many times does each writer top the joke?

> Actually Andy's car was a hardly a roadrunner; in fact, it was an early 1980's Monte Carlo SS with all the trimmings: tinted windows, spoiler, mag shields, a crank-it-up-pull-out stereo, and to top it off, a Penthouse air freshener which had one side depicting two naked girls intertwined with each other and the other side with a girl touching herself in less than prudish ways.
>
> PETER D. DRANOFF

> I delivered the local rag, which, as most customers told me, didn't have enough news to wrap a fish in. They were right. The daily paper was rarely more than five pages long, and carried headlines such as LOCAL SCHOOLS CLOSED TODAY: TOO MUCH SNOW, while stories such as NEW PRESIDENT ELECTED were printed somewhere behind Dear Abby. The paper's motto was "Yesterday's News Today," and once during a reporters' strike became "Tomorrow's News Sometime Next

Week." The most upsetting thing about the whole situation was that the customers blamed me for the bad journalism. As if I, a semi-educated sixth grader, who couldn't type any more than forty words a minute, was capable of writing such garbage.

RUDY RUIZ

SUGGESTIONS FOR WRITING

Arranging the details so that the most important or most clever is last, sketch one of the following:
1. A scene where you were tricked by your friends into dancing on stage for a local pie-eating contest.
2. A moment when you were thrown out of your place of work.

Exaggeration (Understatement)

In *low exaggeration or understatement,* you treat the topic as less important than it is. Mark Twain illustrates this in his famous quote: "The reports of my death have been greatly exaggerated." You create understatement by switching from something important to a statement, action, or detail that is much less important. You get the effect by the speaker's tone or by reducing a complex issue to a simpler level.

Stan Laurel mixes up major and minor priorities in the film *One Good Turn.* Oliver Hardy is washing underwear in a stream next to their campsite. Laurel runs back and forth to a pump by the stream, filling a cup with water and splashing Hardy as he rushes by. Hardy does a slow turn. Laurel stops. "You haven't got another cup, have you?" Laurel asks. "What for?" asks Hardy. Laurel casually responds, "Tent's on fire."

Lou Costello, in *Meet the Killer,* scores with a one-line understated joke at the end of a convoluted slapstick scene. Freddy (Costello) cowers into a dark, foreboding cave. After encircling the pathways and becoming more and more confused, he enters an extremely dank, cold area, then suddenly and frighteningly slides down a patch of ice and over a craggy ledge, facing certain death from a plunge into a bottomless pit. Fortunately, the ice flings him over the precipice onto an opposite ledge, landing him on a huge stalagmite which sticks up, strategically placed, between his legs. Temporarily relieved that he's still alive but pondering his dilemma, Freddy looks at the stalagmite and says to the camera, "This could be serious."

His life in extreme danger, Freddy's only concern is the preservation of his testicles.

Another example: In Monty Python's *Search for the Holy Grail*, Lancelot is being held prisoner by his father until he agrees to marry his father's choice for a bride. He shoots an arrow out the tower window with a message for help attached. As Arthur and his squire romp past, the arrow strikes the squire directly in the chest. Doubling up in excruciating pain, the squire says to Arthur: "Message for you, sir."

The squire directs attention not to his life-threatening wound but to the paper at the end of the arrow.

Low exaggeration or understatement can also set up a *series of threes* where the third member of the series is intoned to be the most important, but the joke rests on its trivial importance. The images drop from the significant to the inconsequential or from the reasonable to the ludicrous. The old college cheer that circulated when the first George Bush was president is an example: For God, for country, and for Yale. For non-Yalies, the puffed-up value of Yale collapses into satire, although some Yale students would argue that their school stands as the most important of the three. You can apply this technique in narrative, too, as in this description of a disastrous week:

> Sunday finally arrived and I reviewed the events of the previous six days: I had lost my wallet, my husband—and seven strands of my newly highlighted hair.

A series of threes can appear too mechanical if overused, but if it's well placed within a larger context, it can spice up the dramatic movement of a scene within a scene and effect a closure for the audience.

Examples

In the following description, how does Rudy Ruiz use understatement to drive the satire?

> Father's sermon asked for money to repair damages to the school gym from a week earlier. It seemed that before bingo, someone put up a No Smoking sign. The women present vehemently disagreed and showed themselves by crying "mutiny" then lighting the stage on fire. No one was hurt, but several numbered ping pong balls were melted onto the floor. Somehow, the concession stand still made a profit for the evening.

In this next description, how does the understatement in the last sentence reveal the character's puzzlement about her father?

> Jody picked at her hair with a wide-toothed comb. Her attempts to enlarge her stature and political presence by heightening her head were futile, and her feathered crest weakly leaned to one side, tottered for a second, then fell down in flat, resolute, and abject defeat. Her father, sporting a tan and deep purple contacts, would be arriving in ten minutes, prepared to drive her home and to register his disapproval at her behavior by appointing himself the family major domo: autocrat, disciplinarian, authority, expert, and wise man, minus of course the frankincense and myrrh. After all, she was no kid in the manger, and he wasn't coming to worship her birth. Still, his trip was curious and Jody wondered why her dad, a four-term mayor of Kennybute, New York, kept changing the color of his eyes. Maybe she could figure it out, she thought, if she concentrated on a cuticle.

SUGGESTIONS FOR WRITING

Understating is more difficult to write than overstating, so if this exercise isn't working for you, don't panic. Doing it on command can be tricky. If you can't get it, go on to other exercises because forcing a technique when it's not coming might cause you to lose confidence in yourself, and that can result in writer's block. But don't skip this warm-up exercise. It's really important that you try since it adds to your humor immeasurably. Write at least a paragraph.

1. Brainstorm about a moment when you (or your character) stole something, creating a situation that could have been serious but turned out to be trivial.
2. Write about a moment when you had a conflict with a neighbor who took the conflict seriously and you saw it as trivial.

Reversals, Opposites, and Contrast

Contrast of appearance and personality was the hallmark of comedy teams, and the laughs coming from something so basic as "differences" was the reason so many comedians decided to work in twos. Stan Laurel—thin, remorseful, nervous, quiet, and lacking confidence—complemented his partner Oliver Hardy—a fat, loud, boisterous, temperamental, and self-assured buffoon—and the audiences loved it. George Burns and Gracie Allen got knee-slapping laughs with their *opposite* personalities—she with her patrician beauty and literal language and he with his puzzled expressions and cigar.

You can create humor by *reversing, opposing, or contrasting* characters, expectations, actions, words, tones, images, and settings. The silents understood this comic power: In Laurel and Hardy's *Blotto*, Stan Laurel throws a piece of paper with a forward thrust—it falls back over his shoulder. In Chaplin's *Easy Street*, in a reversal of failed expectations, Charlie runs to embrace the girl of his dreams but trips over a drain hole. You can create misunderstandings when one character thinks in opposite ways from another character. In *Way Out West*, Stan Laurel sings a few lines of "In the Blue Ridge Mountains of Virginia" in a high, squeaky voice. For the next line or two, he dips into a deep resonant voice. Annoyed by the new sound, Hardy slaps Laurel on the head and he returns to the high squeaky voice. A variation of this routine is repeated in numerous stage shows by Abbott and Costello, where Abbott gives directions to Costello, who's playing a stagehand, to lower or raise the curtain as they prepare for a performance. Costello thinks Abbott is giving him directions on how to sing a song, and he lowers and raises his voice accordingly.

Nowhere is reversal more powerful than in Chaplin's *The Great Dictator*: In this film, the Jew (Chaplin), bears a remarkable resemblance to Herr Hynkel, the dictator of Tomainia (also played by Chaplin). Upon his escape from a political prison and now an amnesiac from his brutal treatment, he returns home where he is mistaken for the dictator and given a leader's reception. Herr Hynkel is later mistaken for the Jew and hauled off to prison. At the end of the film, the Jew gives the people of Tomainia their final, triumphal speech that urges peace.

Reversals, contrast, and opposites work in the language of jokes, too. In Oscar Wilde's *The Importance of Being Earnest*, Lady Bracknell turns a biting wit to Lady Harbury's gold-digging qualities: "I'm sorry we're late but I was obliged to call on dear Lady Harbury," says Lady Bracknell. "I hadn't been there since her poor husband's death. I never saw a woman so altered; she looks quite twenty years *younger*." Algernon responds, "I hear her hair has turned quite *gold* from grief," a reference to her large inheritance.

Earlier we saw how understatement accelerates a series of threes, but contrast can be used in a series, too. In *Frank's Place*, Frank has tried everything to get rid of the derelict standing at the front door of his restaurant and offending customers. Miss Marie offers advice to Frank:

> "You can always catch more flies with honey, son. Why don't you try a little kindness?"
> "I tried that," says Frank.
> "Well, then, try reason," says Miss Marie.
> "I did," says Frank.
> "Well, then," says Miss Marie, running out of reasonable suggestions, "send Big Arthur out and get this thing over with."

Examples

How do these writers use contrast, opposites, or reversals to create the humor?

> Yep, just as I figured, there he was, shopping at Home Depot, the former president himself, still wearing a hidden mike embossed with the presidential seal tucked neatly into his back collar. Oh, the blown-dried hair sat in place all right, stained grey-ish with non-toxic Grecian Formula as advertised on Ebay, and his hand-tailored suit with the obligatory primary-color tie spouted the dignity of the office, but what struck me immediately was the pitiful wave of his hand as he stood in the center of aisle four, next to the circular saws and wall brackets, and ordered up his 2×4's. A half dozen of them. After all those patriotic years in the White House, what could possibly be left for an "ex-president" except crafts and workshopping.

> *Day 10 of my employment (at Disney World):* Today I went around as one of the chipmunk twins. I played Dale. A monstrous little boy would not leave me alone. He kept taunting me by explaining how he knew I was probably some kid who couldn't get a real job out of college. He threw popcorn all over me. I was reprimanded for getting the suit dirty.
> Scott Levy

> Of all the great philosophers the world has known, Aristotle, Plato and Socrates, for example, one has been continually overlooked in history. I speak, of course, of the great American-born philosopher, Monroe Snively. . . . At age seven, Monroe tried to enroll at the University of Illinois to obtain a degree in philosophy, but college officials said he was too short and that he had trouble spelling the word "Zeppelin." So instead, Monroe enrolled in the Ernie Lufkowitz School of Karate.
> Paul Nelson

SUGGESTIONS FOR WRITING

Rap about the trials and tribulations of two opposites: teacher/student; parent/child; customer/clerk; athlete/non-athlete; hard worker/goof-off. Write in the voice of the "loser" as practice for getting inside the minds of different kinds of characters.

Similarities and Comparisons

Similarity occurs when you envision two things that are not usually associated with each other and you find at least one point in common. Working with this one common point, you create an image: In Chaplin's *Modern Times,* the opening shot pans a flock of sheep crowding into a corral; the next shot unrolls a similar crowd of men jamming together into a factory entrance, rushing to work before the late bell sounds. Chaplin jabs a satiric, political point by merging the image of men who labor day after day in a factory with sheep being corralled for the slaughter.

A similarity good for belly laughs is Charlie's drying dishes by rolling them through a washing machine wringer in *The Pawnshop.* He repeats the same concept in *The Rink,* where Charlie, a waiter in a restaurant, cleans and presses his hat and coat by warming them in the restaurant's oven.

Similarities work in jokes, too, like this one told by an exuberantly plump person: "I don't know why anyone would want to sleep with a skinny person. It's like sleeping with a batch of coat hangers."

Examples

How effective are the similarities in the examples below? What connotations are the writers trying to elicit?

> His *pug* nose and *clam-on-the-half shell* cheeks made Dr. Wiggle the most wrinkled being on the face of this, or any other, planet.
>
> TODD TIBBETTS

> The first time I saw her was the first day of seventh grade English class. She walked in with a crowd of admiring girls, tall and individual *as a clipper ship,* and I was immediately smitten. She managed to stand above *the sea of* blue jumpers and white blouses, the required girls' uniform of the day, everyday. She

stared at me across the room and The Writer apparently was moved by The Orphan, for she smiled *like a beacon* into my eyes, sending me *sounding for shelter* below the desk, a fairly easy dive, owing to my great shortness.

RICHARD ANDERSON

Try practicing variations until you get one you like.

Example

WEAK?

He has cute eyes.

BETTER?

His sexy eyelashes flap *like the fringe on a Tiffany lampshade.*
His eyelids snapped up *like a broken window blind.*
He took the drink and his eyes flipped *like a pinball in a Doctor Who arcade game.*
He had the most dazzling eyes you ever saw—*like two stained glass windows depicting the death and resurrection of Christ.*

SUGGESTIONS FOR WRITING

Write a character sketch dabbed with humorous similarities. If you're stuck for an idea, try comparing your character to a food (licorice) or an animal (platypus) or a vehicle (motorcycle) or a game (Purchase).

Transmogrification of an Object

Transmogrification of an object means an object becomes something different from its usual self. You see this all the time in cartoons. When a carrot pops up on a table and dances a rumba, it's changed from a food to a human being. When a frisbee tossed into the air effervesces into a cloud then, landing back on earth, plants itself as a flower, its transformation establishes both visual and thematic energy through a renewal of earth by the sky. When you use this technique, you can make the object a character in itself or a fantasy in a character's thoughts.

When you employ transmogrification, you re-image an object or animal into "something else," either another object with its dominant traits or a "human being" with human characteristics and actions. The transformation of an object or animal into a human form is called "anthropomorphy"; in literature, the usual term for this figurative technique is "personification." By this clever re-imaging, you can enhance theme, liven symbols and myths, or electrify a narrative. Most important, we get to experience how that object or animal imagines his world, adding depth and complexity to the personality. Chaplin was a master of this: In *The Vagabond*, Charlie, a gypsy, uses the bow of his violin to wipe his nose. When Charlie prepares a meal for the gypsy girl he has rescued from a brutal father, he modestly sets the table for himself and the starving young woman. He has no tablecloth so he takes a plaid shirt and lays it down on the table, then, eager to please, he carefully rolls up each sleeve into napkins. The scene is set for gracious dining.

In *The Gold Rush*, Charlie has planned an elaborate New Year's Eve dinner party for the lovely Georgia, a dance-hall girl whom he deeply loves, and her friends. While he waits for them to arrive, he imagines himself already at the dinner—and here Chaplin is at his most brilliant—he entertains Georgia at the table with a high kick routine of two baked potatoes at the ends of two forks. By transmogrifying her dance routine with potatoes, imagining her as dancer as he himself dances, he embodies Georgia's grace and conveys the depth and purity of his love.

Later in the film, Charlie and Big Jim are stranded and starving in a freezing cabin during a huge snowstorm. Even though there's no food, the ever-resourceful Charlie plans a Thanksgiving dinner by cooking one of his shoes. He gingerly lifts the shoe out of the boiling water, places it gently on a dinner plate, then ladles water over it with the savoir faire of a gourmet. He sharpens two knives in preparation for some fancy carving by gently pulling off the shoestring and laying that aside. He lifts off the top of the shoe for himself, then gives the sole with its row of nails to Jim. Jim, angry at being served the bad part of the shoe, switches plates, huffs in despair, then reluctantly chews on the leather. Charlie gnaws an edge of the sole and, savoring its flavor, rolls his eyes. Demonstrating the finest of upper-class manners, Charlie gently winds the shoestring around his fork like spaghetti, sucks delicately on a nail as though he's extracting juices from a bone, then holds the nail with a raised pinky finger and asks Jim to make a wish. Jim gruffly refuses.

Undaunted, Charlie continues eating what he imagines to be the finest food. At the end of the meal, Charlie waves his fingers as though they were sticky from luscious meat juices then hiccups to accelerate his pleasant and filling digestion.

Transmogrifying an object adds strong comic dynamics to film because of its visual potential, but it also works well in written comedy.

Examples

> The computer leered at me, flashed its tush on the screen, then slowly but stubbornly, of its own free-yet-predestined will, shut down.

> The itch crawled along my right shoulder bone then pinched and bit into my flesh, like a Amazon leech with both XX and XY chromosomes reproducing into a thousand points of light which, in this case, transmogrified into agonizingly painful static electricity.

> The woman plopped herself down right in front of me, her hat jostling right above her ears, like a huge red peony that first leered at me then transformed itself into a glaring Batman with seven pointed wings, each tip topped with the face of a grinning Seinfeld who sought me out in high frequency radar.

SUGGESTIONS FOR WRITING

Write a scene where you or your character lets an object take on a life of its own: a shoe; a bag of popcorn; a doorknob; a chemistry student discussing an experiment surrounded by various beakers.

The Unusual: Not Normally Done, Said, Accepted, Expected

You can create humor using any detail that's playfully *unusual*. The technique can be applied to physical characteristics like Stan Laurel's ruffled hair (or Phyllis Diller's) or Oliver Hardy's rotund body shape. You can use it for clothing like Chaplin's baggy pants and ill-fitting jacket, which he clutches and tugs when he moves, or his shoes, so worn they flap like alligators' jaws. Physical actions, when they don't quite fit the context of what is normal in a scene, can also make us laugh: Chaplin's shrug of his shoulders, palms out at each side; the flip of his bowler hat when he greets a villain; or his seaman's walk. They aren't what the characters surrounding him expect and their reaction indicates to us that we, too, should see them as unusual.

Sometimes the unusual stretches to the absurd. In *Bud Abbott and Lou Costello Meet the Killer,* the opening credits anticipate the nonsensical premise of the film: Abbott and Costello pop onto the screen as cartoon figures painting a billboard that announces the film's stars and title. As the cartoon figures of Abbott and Costello finish painting "Bud Abbott" and "Lou Costello" on the billboard, a person off screen shoots holes in it that spell out "Meet the Killer." Costello does a double take, then facing the camera, taunts the gunman. "Ha, ha," he says. "You didn't dot the eye."

The off-screen response is a high-speed dagger, barely missing Costello's nose, that dots the *i.* As trembling Costello struggles to vocalize a choked scream, the vibrating dagger drops blood that spells out "Boris Karloff."

Examples

How do these writers create voice and character through unusual details?

> They immediately kissed each other and remained clasped in each other's arms for about five minutes. The kisses they exchanged were so powerful that their front teeth ached for the rest of the day. Manilov was so overjoyed that only his nose and lips remained on his face, his eyes having completely disappeared.
>
> "Dead Souls," Nikolai Gogol

> Petco was indeed open, and Jim noticed many customers had their leashed dogs with them in the store. "I should have brought Chico," Jim said to a woman with a parrot on her shoulder. Neither responded. Jim regretted leaving Chico home, even though he did keep the TV on Animal Planet and the pantry open in case Chico was hungry. Next time, definitely, Jim would bring Chico with him to the store. But first the little dog would need a leash.
>
> Forty-five minutes later, Jim had two leashes, forty pounds of kibble, flea powder, a squeaky hedgehog, doggie breath mints, and a small knit sailor outfit for dogs under ten pounds.
>
> Laura Klink

> "Put this in your notebook, freak," Dunn shouted at Judy as they passed. Before Judy could reply, a loogie had been effectively

hawked from Dunn's facial orifice, landing with remarkable accuracy on the yellow page in front of her atop the earlier sketch of him. The ink, still wet, began to run down the page with the fresh saliva. The portrait quickly became unrecognizable, streaking the lines of his face and limbs into a grotesque mutant. Soon there was nothing left of him except a shallow collection of mucus and blue, which reminded Judy of the hot thin soup Mr. Berman taught them about in biology.

"This," he had told them, pointing to an old projector image, "is the primitive tide pool out of which all life will eventually grow."

Greg Tebbano

Suggestions for Writing

1. Write a descriptive scene using unusual details or dialogue where some people are gathered at a Pepsi machine. Next to it is a Coke machine. Your main character wants a lemonade.
2. Write a scene describing the items your character carries under his arm.

Obvious and Literal Logic (Using Language Literally)

Using obvious and literal logic means having a character interpret the denotative (literal) meaning of language rather than the connotative (figurative) usage. If someone says to you, "shake a leg," they want you to hurry (literally), not to actually wiggle your leg (figuratively). If Suzy says to Joe, "You have bats in your belfry," she figuratively means that he's not thinking clearly (comparing flying bats to fuzzy thinking), although someone like Monty Python would visualize this literally and draw a clip of a man with bats flying out of his ears.

Bud Abbott and Lou Costello, among others, use literal language for comic purposes: Tubby and Flash (*Hit the Ice*) casually enter a bank immediately after it has been robbed. Oblivious to what has happened, they register bewilderment.

"Door's open," Tubby calls to the tellers. No one answers. Tubby tries again.

"Hey anybody!" (Whistles.) "It's after 3:00. You want this door open?" He scans the room for the vanished tellers. "Wait a minute. Where is everybody? It's a wrong way to do business," he says to them. "Somebody might come in and rob the joint."

In *Meet the Killer*, Freddy (Costello), a bellboy at Crandall's Lost Cavern Hotel, gets fired by the hotel manager for his clumsiness. He has dropped Mr. Strictland's baggage and broken his glasses. Strictland and Freddy get into an altercation.

Strictland asks, "Are you threatening me?"

Freddy answers, "In words of one syllable: yes."

Later in *Meet the Killer*, Freddy discovers a body and shudders as he slowly backs away from the corpse. "Come on," says Casey (Abbott), trying to get Freddy to move faster, "get some *life* into it."

Freddy jumps nervously at the suggestion, stupefied by the dead man. "Don't you think that's asking a little too much?" he says.

The writers never stop. Near the end of the film we see a hilarious split-scene effect where the Assistant Inspector says to the Inspector: "I still think if you let me *sweat* that bellhop a little bit I'd get a confession out of him." The scene quickly switches to Freddy who is in desperate trouble trapped in a steambath and screaming for his life.

Examples

How do these writers use literal logic in these "worst opening lines" to create the humor?

> He caught the ball clean, kind of like when you play receiver for the Giants against the Steelers right after you've taken a shower.

> She was called "Slim," not like when Humphrey Bogart called Lauren Bacall "Slim" in the movie *Key Largo*, but more like in the 1960s when Hubert Humphrey called my neighbor Gladys "Slim."

> The only time the spleen gets any attention at all is when someone says they need to vent it. "I have to vent my spleen." Of what? What exactly is inside your spleen that needs venting?
>
> DAN AMRICH

SUGGESTIONS FOR WRITING

Write a scene where your character wears a t-shirt with a logo that a person from another country interprets literally. Create some dialogue between them as the person tries to figure out the meaning implied.

Focusing on the Wrong Thing

Focusing on the wrong thing or switching off from the main point is an easy way you can shape humor that's illogical:

> In Chaplin's *The Gold Rush*, the character Jim, an Alaskan prospector who's just become a millionaire with Charlie from their discovery of a gold mine, decides to get a manicure; but when the manicurist approaches Jim, he says, "Not my nails . . . my corns."

By drawing our attention to the corns, we're reminded of Charlie's and Jim's hard lives and humble beginnings, and we see that their behavior and character won't change, even with all the gold.

Klinger and Hawkeye, in television's highly successful series *M*A*S*H*, often exchange nonsequiturs by focusing on the wrong thing: "Captain, may I be excused from this detail?" asks Klinger, scrubbing the floor outside the operating room. "My nylons are bagging around the knees." Without batting an eye, Hawkeye replies, "Get bigger knees."

Examples

Where does Rudy Ruiz focus on the "wrong thing" to create the humor in the scene below?

> Our regular church organist was always coming down with dyslexia, and had to be replaced with the organist from the local baseball stadium. On her first day, the opening hymn was "The Star-Spangled Banner," during which people became confused as to whether to make the sign of the cross or keep their hand over their heart. After Father Pilfer's sermon, she played the charge rally, to which one man yelled "Amen." Her exit hymn was "Sweet Georgia Brown," over which she sang the words of Ave Maria. It was a big crowd pleaser.

SUGGESTIONS FOR WRITING

Write a scene where you had to hide something you shouldn't have had in your pocket. Try to include a switch to a different object from the main object in question.

Concreteness

Like all good writing, good humorous writing is concrete. If your writing isn't as funny as you want it to be, write more concretely. What do we mean by that, you ask?

A *concrete detail* is a word that names a tangible object, one that we experience with our senses—sight, sound, taste, touch, smell. It describes an object so specifically that we can arrive at a consensus about its meaning almost immediately upon hearing the word. *Abstract words* are those that designate qualities or ideas; *general words* are those that designate classes or categories to which objects belong; *concrete words* refer to sensory images.

Let's say I ask each of twenty students in my writing class to bring in something "sweet" the next day. Since "sweet" is an abstract word, the communication between us isn't very precise , and one student would bring in a cake, another a valentine card, another his puppy, and so forth. If I then asked each one to bring in a sweet food, "food" being a general word, our communication would be clearer, and students would bring in a pie, a cake, a stick of sugar cane, prunes, or candy. Our understanding of what I wanted would be less cloudy. If I then said, bring in a candy bar, we would get a pecan nut roll, a chocolate bar, and so forth. Here the communication would be even more precise.

If I then asked each student to bring in a ninety-eight-cent Hershey bar with almonds, I would be speaking in very concrete language and the communication would be extremely precise since each student would arrive with exactly the same object.

Words, thus, can range from abstract to concrete on a continuum, and to get humor, you generally want to be on the right side of the following diagram:

ABSTRACT		GENERAL		CONCRETE
sweetness	sweet food candy	chocolate Hershey bar	98¢ Hershey bar w/almonds
creative work	literary work	book	novel	*Don Quixote*

Concrete details conjure more humor than abstract or general ones because their incongruities clash more directly with normalcy; with abstract or general words, the incongruities disperse and the out-of-focus meaning mellows the humor, creating a weaker effect.

Of course, you don't have to use concrete words all the time to create humor; sometimes the writing calls for abstract or general language, depending on your artistic intention, and besides, if abstract and general words were totally useless, they would quickly disappear from the language. Use them when the context calls for them. For the most part, however, concrete language enlivens your writing, helps us understand the meaning more easily, and creates more dynamic humor. If you have a tendency to write in abstract or general words, never fear. It's easy to revise.

Ways to Get Concrete

Substitute a Concrete Word or Words for an Abstract, General, or Vague One

Look at the italicized words below. How would you make them more concrete to enhance the incongruity?

REVISE?

> As he left the end of the broomstick soaking in a can of gasoline, my dad ran in the house to grab some *food*. It was finally time to kill the bees. . . . My father staggered back into the house carrying his tools. He had a *smile* on his face. He grabbed some more *food* and settled down in front of the TV.

We might smile at the grungy cute dad, but the action could be funnier.

MUCH BETTER?

> As he left the end of the broomstick soaking in a can of gasoline, my dad ran in the house to grab a quick *bologna sandwich and a Yoo-Hoo*. It was finally time to kill the bees. . . . My father staggered back into the house carrying his tools. He had that *"do it yourself and save money"* smile on his face. He grabbed a *frozen Milky Way* and settled down in front of the TV, *just in time to catch the last quarter of the Penn State game.*
>
> CATHERINE CARCHIA PHILLIPS

REVISE?

> Danny's audition left me gnawing at my *nails* and forced me to bravely down a cold, yet refreshing *drink* for lunch to alleviate my *nervousness.*

BETTER?

> Danny's audition left me gnawing at my *ten bleeding nails* and forced me to bravely down a cold, yet refreshing *bottle of Pepto Bismol* for lunch to alleviate *the runs I began to feel drip down my pants.*
>
> STEVE SIMONS

REVISE?

> Mr. Daily was the history teacher. His brows were sometimes average and sometimes not, but they always made a clear point. His brows changed according to *whatever period of history* he was discussing.

BETTER?

> Mr. Daily was the history teacher. His brows were predictable and sometimes adventurous, but they always made a clear point. *Mr. Daily's eyebrows started out black and grew increasingly grayer when he told the class for the fiftieth time about the theories of Darwin and evolution. His brows seemed to get bushier when he talked about Cro Magnum men.* Now they had some serious browage!
>
> JULIE SWITZER CAPLAN

Don't Forget Spiffy Verbs

Nothing spices up a sentence like a spiffy verb. Use the more general "to be" verbs or non-action verbs sparingly: *is, are, was, were, smell, feel, taste, seem, appear, become, look,* and *turn.* Also, don't overdo *has, have, had, do, did, done.* If you can't recognize these immediately, memorize them. It'll pay off in the long run.

There will be times, however, when you'll use "to be" verbs; obviously they exist for good reasons and have purpose in the language. But if, let's say, more than 80 percent of the verbs you're using in every paragraph are "to be" verbs, you're probably squelching the humor, and you'll want to substitute concrete verbs for some of the vague ones. When you do, you'll energize your sentences and the imagery will soar. One caution here: Don't overdo it and use all kinds of fancy verbs that flit over the meaning. When writing becomes excessively concrete, it's described as "fine writing," which means that its fussy style dominates content. Because that's confusing, that's not good.

Which is the funnier writing below?

REVISE?

> Lisa *was* close to John, hoping to somehow meet the boy who *had* firm bulgy biceps and who *was able to put* a ping-pong ball in his mouth and who *had* the skill *to make it appear to move* forward with amazing accuracy and speed. Because of his flamboyant style he *was* always above the rest of the crowd.

BETTER?

> Lisa *edged* closer to John, hoping to somehow meet the boy with the firm bulgy biceps who could *stuff* a ping-pong ball in his mouth and *pop* it forward with amazing accuracy and skill. His flamboyant style always *projected* him above the rest of the crowd.
>
> TOM LONGO

Add Concrete Words to Abstract, General, or Vague Ones

Sometimes you'll want to keep the abstract or general words in your writing and add concrete words to them. This works especially well when you need the abstract or general words for clarity or transition.

General Word + Details Added to the General Word

> He was *terrific*: he had *wavy brown hair, jet blue eyes and two freckles on either side of his pug nose.*

> When I turned around and saw you sitting there with your ringlets of red hair, light blue sweater, and caramel jacket, I felt *something*. It was a sharp *pain, a lightheadedness*, and a fluid, fuzzy warmth, all converging at my upper intestines. I think it was love, but it could have been *indigestion, since I did have the Quixote quiche for supper that day.*

NEEDS SOMETHING MORE?

> Quite accidentally John Hiss met his dream girl at a *fair.*

BETTER?

> Quite accidentally, John Hiss met his dream girl at the *tenth annual Earl L. Vandermuhl "tug-in-da-mud" fair. A tug-in-da-mud is one of those cultural happenings where two four-wheel drive Leviathans have a tug-o-war in a manmade mud puddle for plastic beer hats and a year's bragging rights.*
>
> TOM LONGO

MORE?

> The lecture continued and class was almost over. We had just sat through one of the *most boring* lectures on the economics of the developing nations of the world, but I got a lot of work done though.

BETTER?

> The lecture continued and class was almost over. We had just sat through one of the most boring lectures on the economics of the developing nations of the world, but I got a lot of work done though. *I did my Spanish, my calculus, planned my parents' twenty-fifth anniversary party which was to occur in about three or four years, and counted all the bricks in the wall, all the tiles of both the floor and ceiling, and all the hairs on my fingers just above the knuckles. There's one hundred and thirty-seven on each hand. It's fascinating how both hands had exactly the same amount.*
>
> KENNETH M. AYOUB

Deliberate Abstraction

Concrete writing easily generates humor, but sometimes you might want to be deliberately abstract to suggest a character's personality or to hint at your theme. Abstract words can be funny if their obvious vagueness sets up humorous incongruity within the text.

Examples

> We gazed at each other's eyes in a passionate moment of *uncharted exploration.*

> Then there's me . . . I did not really stand out among my classmates like Danny and Priscilla. I was pretty much like the rest

of the class: *obnoxious, rowdy, loud, adventurous, and in sixth grade to have fun.*

STEVE SIMONS

And here, along with parallel sentence rhythms and repetition, the writer uses general words to suggest the poignant life of the hero.

Arnold Cheezer was tall, slender, had curly brown hair and baby blue eyes. His only major fault was that his nose was *extremely large*. He also had a *mild skin condition*.

Andrea Swift was Arnold's dream girl. He had spoken to her often, but that was the extent of his relationship with her, although he walked by her house whenever the opportunity presented itself. Andrea had long, blonde hair, sparkling blue eyes, perfect teeth and, in Arnold's opinion, a perfect body. *She did not have a large nose or a skin condition.*

PAUL NELSON

SUGGESTIONS FOR WRITING

Using concrete details, describe any of the following:
She had *a strange way of figuring out* that we did *it*.
I like *variety* to my Friday nights.
Many *different kinds of supermarket carts* obsess me.

Show, Don't Tell

When you're writing stories (comedies), *show* what's happening rather than *tell* it, because showing intensifies concreteness. "Showing" (or "dramatizing") a scene means you let us see and hear the characters in action; "telling" a scene means you just summarize the characters' actions. When you show a scene, you emphasize it, and thus the reader sees it as important because you've lengthened its space. Though you won't do this for every scene you create (making everything equal deemphasizes everything), you should usually expand your most important moments.

Sometimes you'll just tell a scene. Telling a scene is appropriate for transition paragraphs where you want to move through a point in time quickly to arrive at another more important point. You might also tell a scene to convey essential information quickly, and some essays, short stories, or joke monologues are structured aesthetically in ways that require no dramatization. As the writer, you have to decide the intention of a scene and its appropriate shape or length, and whether or not it should be shown or told.

Generally, though, you'll want to show (dramatize) your most important scenes, especially those that draw on emotions, because the audience needs time to experience what you hope they'll feel. If you plan to show a scene by expanding it, be careful that you just don't add scenes on. Showing a scene isn't creating a chain of rubber bands; showing a scene is the s-t-r-e-t-c-h-i-n-g of a single rubber band so we see it expanded to its fullest.

To show a scene, stuff it with any combination of the following:
- description (physical, place, etc.)
- background information
- dialogue
- thoughts (your character's or your narrator's)
- action description

Look at the following examples. What does the "show" scene offer us that the "tell" scene doesn't? What effect do they have on your emotions as you read them? How do they reveal character?

Tell

> The Terry Town High gymnasium was set for the dance. As they entered the gym, a couple of students gossiped about Chuck Holt, the school basketball hero.

Show

> Terry Town High Senior Gymnasium was not without its share of drama. There was not a local in a thirty-mile radius who would forget the Class C title game against Vicksburg where Chuck Holt had played through a broken wrist to bring home the State Championship. So inspiring was his performance that they had kept the cast, still embalmed with the air of that magical night back in 1974, and enshrined it in the lobby trophy case, right beneath a post-game picture of Holt with his hand dunked in ice, Afro reaching towards the sky. Sometimes kids would stop by to look at it, not to read the story of that famed evening etched in low class pewter or to memorize the statistics that had

put all other school athletes since then to shame, but to marvel at how one man could support so much hair.

"Sure it's real," Judy said. "Just look at where root meets the scalp. You don't get that kind of authenticity with rugs—not even the sew-in kind."

"I'm sorry but that's like forty cubic ounces of protein up there. If that shit's real, I'd hate to see the man's shower drain." Samantha was a bit of a closet conspiracist. She was still sure that the Righteous Brothers were black.

"Come on, you think he'd put that thing on to play basketball? It'd be like wearing a dead mammal." Judy's eyes cut sharp logical paths to Sam's. "You know you're wrong and anyway, I'm sick of standing out here when there's a dance going on." She grabbed the other girl's arm, ending the conversation, and wheeled them both into the gymnasium.

Greg Tebbano

Tell

When Uncle Perk had his leg amputated, the church said we had to bury it.

Show

But how to move Uncle Perk around wasn't the problem. The big thing we had to decide was the funeral. Father O'Donovan came down and said the leg had to have regular burial, with prayers and a coffin. That was the Church's law and not only for the Irish. (We asked that to make sure he wasn't giving us Slovaks just some old Irish rule.) Anyway, it seems that us Catholics have to have respect for all parts of the body, whether they're still a part of you or not. To have respect for the spirit that belongs to the whole spirit, Father O'Donovan said. And that would mean burying any part of you that died.

So we all went to see Uncle Perk in the hospital to tell him about what Father O'Donovan said. At first the whole family, all eight of us, went in together, and it was hard to know what to do with everybody just saying hello and nothing else. We just looked at him for a while, then the nurse brought his teeth, maybe to make him feel better, but he said no, he didn't want them, he never wore them at home. He said his gums were sharp enough to tear at meat and he never used his teeth from the first, so that when he didn't have them in, it wasn't too bad since his face didn't sink inward.

He was quiet for a while, with all of us just standing around, but then when we told him what Father O'Donovan said, that was the first time Uncle Perk really showed us to be himself again. He was yelling so hard Jerry heard him all the way down by the hospital souvenir shop.

"I ain't goin' to my own leg's funeral."

"Perk," my Aunt Kate said, "you can't look at it that way. You have to look at it like Father O'Donovan. You have to have respect." She pulled at the sheets Uncle Perk kept wrinkling. "You just can't always do what you want."

The rest of us stood around the bed quiet. Uncle Perk was mad. He kept bending his bad knee up in bed, which he wasn't supposed to do because it cut off the circulation.

"When Lizzy Zablonski had her goiter taken off," he yelled, "they didn't bury it."

My aunt was mad, too.

"Perk," she said, "that goiter was small. A leg is big. It goes by size."

After that, the nurse made us all get out because we were making too much racket for the other patients and we could only come back one at a time.

MARY ANN RISHEL

5

One Month Later: Still Nobody Laughed. What Then?

So what happens when you've written your heart out, revised ad infinitum, measured and perfected your timing—and no one laughed? OH LORD, OH LORD, SAY IT ISN'T SO. Yes, it's true. Failure. Awful-deep-down-in-the-gut-you-know-it's-true-oh-my-god failure. Now what?

Well, it happens. If you want to write humor, you have to take risks. And some experiments fail. That's just the way it is.

"But my heart aches," you say.

Well, OK, let yourself droop for a day or two, but if you're serious about writing humor, you'll turn on that computer (or get out that pencil and paper if you're not technologically inclined) and try again.

Now you could throw away that awful first draft and begin anew, but sometimes starting over without analyzing that previous effort could entrench bad habits, since you might just repeat the same mistakes. So if you can bear it, look at your first attempt to see what happened. If no one laughed, it could be the audience lacked a sense of humor, or it could be (I'm sorry to say it—I know this is hard to take) that your writing wasn't really funny.

"What can go wrong?" you ask.

Well, a couple of things. And the good news is that you can revise.

Let's compare the different versions below. (The not-so-good versions, as is true throughout this book, are exclusively my invention; the authors get the credit for the good ones.)

Not Concrete Enough—Writing Is Too Vague

We discussed concreteness in the previous chapter, but it's important enough to bear repeating. *Words that aren't (playfully) concrete often generate a text that's not humorous, and this is the most common reason why writing isn't funny.* Vague words distance us from whatever humorous (incongruous) impact you're trying to set up because they don't excite the senses and they don't kick above the normal enough to be perceived as humor. Solution? Simple. Slog through your text inch by inch, locate abstract or general words, and change them to more concrete ones.

LESS CONCRETE AND NOT SO GOOD

> And there's my boyfriend in nothing but his shorts, standing in the den, watching a football game and drinking a cold drink.

Because the boyfriend's in his shorts and it's not the usual way we dress in front of people, we might laugh, but we could tap more vivaciousness from this line. Which words would you strengthen?

MORE CONCRETE AND BETTER?

> And there's my boyfriend, wearing nothing but *Bon Ton boxer shorts and one Nike sneaker, standing in the den with one eye on the Steelers game and one eye on his beer.*

Can you see how the language takes a humorous direction by topping the images with tongue-in-cheek concretes?

LESS CONCRETE AND NOT SO GOOD

> Lights came up in different colors as the music announced their entrance. The decorations in the gym were staged in winter white and as the music began, everyone started dancing, only slightly resembling their daytime selves. They weren't really suited for dancing, Judy noticed.

Is there any tang to the imagery? Do you feel an urge to push the humor deeper? Review how Gregory Tebbano's use of concretes spikes the wit.

BETTER?

> Lights came up *pulsing primary colors* all around them as the opening *trumpets to "Superstition"* announced their entrance. *Cotton ball snow* and *15 watt stars paraded* around the edges of a *fake indoor winter. Black and white mannequins of Terrytown* students were *shuffling their limbs* in groups or pairs, only slightly resembling their *geeky lunch-box-carrying originals.* Their *plastic appendages* weren't particularly well inclined for such movement, Judy noticed. Well, dances did that to you.
>
> GREGORY TEBBANO

Not Exaggerated Enough—Writing Is Too Real

Sometimes your words will be concrete, but they won't be exaggerated (incongruous) enough to get a laugh. Since unexaggerated words rarely clash with normalcy (because everything is normal), they aren't humorous. To rework this, study the words in your writing, including the concrete ones, to uncover places you might "exaggerate.

EXAGGERATED ENOUGH?

> As Marcy and I moved to the party, the neon light read: "Bubbles and Mikey's Deli and Restaurant." The DJ, blasting Madonna at *fifty watts*, pulsed trebles and bass through the soles of our feet as we entered the Deli's double doors. . . . My hair was so sweaty *it dribbled rivulets along my cheeks.*

Not bad writing since many of the words here are concrete: *Marcy, neon light, Bubbles and Mikey's Deli and Restaurant, DJ, Madonna, fifty watts, pulsed trebles and base, Deli's double doors dribbled rivulets.* But the description would kick a little more if it were exaggerated. The last image, especially, needs to demonstrate his predicament more than it does.

BETTER?

> As Marcy and I shuffled closer to the party, the neon light display *flashed red and orange*: "Bubbles and Mikey's Deli and Restaurant." The DJ blasted Madonna at *seven hundred watts*, which *exploded* trebles and bass throughout *our neuronic cranial circuitry*, and after three hours my hair became so sweaty it dribbled rivulets down my cheeks, *not unlike primordial erosions, both glacial and pre-glacial, of the Grand Canyon* or the *Snake River.*

In this version, we spiced up the middle and tightened the wit of the last image, ending it with an exaggerated description of the narrator's anxiety and exhaustion. Do you agree that it's better?

EXAGGERATED ENOUGH?

> Walter was an older man in his late sixties. His complexion was a delicious color of cream, *with purple lines where veins ran through the skin.* His *swollen eyes* were set deep in the back of his head, and for all you *fantasy fans*, he resembled a *woodland creature.* For all you non-fans, trust me, the dude was beautiful.

Some of you might give thumbs up to "woodland creature" and the last line. But what else could you do with "purple lines where veins ran through the skin"? Could you add an image that would exaggerate "purple"? Can you get more clever than "swollen"?

CONCRETE AND EXAGGERATED

> Walter was an older man in his late sixties, *pushing his late nineties.* His complexion was the delicious color of cream, *mottled with purple spots, sort of like an old raw sausage.* His *froggy* eyes were set deep in the back of his head, and for all you *J. R. Tolkien* fans, he resembled *the creature, Gollum.* For all you non-fans, trust me, the dude was beautiful.
>
> CHRISTINE DECKER

Concrete and Exaggerated, But Not Unusual Enough—Too Flat; Too Non-original; Too Dull

When a slapstick comedian struggles to climb onto a horse, we pretty much guess that he'll fall off the other side. When he does, the action is so clichéd that we yawn rather than laugh. In theory, the idea is funny, especially if the comedian executes balletic motions, but in practice it's so overdone we aren't surprised. If the horse could jack up the comedian's suitcase with its tail as the comedian flips onto its back, then that might be more interesting to us just because it varies an old routine. Bad slapstick comedians are most guilty of this where the routines have no direction or meaning beyond the physical, but humor writers, too, can get caught up in this artistic quagmire if their thinking fuzzes.

What happens when your writing is both *concrete* and *exaggerated,* and people still don't laugh?

Writing can be both concrete and exaggerated, but if it isn't *unusual* or *original* enough to create a surprise incongruity, the sensory value in each image equals the previous one, the spark implodes, and we don't laugh. As in an overused slapstick routine, the majority of readers will accurately guess the next image and, therefore, no one is tossed off balance, as they should be. What we get is what we expect to get. Writing that's not unusual enough or not original enough lacks pizzazz. Nothing sparkles; nothing delights; nothing gives new insight, color, or depth. Writing that isn't very original is said to be *clichéd* because the writer employs overused expressions with long-lost emotional impact, resulting in dull, flat writing. Not good.

CONCRETE

How effective are the concrete words? The main character of the story is an eleven-year-old boy who is forced to play Cinderella's wicked stepsister in his sixth-grade school play.

> The week of dress rehearsal was miserable. My *dress* was too big. It kept falling down, *leaving me embarrassed*. I had *runs in my nylons*.

Dress rehearsal, dress, and *runs in my nylons* stir up images but the sentence hardly bubbles.

CONCRETE AND EXAGGERATED

If you agree that this version is better than the previous one, why?

> The week of dress rehearsal was miserable. My *dress seemed to be made for twins*. It kept falling down, leaving me standing embarrassed at center stage in my *oversized jockey shorts*. The runs in my nylons raced *down my legs toward my shivering toes cramped inside the size seven ballet shoes*.

A *dress seemed to be made for twins* extends an irony, and it's followed by *oversized jockey shorts*, which pictures his embarrassment. The last line spills forth some energy, with the nylons racing toward shivering toes. But the toes are cramped inside size seven ballet shoes, a concrete detail but obvious, because we normally wear shoes on our feet. As is, the laugh centers on the guy who yearns to impress a girl with his "maleness" but who's forced to wear women's ballet shoes in front of his classmates. Not bad, but it could be better.

CONCRETE, EXAGGERATED, AND UNUSUAL—BEST?

> The week of dress rehearsal was miserable. *My dress seemed to be made for twins*. It kept falling down, leaving me standing *dumbfounded* at center stage in my *Fruit of the Looms*. The runs in my nylons raced down my legs toward the grand surprise, foot odor.
>
> STEVE SIMONS

True, foot odor and nylons are based on the same image but now his embarrassment has intensified with incongruous tension, and that makes it funnier. The narrative continues.

CONCRETE

I didn't have breasts yet. They would suddenly develop the night of the show. I insisted on *big breasts,* but my teacher said that sixth graders should have *smaller ball-like ones.* Mine would be *small.*

CONCRETE AND EXAGGERATED

I didn't have breasts yet. They would suddenly develop the night of the show. I insisted on *big balloons,* but *Mrs. Glick* told me sixth graders *either were flat or semi-rigid.* My little ones would consist of *two little balls sticking out at right angles from my chest.*

CONCRETE, EXAGGERATED, AND UNUSUAL—BEST?

I didn't have breasts yet. They would suddenly develop the night of the show. I insisted on *big bazooms,* but *Mrs. Glick* told me sixth graders *either were flat or semi-rigid.* My little ones would consist of *cold, wet dish towels, so they'd keep me firm and stimulated.*

STEVE SIMONS

CONCRETE

John caught *Lisa's* eye as he tried to toss a *golf ball* into a *fishbowl* at a local *restaurant.* There seems to be a *ritual* in my *town* where *boys swallow goldfish* and take the consequences.

CONCRETE AND EXAGGERATED

John caught *Lisa's* eye as he *gallantly attempted to toss a golf ball* into a *fishbowl* at the *Fish Fry run by the local Italian restaurant.* There seems to be an *adolescent ritual,* in *Jagger Heights,* where *boys swallow goldfish whole to see what they do to their digestive system.* Rumors of angry goldfish have always managed to dissuade children from playing near septic tanks.

CONCRETE, EXAGGERATED, AND ORIGINAL

John caught *Lisa's* eye as he *gallantly attempted to toss a ping-pong ball* into a *goldfish bowl* at the *Pong-O-Fest, run by a local full service Italian restaurant.* There seems to be an *adolescent ritual in Jagger Heights where boys swallow goldfish whole and still flopping, preferably head first, and count the days until they see the fish again.* Rumors of giant man-eating goldfish have always managed to dissuade children from playing near septic tanks.

TOM LONGO

Not Intellectually Challenging Enough—Too Patronizing

Humor that isn't intellectually challenging enough bores an audience, and that might be a reason why writing isn't funny. If your writing treats the audience like children when they expect to be treated as adults, they're miffed rather than amused. This occurs when the writer announces then interprets the obvious, spelling out everything far beyond what's necessary to understand the point. Since the writer doesn't have enough awareness of the audience, sometimes this problem is hard to spot; if you aren't sure about your own work, ask a friend to check it, but take this suggestion cautiously. Some major writers—Cervantes comes to mind—use extensive explication as a literary device for a character's thoughts, and when explication is intellectually complex, it's perfectly fine to expand it. This is different from what we're talking about here. Here we're talking about the overbearing stuff.

OVER-EXPLAINED?

What's being repeated in this example?

> Death is a complex thing. Everyone spends a lot of energy thinking about it because it's so complex. Except for people thinking about Elvis's death. Thinking about his death doesn't cause anyone to lose energy. Even Elvis doesn't lose any energy.

Can you see that the sentences don't expand the substance? How does this writer achieve an ironic sophistication in the passage below?

> Death is good once in a while, but it takes a lot of energy. Except for Elvis. He's been dying and resurrecting for decades now and it hasn't done anything for his weight problem.
>
> LISEL GORELL

What is Lisel Gorell satirizing about society's views of Elvis? Can you see how she climbs from one ironic tone to another? In a passage both philosophical and illogical, she teases Elvis fans who desperately want to resurrect him, and she achieves this by respecting the audience's intelligence.

OVER-EXPLAINED?

> The ticket master floated about the passenger cab like Saint Peter, black gloves tearing tickets as if performing benediction. *He implied that he intended to give a blessing.* As serrated edges came apart, validation lit up the faces of those who had been received and they clung to their stubs like they were birth receipts. *There was a sense of going to heaven, which would be a rebirth.* An attendant trailed him, pasting little yellow tags on overhead compartments with each passenger's destination until the aisle read like a long litany *of prayers* of international city abbreviations spelling out America.

Does the extended metaphor need to be explained to the audience? Might the over-explanation weaken the wit?

BETTER?

> The ticket master floated about the passenger cab like Saint Peter, black gloves tearing tickets as if performing benediction. As serrated edges came apart, validation lit up the faces of those who had been received and they clung to their stubs like they were birth receipts. An attendant trailed him, pasting little yellow tags on overhead compartments with each passenger's destination until the aisle read like a long litany of international city abbreviations spelling out America.
>
> GREGORY TEBBANO

Not Fast Enough—Too Boring

When writing chugs along too slowly, its pacing skews. This often occurs in the introduction. (Royalty aside, most of us don't tolerate a lot of fanfare.) Slow writing also ensnares petty details, creating anti-narrative. If anything moves in this writing, it slogs along, burdened by the weight of language, a dead action that curdles at the surface like scum on a cauldron. Instead of laughing, most of us fall asleep. The best way to locate slow writing is to read your work aloud. Once you spot the problem, trim the excess, reread it to sound it out again, then subtract accordingly. Remember that there are no right or wrong answers to good pacing (it's like a song, you have to experience it), and in the examples below you might choose a different design that would work equally well for your purpose. But these passages will give you a sense of what happens when rhythms are too slow.

T-o-o-o Slow

Where does the action of this passage really start?

> He beckoned me inside and I followed. I walked slowly through the door, observing that the door knocker was a lion with an opened jaw, then closed the door behind me. It creaked and I had to push it shut three times before the latch took hold. The door knob needed some oil. I entered the hallway that had no furniture except a long tattered rug. He beckoned me into the living room. His house was a mess. Everything was in chaos. From the chairs to the floor, all was covered in all kinds of junk. I couldn't even find a place to sit down. Gross piles of potting soil and inflatable Ed McMahon dolls littered everywhere with a weed whacker or two thrown in for good measure.

Although you might think the main action deserved a slow lead-in and you might select a compromise version, consider this writer's fast-paced approach, which sets the satiric jabs in the last sentence.

> He beckoned me inside and I followed. His house was a mess: gross piles of potting soil and inflatable Ed McMahon dolls littered the room along with a weed whacker or two thrown in for good measure. Sweepstakes envelopes and Victoria's Secret catalogues were everywhere. I guess he got on those goddamn mailing lists too.
>
> Dave Vergano

Too Slow?

Is the long introduction in this passage necessary?

> First there was fire. Then came the wheel. Yes, history has counted many different kinds of inventions, some discovered by accident and some found after years of hard work; and while some of them have proved useful, some of them have gone by the wayside as people no longer found them of any use. Somewhere between the advent of the wheel and "Spam Lite" came the elastic strap on underwear. We all take this milestone for granted these days, but think how many tragicomedies Shakespeare could have created about the elastic underwear band and love that was not meant to be.

FASTER

> First there was fire. Then came the wheel. And somewhere between the advent of the wheel and "Spam Lite" came the elastic strap on underwear. We all take this milestone for granted these days, but think how many tragicomedies Shakespeare could have created about the elastic underwear band and love that was not meant to be. I can (almost) see a packed festival crowd taking in a production of *The Taming of the Loom.*
> MIKE SIMONOFF

Not Emphasized Enough—Too Hidden

And then there's the kid who cowers under a baseball cap because he's shy, the same kid who mumbles hello under his breath when he passes someone in the hall, or worse yet, chews triple-sized wads of bubble gum so he never has to speak. Yet underneath that bashful behavior simmers a bravery waiting to explode.

Sometimes humor writers write the same way. They smother the best parts of their work with too much surrounding information. The punch lines, the toppers, and the biggest surprises are so buried that the audience has to dig for them. Padded writing, through sluggish pacing and muddled rhythms, distracts from the sharpest part of the joke and disperses its intensity.

This problem is easily solved: shuffle the deck of words and phrases, and place the best details in more prominent spots: beginning and end of phrases, sentences, paragraphs, or in scenes of dramatic intensity. This focuses the pacing, which guides the audience to the details you want emphasized. No, I'm not suggesting these details appear only at the ends of sentences or paragraphs. If you do that, then your structure will be too patterned, and it'll read like a list of items. Vary their placement, but scatter clues so we can find them. Readers won't jump for joy if they're standing on a gold mine but don't know it.

If shuffling phrases won't help, shave off some humdrum details to highlight the important words.

JOKES HIDDEN?

> The principal didn't want us to know he wore a hairpiece so when it began sliding down on his face he tried to push it back hoping we wouldn't notice what was happening. He kept trying to push it back up and that was really funny. Sometimes he wiggled his nose and sometimes he nudged his eyebrows upward

slowly, moving his eyes in a way he hoped we wouldn't notice, trying to stem the tide. We were really laughing and trying to hold it in. Sometimes he moved his eyebrows.

BETTER?

The principal felt his hairpiece slide forward a tiny bit as he smiled; he nudged his eyebrows upward slowly, trying to stem the tide.

DAVE VERGANO

JOKES HIDDEN?

His name was Clade, and he didn't like people who made fun of his face which became a face on a drawing his father had once commissioned for a hot tub party, which was really strange since the face in the painting didn't have features.

BETTER?

His name was Clade, and he didn't like people who made fun of his face. This was because he didn't really have a face, just the remnants of a drawing his father had once commissioned for the opening of the family's hot tub.

DAVE VERGANO

JOKES HIDDEN?

I believe that society has made a serious *faux pas* by overlooking the plight and purpose of the high standing brow line as depicted by the humor of Groucho Marx or the powerfully deceitful and slimy Richard Nixon of Watergate fame. The brow line is as much a part of facial hair story as the mustache, earlobe hair, and long, lovely luxurious eyelashes. Think of the famous brows you know. Can you conceive of life without them?

BETTER?

I believe that society has made a serious faux pas by overlooking the plight and purpose of the high standing brow line. It is as much a part of facial hair story as the mustache, earlobe hair, and long lovely luxurious eyelashes. Can you conceive of life without them? Think of the famous brows you know: Would Groucho Marx be as humorous without his? Or would Richard Nixon be as powerfully deceitful and slimy without that Watergate brow?

JULIE SWITZER CAPLAN

Not Slow Enough—Too Invisible

Sometimes writing won't be perceived as funny if it's too fast. When writing races from one point to the next, not enough time transpires for us to grasp the meaning. With this writing, our minds haven't had time to register the information so that our emotions can react. Since each molecule of humor must pass through a series of steps for us to laugh, when any step is missing, the humor fizzles.

To get in touch with overall rhythms, read your work aloud, tuning in to its rhythmic flow. Don't cheat and read it under your breath. You have to read it aloud. That way you'll catch its speed. Which of the two versions do you prefer? Why?

TOO FAST?

> So now it's easy to imagine many things. In your hand the pebble looks like a miniature Earth, but you don't feel quite like God. This could be what God would see on the merest literal and physical level when He wakes up in the morning before having His coffee.

BETTER?

> So now it's easy to imagine many things. In your hand the pebble looks like a miniature Earth, but you don't feel quite like God because of the lousy sex you had that morning. Still there is a certain sense of possibility that this could be sort-of-kind-of-a-little-bit-like what God would see on the merest literal and physical level when He wakes up in the morning before having His coffee. You decide God's coffee machine in all probability makes many more cups than one at a time, if He feels like it. Of course the truth of the matter is sometimes one cup is enough even for God.

Though you might prefer the faster version, can you sense that the easier pace magnifies the jokes?

Too Excessive—Too Silly—Too Fussy— Too Effusive—Bubblegum Writing

Sometimes writers struggle so hard to be funny, they become effusive, and when a work strains the humor, the audience feels embarrassed for the writer instead of laughing at the jokes. Excessive humor confuses us and juggles itself into the plain silly.

Don't let yourself get carried away by pushing a point too far that is, becoming too incongruous, or you might lose your audience.

EXCESSIVE OR NOT?

> Suzie Sandra Airhead, daughter of Aretha and Arthur Airhead and Suzie (Swizzle) Whiskeyfire, of 69 Cherry Cove, Dripping Diamonds Beach, Long Island, and Rich Man's Bluff, Miami, Florida and Reginald von Harvardsniff, III, son of Reginald and Muffy von Harvardsniff of Palatial Palace, Beverly Hills and Giomono's Palace, Las Vegas, were united in marriage on January 3, Saturday, at seven-thirty-nine past the hour of seven in the evening by Rev. Zizzi Moneybags at the Church of the Holy Dollar and Emerald Cross, in downtown Las Vegas.

A play on names made drop 'em dead humor in the fifties, a naive decade for social satire, but some readers now would find this too simplistic, like the obvious implications in the word play of *Airhead, Whiskeyfire, Cherry Cove, Dripping Diamonds Beach, Harvardsniff,* and *Giomono's Palace, Las Vegas.* For many people, the obvious satire of puffed-up social behavior so contorts meaning that it erases the intellectual base. We're not saying you shouldn't ever write this way, and you might want to do it for some zany effect, but be aware of its limitations. For this to work at all, its context would have to be extreme, like the humor of Monty Python. Sid Caesar, Lucille Ball, Carol Burnett, and Vicki Lawrence have also created routines on this humor, as did the television show *Hee Haw.*

As we'll discover throughout this book, not everyone agrees on what is humorous, so one way to understand an audience's reaction is to examine the meaning it generates. Whatever you decide about the weaknesses in your first drafts, however, don't let that knowledge intimidate you. Don't be afraid to fail. You can always throw that awful stuff away, and at least you've written something. And chances are that your work was much better than you thought.

In any case, shy or daring, grab that computer or pen and try again.

Comedy

How Come, When Our Heart Breaks, That's Comedy?

Like the word *humor,* the word *comedy* refers to anything amusing. *Clowning, jesting, joking, witticisms, slapstick,* and so forth, are frequently described as *comic,* and the words *humor* and *comedy* often interchange. We reviewed the reasons for the lackadaisical attitude toward a precise usage of "humor" earlier; similar reasons for overlapping meanings occur for the word "comedy," and thus the confusion for writers.

To begin our definition, we return to the major source for the most common meaning of "comedy," its home base so to speak: drama. From ancient Greeks to the present, the play encompasses comedy's most customary form, and a glance at its literary history and its variants might help you see why writers for centuries so often summoned it as their artistic voice—and why comedy usually aches from a broken heart.

Cartoon 1. PEANUTS, reprinted by permission of United Feature Syndicate, Inc.

History of Comedy

Antiquity

Western comedy derives from ancient Greek wine festivals that celebrated nature, harvest, and fertility. The Greek word for comedy, *comos,* meant "revel"; singing, dancing, and drunkenness made up these fertility rites, accompanied by obscene joking with jesters sporting enormous leather phalli as part of the fecundity themes. One famous festival honored Dionysus, god of wine, and another commemorated Demeter, goddess of grain. The Greek fertility rites and the accompanying sexual joking formed centuries of precedent for romance and sex as the traditional themes of comedy. Thus the broken heart.

Ancient Greek comedic plays date after the first performances of tragedies, but they both came from the same Dionysian traditions. Since the Greeks, especially Aristotle, believed that laughter existed as a social corrective, the comic plays of the time were mainly satires of well-placed and rich Athenians. Aristophanes (c. 448–c. 380 B.C.) is the renowned comic playwright of this period, and one of his best-known plays, *Lysistrata* (411 B.C.), celebrates women's attempts to end the Peloponnesian War by withholding sex until the men cease fighting.

The *Romans* continued the themes of Greek comedy, especially the troubles of youthful love, and the best-known writers of ancient Rome who extend these ideas are Plautus (c. 254–184 B.C.) and Terence (190–159 B.C.). Plautus coined his play *Amphitryon* a "tragicomedy" because it contains characters from both the upper and lower classes, even though ancient classical writers believed that comedy and tragedy should be separate.

Middle Ages

During the Middle Ages the Catholic Church suppressed the theater, but people's appetite for comic drama was fed by skits of circuit actors who performed on impromptu stages in front of wagons at local market squares. The Church did permit, however, comic interludes within the serious religious plays of the time. These interludes provided welcome relief from the long performances of the serious dramas, which often lasted seven or more festival days, and the Church allowed for satiric barbs at the clergy, a common theme of the interludes. The plots on occasion were obscene, especially those of the cuckolded husband duped by the devious lover. In addition to the theater context, a comedy during this time also referred to a poem with a sad beginning and happy end, although its treatment wasn't necessarily humorous. Dante's *Divine Comedy* falls into this category.

Seventeenth Century

By the early seventeenth century, Shakespeare included scenes of comedy and tragedy in his serious plays, such as the gravedigger scene in *Hamlet,* where the gravedigger intensifies Hamlet's pain by his punning banter. In *Henry IV* parts I and II, the boastful Falstaff, considered by many to be Shakespeare's most brilliant comic character, nettles the emerging nobility of Prince Hal by tempting the moral code Hal must eventually claim as king. As for Shakespeare's comedies, these extend from romance to dark fantasies. In the romances, characters disguise themselves as the opposite sex, and the action unfolds on the subsequent confusion over sexual identities and sexual attractions (magnificently foreshadowing the sexual dilemmas in plays of today); the dark fantasies involve encounters with strong forces of nature.

At the same time in Spain emerged perhaps the most brilliant comic novel to date: Miguel de Cervantes' *Don Quixote* (1605). The knight Don Quixote searches for windmills in the midst of reality and illusion, although the cornucopia of themes in this great work can hardly be summarized in one sentence.

Ben Jonson (*Volpone*) in England and Molière (*Tartuffe; Le Misanthrope*) in France also represent the finest writers in this period.

Eighteenth Century

Comedy of manners typified the comedy of the early eighteenth century. Characterized by witty, cynical repartee over illicit love, upper-class couples vied for the upper hand in amoral relationships. William Congreve (*The Way of the World*) and Richard Sheridan (*The School for Scandal*) are two outstanding playwrights of this period. This century also saw the emergence of the English comic novel, usually parodies of other novels or the misadventures of a loveable rogue, like Henry Fielding's *Joseph Andrews*, and although few major poems can be described as comedies, Alexander Pope's *The Rape of the Lock* shines as an excellent exception.

Nineteenth Century

In the nineteenth century, sentimental comedy or melodrama contained characters and plots of emotional extremes, adding Gothic components like blood and violence and beastly villains in black capes and tall hats. Written primarily to tug at our heartstrings, these stories witnessed goodness triumphing over evil after overcoming incredible odds, and virtue and purity exemplified models to live by. Coincidences drove the sensational plots, and endings were artificial or improbable, with illness or death lingering for the maximum amount of sobbing. Some melodramas meant to be serious are so contrived that we now laugh at them instead of cry. Besides theatrical melodrama, many old silent films savored static patterns, such as those where the heartless villain throws a poor, pathetic, starving family into the freezing cold. Chaplin occasionally enjoyed playing up to these heightened emotions.

For the lower classes who didn't have access to literature, vaudeville theaters provided the broad humor of rough-and-tumble buffoonery. A person rudely pushing his way through a crowd would be typical, and in the end he would receive comic justice by being pushed back to where he began. From the eighteenth century onward, other genres competed with theater for the nomenclature of "comedy" quite successfully in both popularity and literary quality. In the nineteenth century we add the novels of Jane Austen (*Pride and Prejudice*) and, of course, those of Mark Twain, who wrote the quintessential American novel, *Huckleberry Finn*.

In the latter part of the nineteenth century, musical comedy drew thousands of fans each year to white barns throughout the country for stage plays, and then to Broadway. Gilbert and Sullivan's comic operettas represent some of the best.

Twentieth and Twenty-First Centuries

The twentieth century continued the shift in the meaning of "comedy" away from its exclusive identification with the stage, and as we see in our present century, the definition now extends to films and television productions as well, and it is probably best known by the public in that popular reference. So many film and television comedies have been produced that it's possible to mention only a few: the silent films of Chaplin and Keaton; the comedies of Preston Sturges, Mel Brooks, and Woody Allen; and in television, *M*A*S*H*, *All in the Family*, *The Bill Cosby Show*, and *The Mary Tyler Moore Show*.

The twentieth century also produced many comedic (or tragicomic) short stories, such as those written by Frank O'Connor and Flannery O'Connor, and novels employing broad satire like Joseph Heller's *Catch-22* or sophisticated satire like Alison Lurie's *Foreign Affairs*.

Because the public has always believed that comedy belongs to them, audiences use the name loosely for anything that makes them laugh. The meaning of comedy therefore fluctuates. It's classified by its literary form (comic poetry, comic plays, comic monologues); subject matter or style (comedy of manners, romantic comedies, situational comedies, comedy of humours, comedy of ideas); or author's attitude toward the subject (satiric comedy, genial comedy, bittersweet comedy). When referring to a literary genre like a novel, poem, or story, however, we still usually say "comic novel" or "comic poem" rather than just the word "comedy." If you call these other genres "comedies," you may be understood to mean "drama."

High and Low Comedy

Another classification of comedy is its division into *high and low comedy*. *High comedy*, coined by George Meredith in *The Idea of Comedy* (1877), is witty and intellectual. See any play in Restoration Comedy or Katharine Hepburn in the 1930s film *The Philadelphia Story*.

Low comedy is physical instead of intellectual: it's the pie in the face, the sliding on a banana peel, the car chase, the drunken stagger, the fight. Broadly done, we admire it as ballet because of the grace and athleticism of the actors. When it appears in writing, as in James Thurber's *The Night the Bed Fell*, we enjoy imagining the entanglement of the physical gyrations. Low comedy appears in literary works as well as vaudeville. See Chaucer's *Canterbury Tales*, Shakespeare's *Henry IV* parts I and II, Cervantes' novel *Don Quixote*, and Isaac Babel's short stories.

Non-Western Comedy

Other cultures see comedy differently from Western writers. In India, a happy ending in Sanskrit plays would be a spiritual balance. In Chinese and Native American creation myths, overcoming an enemy by ruse rather than valor would be seen as serious, but Western literature would attribute this talent to a comic hero.

General Meaning

Finally, in addition to all its specific uses, comedy has come to mean—in a general sense—happiness, joy, a celebration of life, or amusement.

"So why, then," you ask, "does comedy always deal with broken hearts?"

Because pure comedy speaks to a reaffirmation of the human spirit through rebirth, thus its emphasis on romance and sex. It also acknowledges our human limitations and flaws through our yearning for the all-powerful yet elusive love.

That's why comedy both hurts—and triumphs.

"That Was a Good History of Comedy," You Say, "But How Do We Write One?"

Definition

As we noted before, since the word "comedy" in its broadest sense means anything amusing, we use it to describe a joke monologue, a Chaplin pratfall, a waddling puppy, or a hat with a decorative goose. It signifies the verbal pyrotechnics between Katharine Hepburn and Spencer Tracy or a pun in a Monty Python routine, and we spin it with many derivations as in "comedians," "comic actors," "comics," and "comic strips." But the word "comedy" also carries a more specific meaning, and because of this definition's particular value to the writer, in this chapter we'll define it as follows: *A comedy is an amusing narrative.*

The key word here is "narrative." A comedy always tells a story. The narrative isn't limited to any particular genre, as it can assume the shape of a short story, tale, personal essay, public essay, poem, monologue, novella, novel, play, film, or television sitcom. It can be written or oral. For a writer, however, the major distinguishing feature of a comedy is narrative, that is, it tells a story. To tell the story, a comedy has characters and a plot, and the plot usually has a beginning action, several high points or crises, and a closing action.

The most common structure is shown in Figure 6. Besides this linear three-crisis structure, as Gerald Mast points out, comic plots might magnify something absurd, then reduce the action to chaos, like a whole film about a character trying to pick up

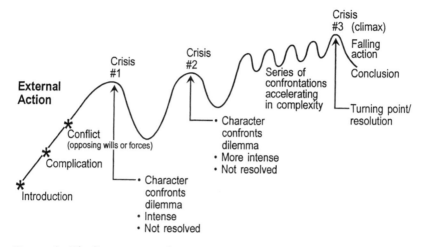

Figure 6a. Plotline—external action

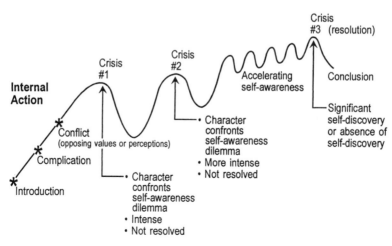

Figure 6b. Plotline—internal action

a quarter from a sidewalk (a reduction to its most absurd) who then pulls up the cement; or a plot might "riff" on miscellaneous bits of action or improvised gags, like the Keystone Kops chases, where the increasingly accelerated pace unifies the skit.[1] In other plots a character confronts an insurmountable task, such as man versus inanimate object, and the dramatic line is pulled by solving a problem. John Morreall notes that some comic plots center on enormous effort yielding little result or little effort achieving an enormous result.[2]

Although a writer can take great liberty with comic plots, a comedy of high artistic value has a unifying theme, and at the end, the main characters learn something about themselves they didn't know at the beginning. A comedy can be told from any point of view—first, second, or third—and it can be true as in a personal essay or imaginative as in fiction. A comedy can appear in other art forms besides "literature." Musical compositions can tell humorous stories, and comedy can form the visual components in a narrative painting, a cartoon, or a comic strip. A traditional "comedy" differs from farce or burlesque in that it contains complex characters, a more structured plot, and less buffoonery.

For a narrative to be a comedy, as opposed to a serious or tragic story, the author's attitude toward the characters or theme has to be genial and the majority of the "clues" must be perceived as nonthreatening.

Writing the Comedy

Let's look at the elements that make up different comedies and the creative process for your own writing. This chapter includes discussion of romantic and bittersweet comedy, nontraditional sex comedy, comedies other than romantic or satiric comedy, multiplot comedy, and tragicomedy. *Hint:* The major element in good comedy is *character.* Don't focus exclusively on plot. Let your character be more than a person who zombies through plot, because a strong character marks the universality of the story. Ask yourself, what's the main character like? Why is he acting this way? Why does she say what she does? Once you establish the character, the plot takes care of itself.

Writing the Romantic Comedy

In the *romantic comedy,* a narrative about *romance* or *sex,* the author *likes, respects, identifies with, or sympathizes with* the main character or characters. In a traditional romantic comedy, the main lovers must overcome many barriers before they find happiness together, and the ending is always a happy reconciliation of all the main characters.

CHARACTER(S)

Choose a character. That character could be you, someone you know, or a fictional person. If you're a novice writer, selecting a fictional "you" as the main character works well because that's the person with whom you're most familiar, and you would, therefore, discover much to say.

Think about all the people you (or your character) have loved. Think about romantic and comic sexual encounters. Think about your best friend, a salesperson, a sewer worker, a business person, a storekeeper, a bartender, a truck driver, your high school teacher, your college professor, or someone you briefly passed on the street. In a romantic comedy, the main character(s) should have romance or sex as the main thing on his/her mind, but the person could be shy, promiscuous, or somewhere in between. Sometimes, other things on his mind, the character is only remotely involved in romance.

PLOT

Put the character in a difficult (but not tragic) situation: an obstacle needs to be overcome; a problem needs to be solved. Remember that the situation or problem should be related to romance or sex and ultimately shouldn't threaten: for example, a first love; a first kiss; a first playful sexual experience; a first playful nonsexual experience (as most of our first sexual experiences turn out to be); falling in love forever; the senior prom; a most embarrassing sexual/romantic moment; a second love (and what the character learned about being in love the first time). Maybe the action is limited, like walking past the *crush* without blushing—or outstaring the competition; maybe it's earthshattering, where worlds will collide if she doesn't solve the mystery of his presence. Traditional conflicts have included misunderstandings, perplexities, struggles to succeed, unbelievable coincidence, mistaken identities, self-deceptions, cross-purposes, freak accidents, misplaced objects, searches for clues, secrets, trivial misfortunes, or embarrassments; others center on a moral conflict.

Imagine the action. How do you want your action to move from beginning to end? If it helps, draw a plotline.

COMPLICATIONS

Provide complications for the character, getting the character as entangled or confused as you want. Speed up the pace and action as you move the plot along, building intensity at the crisis points. Maybe, for example, your character tries to catch a glimpse of the perfect guy by walking by him; when that doesn't work, she climbs a chair. When that fails, she flashes trick mirrors; when that fails, she climbs a roof. Each attempt raises the difficulty and absurdity.

Of course, if you want the opposite, then slow down the action until it stops or fizzles.

Getting the character(s) out of the complication could be arbitrary or clever. A clever resolution speaks to the intelligence of your character's comic mind; an arbitrary ending tosses your character's fate to the winds.

TONE, IMAGERY, ATMOSPHERE, VOICE

Keep these light, happy, friendly, gentle, sympathetic, joyous, or kind. Don't let your voice or tone become bitter, cynical, or sarcastic. Remember, you're writing a traditional romantic comedy.

ENDING

Resolve the action or problem *happily.* Gather everyone together at the end for an explanation and a big party. Let *everyone* be happy! Join all major and minor characters, both heroes and villains, to celebrate, gather, regroup, renew friendships, fulfill themselves sexually, or marry.

This excerpt from Chris Capozzi's "Self-Confidence Man" is an example of light romantic comedy.

Self-Confidence Man

CHRIS CAPOZZI

Sixth grade not only meant that one's feet grew every two days, it also meant that one was more aware of creatures of the opposite sex, namely Stephanie Fitzgerald, who had the best set of tits in the whole sixth grade. Dickie Lyons brushed up against them once as he walked by her and he said they felt soft, like they were filled with grape jelly. Although looking at girls and even brushing up against them was socially acceptable behavior, talking to them was indeed forbidden. . . .

As I approached Cindy, the eyes of every girl near her looked at me with a romantic inquisitiveness, as if they were all wondering if I was really going to go through with it. I stood before her, and she looked up with her big brown eyes and my brain immediately disengaged. My throat became extremely dry, as though I had just swallowed a spoonful of baby powder. I don't know where the words came from, but I was able to barely mutter, "Would you like to dance?" and as I did so I extended my hand. I don't know where I got the idea to extend my hand. I think it was from watching the ballroom scenes in old Abbott and Costello movies, in which the handsome gentleman always extended his hand when asking the young debutante if "she cared to dance." Cindy responded with a soft "yes" and started to get up, but I did not feel at all relieved by her response, because I knew deep down inside that there were still plenty of time to make a complete fool of myself.

I nervously led her to the dance floor and found ample space for us to dance. I then turned and we put our arms around each other, hers around my neck, and mine around her waist, just as Chuckie had instructed me and the rest of the sixth grade boys. I felt a sudden warmth and I loosened and relaxed from my previous stiffness. . . .

Finally, I began to slowly glance her way. Our eyes met and we both smiled sheepishly. As I looked at her, I noticed for the first time that Cindy had freckles. A light brown, they dotted the upper portions of her cheeks. Up until that point I had always thought that freckles were the ugliest thing that God could place on a person's face, aside from a big protruding wart like the one Mrs. Demic, the lunch lady, had on the corner of her mouth, of course. But these freckles were beautiful. They were perfect. They were like the crushed peanuts on top of a hot fudge sundae; sure the sundae would still look good without them, but with them it looked better than good, it looked perfect.

Writing the Bittersweet Comedy

Now, you might be thinking that a traditional romantic comedy is too corny, given your own bad luck with romance. Maybe the too-good-to-be-true philosophy doesn't suit you; after all, like most of us, your heart may have been broken in first grade, then again in junior high, then again as an adult, then again as an even older adult, more times than you want to think about. If so, your instincts might lead you toward a bittersweet view of romance.

No problem. If you want to write bittersweet, just consider the following.

TONE, IMAGERY, ATMOSPHERE, VOICE

Mix some sadness in with the happiness. The general tone might be light, but a touch of melancholy signals that this character isn't so lucky at love. Sprinkle the writing with sadder images; instead of having your character munch on a chocolate candy bar have her bite into some hard candy that breaks her tooth.

ENDING

End with a not-so-happy ending. (But don't conclude with a sour or tragic event.)

In Richard Anderson's "Memories of Mimi," an example of bittersweet comedy, what element in the hero's personality makes this poignant? How does the second thematic element merge with the first? How does imagery work in this essay (pumpkin, nature, sea)?

Memories of Mimi

RICHARD ANDERSON

When I was thirteen I was short, fat and in love with Mimi, who was tall, rich, and, I thought, in love with me. Mimi wanted to be a writer, so the Dickensian colors of my life may have been the spur for her attention. My mother died when I was a year old, and my father shortly remarried a no-nonsense French Roman Catholic, whose charity did not extend to used children. So, for a decade I drifted from one foster home to another until the tide dropped me in St. Patrick's Parochial School and (for me) Orphanage, where I met the redoubtable Mimi.

The first time I saw her was the first day of seventh grade English class. . . . By Christmas time we had become a couple in the eyes of the class and we had yet to exchange a word. We exchanged notes all the time, however, which several times landed us in trouble. The punishment was staying after school and writing 100 times on the blackboard, "I will not write notes to Stringbean in class" (mine), and "I will not write notes to Pumpkin in class" (Mimi's). Mimi's columns marched straight down the blackboard, while I spent a good deal of time erasing my bottom quarter and starting over. Thus she was done and gone long before I was finished, and it seemed our relationship was destined to be literary forever. Especially when some unknown welfare worker, needing more paper work to shuffle, decided to have me placed with a farm family some 30 miles and a few light years away. . . .

Some ten years later, home from college for the Christmas holidays, I was about to leave yet another boring party when Mimi walked in. She was surrounded by admiring men, who looked shipwrecked from the round of parties she had obviously led them on. She saw me across the room, and after a long look of appreciation at the fine, lean specimen the Pumpkin had grown into, she came over. Without a word, we left the party and walked for a long time through the winter streets of a town which was not ours anymore.

Mimi was a Senior Creative Writing major at U.C.L.A. She was working on a novel which would be "a kind of Northern Thomas Wolfe, you know, with the sights and sounds and smells of a small town childhood, and growing up there, and falling in love, and leaving." She seemed politely interested to hear of my impending graduation from St. Olaf's with a degree in Animal Husbandry.

I called a taxicab and we sat for a long time in front of the doctor's house which I had never set foot in. We exchanged addresses, made plans to meet again over spring break, and still delayed saying good-bye. Finally, under the guise of arranging her collar against the blasty wind, I kissed her once, chastely. I never saw her again.

Writing a Comedy about Nontraditional Sexual Experiences

To twist the usual romance, visualize an unconventional approach. Phil Cormier discovers perfect love with his first-grade teacher.

Miss Fisher

PHIL CORMIER

It didn't seem to matter that Miss Fisher was 25 and I was only 6. . . . I was determined to marry my teacher, Miss Fisher.

A short blonde pixie haircut hugged her face, which was highlighted by bright blue eyes and a small, yet sensuous nose. She usually dressed in pretty skirts and fluffy blouses with a color-coordinated bow at the collar. Around her neck she wore a small gold watch on a chain that hung between her "bumps." Unlike the other teachers, Miss Fisher was young and sweet, and there was no flab under her arms to wag back and forth as she showed us how to make 4's on the blackboard. . . .

It wasn't merely coincidence that Miss Fisher held up my drawing of a baby buffalo for the class to admire AND gave me the only pack of crayons containing all 8 colors. She was coming on to me. Yes, these were subtle advances, but she gave herself away when she chose me over Charlie Denny to be her dance partner for Jump-Jim-Joe.

There was something about my chunky 4-foot frame that really turned her on while we danced. I know this because her hands were cold and clammy. I became so excited that I had all I could do to keep from peeing over the room. Apparently my hunched-over body and locked knees gave this away, as Miss Fisher quickly led me out the door and down the hall to the boy's room. I walked in to find 6 wall urinals, the long kind that extend all the way to the floor for the very short boys. I stepped out of the bathroom and, trying my best to be cool, gazed up at Miss Fisher with a blank face and said, "Miss Fisher, I've never peed in those before."

She followed me back in and positioned me in front of the second urinal. "Just pee, Philip," she said in her soft voice.

I tried and tried, but it just wouldn't come out. There we stood, side by side, my right hand holding Miss Fisher's hand while my left hand held my ever-so-shy tinkler. A very long 3 minutes passed with still nothing to show. I realized then that I was in love.

Writing Comedies with Other Conflicts Besides Love and Sex

PLOT

Put the character(s) in a difficult (but not tragic) situation involving something other than romance or sex:

    fighting to get a seat on a subway
    trying to outsmart a two-year-old
    losing your temper at a tailgate party

TONE, VOICE, ATMOSPHERE, IMAGERY

These can be either light or a little sad.

ENDING

The end could be happy, bittersweet, or sad.

In "Kicking It on the Roof," Brett Matthews relates a story of chicanery and youthful violence against animals. The narrator grapples with his own integrity and discomfort with the other boys' antics and, therefore, the action is as much internal as external. How does the narrator deal with his sense of compassion for the birds? How does he try to stay part of the group? What role does the mother play in this? Would you call this a comedy or is that too farfetched a label?

Kicking It on the Roof

BRETT C. MATTHEWS

The roof's hot even through the towel we're sitting on. We're eating Muselix and had lined up three boxes of cereal, several bowls, some Soft Batch cookies, and a full gallon of milk on top of the roof. You see, you can climb on my roof from the deck, so that's why we're always kicking it on the roof. That is, when mom's not home.

We're hanging out eating cereal when my friend Goose decides to get tennis balls to shoot at the birds and the squirrels. My friend Goose loves to shoot things. One time he beaned my sister's friend in the back of the neck with a rotten plum from across the backyard. He was way across the yard, she was running, and when the plum hit her, it splattered all over the back of her neck, and some even dribbled down her shirt. Anyway, he loves to shoot things and my dog Daisy always chews on tennis balls so there's always a ton of them around the bushes for him to shoot.

So Goose gets a bunch of tennis balls, and hands them up to Gary, who keeps them in a pile on the roof. Then Goose climbs up, and him and Gary start to throw them at the birds and the squirrels, who keep eating out of my bird feeder because they don't know that Goose wants to bean them. The bird feeder hangs on a rope from a branch, and the squirrels have to hang upside down to eat. It's the long skinny kind that looks like a plastic tube, and the squirrels have eaten a hole right through the plastic.

Anyway, I start getting nervous because they're both coming real close to hitting the birds and the squirrels. The squirrels seem to be telling the sparrows that Goose is after them, but the sparrows don't want to listen, and they keep coming back for more food. This is when I start getting real nervous. But soon Goose and Gary run out of supplies, because they've both shot so many that all the neighbors' yards are full of my dog Daisy's tennis balls. Well, Goose doesn't want to go into the neighbors' yards to get more tennis balls, because that's too far away, so he starts collecting rocks from my yard to shoot at the birds and the squirrels. I swear he's always wrecking things. One time my mom told him to cut the wood for the fireplace, and he made a mark with the hatchet on every single tree in the backyard. My mom banned him from the house for two weeks.

So Goose gets the rocks, passes them up to Gary, and they try to bean the squirrels and the birds, all over again. Two little sparrows are munching away through the hole, and they seem not to notice Goose and Gary on the roof with the pile of rocks. I tell the birds to watch out, and to get the hell out off the bird feeder, but they just look at me like I'm crazy.

"Goose, I don't think this is a terrific idea," I say, but he just begins winding up.

So I start getting really nervous this time, because the guys are shooting rocks, and the animals are so stupid that they keep coming back for more food. And I know if Goose hits the tiny sparrow's skull with his head aim, he'll knock its head off.

Well, just as the sparrow comes flying up to the bird feeder for more food (sparrows are really dumb), Goose shoots a rock and it flies through the air, whizzes by the fragile skull of the stupid sparrow, and smashes the plastic bird feeder into a thousand little pieces. The sparrow looks at us on the roof like we just interrupted his meal, gives us a few angry chirps, and flies off to the neighbor's bird feeder.

"Geeeez," Goose whistles through his teeth.

Well, now we've really done it. We can't just leave half a dangling bird feeder for those stupid sparrows, so we have to come up with another plan. Goose is still laughing when I ask him what to do, and when I ask Gary what to do, he doesn't know what to think. Gary never knows what to think.

Anyway, I have to be the one to come up with a plan. I swear I'm always the one who comes up with a plan. Mrs. Grosso is a fat lady that lives across the green area, and I know that she has the same kind of stupid bird feeder that we have, that is— the long plastic tube kind. Since she knows my face, I can't go, so I tell Goose to stop his laughing, and that he should steal her stupid bird feeder.

"OK, I'll go," Goose says, "but you guys have to come with me."

Gary says OK, and I think this isn't such a good idea, but I say OK, too. Well, we decide the best plan is for Goose to take a knife from my kitchen, cut the bird feeder down, and then shoot it to Gary. Gary would then run with it, and shoot it to me, and I would hottail it out of there, back to my house.

Well, Goose cuts it down all right, but it falls on the lawn, and all the bird seed starts leaking out all over the place. Then Mrs. Grosso's dumpy husband comes out and starts chasing Goose around the yard. Goose still has the bird feeder, so we aren't too concerned because Goose can run alot faster than Mr. Grosso, because Mr. Grosso has such short little legs, because he's so dumpy. Anyway, Goose outruns Mr. Grosso, and shoots the bird feeder to Gary, who shoots it to me, and I hottail it out of there, hoping little dumpy Mr. Grosso won't catch up.

Well, we all make it back to my house, breathing hard from running so fast across the green area, but we have the stupid bird feeder and that's all that matters. We fill the bird feeder back up with birdseed in my garage, and pick up the pieces from the other one that Goose smashed.

Just as Goose is returning my kitchen knife that he used to steal the stupid bird feeder off fat Mrs. Grosso, I hear my mom pull in, because she has one of those old crappy Volvos that squeaks when you push the brake. Anyway, I tell those guys to quickly hang the new stupid bird feeder up, while I go distract my mom so we won't get busted.

Well, my mom has about a million groceries in her hands, so it isn't too hard getting her to wait in the front hall by asking how her day was, and making a bunch of stupid ding-dong talk so that those guys can hang up Mrs. Grosso's bird feeder. I take the groceries from her hands and walk into the kitchen, hoping those boneheads are done.

Anyway, it's hanging on a rope filled with birdseed, and it looks pretty good. I mean it's full and all, just like the stupid bird feeder Goose smashed in the first place, and it even has a dumb sparrow eating out of the hole. Goose and Gary say hello to my mom and stroll in through the deck door, cool as cucumbers, like nothing happened.

My mom tells them to bring in the bags, and I don't want to seem too obvious, so I go with Goose and Gary to bring in more groceries from our crappy Volvo. Well, when we all come back in through the door with the bags, my mom has that look like something isn't right.

"Where's my bird feeder?"

"What?"

"I said, where's my bird feeder?" (Mom always notices stupid things like if her bird feeder is different. She has an eye for detail.)

"Oh, Goose broke it with a tennis ball." (I'm bad at coverups.)

"Goose, why were you shooting tennis balls at the bird feeder?"

"We were trying to bean the birds and the squirrels."

"What? Well, where did that other one come from?"

"Oh, that one's Goose's Mom's; she had an extra one." (I'm not that bad at coverups, with small things.)

"Brett, you're grounded for two weeks. Goose and Gary, I'm sorry, but if you guys want to wreck things, do it at your own houses. You guys can come back in two weeks."

My mom always busts me for dumb things like our stupid bird feeder. If I replaced the exact same one, she would've said within the first five minutes in the kitchen, "Brett, how come that birdseed isn't at the same level as when I left?" Then I would've tried to make a big lie in my head, but then I would've had to settle for a little one, and say "Oh, we were trying to bean the birds and the squirrels, and we broke the stupid bird feeder, but Goose's mom had another one." We all would have been grounded anyway.

Writing the Satiric Comedy

The difference between *satiric comedy* and *non-satiric comedy* stems from the author's attitude toward the main character(s) or society at large. In a non-satiric comedy, the author likes, sympathizes with, or identifies with the main character; in satiric comedy, the author *disapproves of or dislikes the behavior/values of one or more characters. The author may also address the folly of society at large.* Although the author's critical point of view distinguishes these satiric comedies from romantic comedy, many comedies *mix* tones and merge satire with romance. To write a satiric comedy, combine criticism of your character or society with the comic plot.

In Brett Ross's story, an example of satiric comedy, how does its tone differ from the tone in the previous examples you've read? What's the character like? Why do we identify with him? What's the underlying theme? How does the author feel about the situation?

I Was a Fat Child

Brett Ross

I was a fat child. The only thing worse than being a child in the first place is being a fat child. The only thing worse than being a fat child is being a fat child with an older brother who is a jock. My brother Brian is a jerk. As a small boy Brian was in a tricycle accident that left him paralyzed from the neck up. Brian's idea of fun was taunting with abuse that would go something like:

"Hey Brett, wanna cookie? I mean, I noticed you ain't had nothing to eat in five minutes."

and

"Hey Brett, you ever notice you don't look like mom or dad or me? Know why? You're adopted. But don't tell mom I told you cause you're not supposed to know 'til you get older. Yeah, your real parents didn't want you cause you were fat, so my parents felt sorry for you and let you come live with us."

Being fat is hard at any age, but children are not known

for their subtlety, and growing up was a painful experience. I realized early that the only way I could make it was by being funny. The idea wasn't flawless, though, because I was still spoken of as "that funny fat kid." In school the other children had endearing nicknames for me like whale-butt, pig-face, hippo hips, Godzilla-gut and the witty and ever popular FAT BOY.

School would have been easier to handle if I could have found refuge at home, but Brian saw to it that I enjoyed no peace. As I said before, Brian was a jock and, being three years older than I, was naturally bigger and stronger. When I hit seventh grade packing 155 pounds on a 5'2" frame, Brian was already a freshman and star quarterback of the football team. As luck would have it, my Phys. Ed. teacher was Brian's coach.

Let me take a brief moment to give you my philosophy on Physical Education. First of all, in twelve years of lower education I heard the term physical education only once; on the last day of junior high school when my guidance counselor told my parents that I had given a new meaning to the term remedial physical education. Other than on that occasion, P.E. was referred to as Gym, a word derived from the word Gymnasium, and used in this context so that P.E. teachers might remember where their classes were held. Where Physical Education suggests the process of learning, Gym suggests the process of sweating. The last thing a pubescent fat child needs is a class based on public humiliation that culminates with a shower taken with twenty-three other people. Embarrassing as gym is for a fat child, it is inevitable, and so my story continues.

My gym teacher's name was Mr. Schmidt, an out-of-work Nazi storm trooper whose office was decorated with inspirational slogans like "Quitters are Slime." Schmidt loved my brother, who was the kind of Aryan stereotype that would appeal to any former Hitler youth. Brian won games for Schmidt and the coach naturally assumed that athletic talent ran in my family. This, of course, was not the case. Once, at a birthday party, I fell out a window while playing in a rigorous game of pin-the-tail-on-the-donkey.

If ever there was a brown-nosing teacher's pet, it was brother Brian, and Schmidt was so excited to hear another Ross had come along to win games for him that he sent a letter home to thank our parents for their generosity. When Schmidt walked into the gym, a hush fell over the class as we viewed what appeared to be a Neanderthal man; truly a freak of evolution. I could imagine the Schmidts of only one or two generations before swinging on tires in a zoo in Berlin. Schmidt cleared his voice and started yelling roll call. I expected the disappointment I saw on his face as he got to my name.

"Ross!" he barked.

"Here!" I squeaked.

The man's face sunk.

"Brian Ross's brother?"

"Ah . . . yessir," I replied.

Schmidt frowned as he wrote something in the margin of his pad. Next he ordered us to line up for pull-ups, an activity I so seldom found necessary that I was horribly out of practice. Schmidt was kind enough to tell us that doing less than ten pull-ups reflects directly on one's masculinity. I groaned softly.

My turn eventually came and I wheezed my way to the bar. It stood ominously some two feet over my head. In two evenly spaced places the paint had worn through and been replaced with what was probably rust but what I imagined to be blood.

"C'mon Ross, get the load up," Schmidt yelled.

I jumped up to the bar and felt a sharp pain as my arms fully extended to bear the brunt of my weight.

"I think I broke something!" I cried.

"Don't be a girl, Ross. I wanna see at least one of your chins get over that bar."

Nice guy, I thought to myself. The other kids started to giggle, and I started to feel faint.

"Goodman, Allen, give Ross a hand," Schmidt growled, and as they got under me to help, I lost my grip and crashed to the floor.

"You alright?" Schmidt inquired with feigned concern.

"Where are Goodman and Allen?" someone asked.

Beneath me I felt movement and was relieved that I had not killed anyone. Class was dismissed to make room for the paramedics and their gear, and Goodman and Allen were removed, their bodies intertwined on one stretcher.

The next day I was assigned to Phys. Ed. 102, a remedial class for the "physically and otherwise afflicted." The class wasn't too bad, although most of it was composed of socially backward and morally void children. I later suffered a bout of intestinal flu during which I lost thirty pounds and was deemed worthy of returning to my original class.

While school continued to be tough, throughout my years there I adjusted well to not being fat. I was, however, saddened to learn that in the interim Coach Schmidt had been killed by an exploding keg of beer while at an Octoberfest. This so severely affected my brother that he quit playing football and dedicated his life to baking obscene pastries.

Traditional Satiric Characters

Satiric characters have played a major role in Western drama throughout history. Here's a list of the common types:

- silly or conniving or "upper-class" servants or domestics
- pedants: teachers/students
- professionals: doctors/lawyers/politicians
- cowards
- slobs
- cheats/thieves/con men (or women)
- tricksters
- liars
- braggarts
- fanatics
- sophisticates
- misers
- imposters
- drunkards (These are less funny today, given our concern about alcoholism. Other kinds of addicts are even less funny. The drunkard emerged as a strong comic figure in the past because he—and it was almost always a "he"— defied convention.)

Writing Comedy with More Than One Plot

You can double a plot by weaving two stories at the same time. Although they could be of equal importance, usually one is more important than the other for dramatic emphasis. This main plot and subplot structure appear frequently in traditional drama, as in Shakespeare.

TYPICAL MAIN PLOT

the young couple of *nobility* fall in love (romantic comedy with dabs of social satire)

TYPICAL SUBPLOT

the young *servant* couple fall in love (slapstick and low humor)

EXAMPLE

While you're trying to sneak in the house at 3:00 A.M., a little drunk, you have to get past your parents who are trying to make love on the living room floor. Just as you're a little drunk, your father's a little impotent.

Writing the Tragicomedy

A tragicomedy mixes sad and happy elements. In the television show *M*A*S*H*, we laugh at Hawkeye's sarcasm and groan at his terrible puns, but in the background looms the bombing from the war.

Any one segment of a tragicomedy could be all comedy, all tragedy, or tragicomic, and as our current literary rules crumble, you can vary your stories with impunity. Some critics will argue that comedy is just an extension of tragedy, the obverse of the same coin. There are, however, differences. In comedy, our vulnerability as humans causes us to act foolishly; in tragedy, we humans are essentially good but because of a tragic flaw in character, we do evil.

CHARACTERS

In a tragicomedy, the characters combine both comic and noble traits.

PLOT

The plot should mix the comic and the tragic.

THEME

The theme would mix the light and the serious, the comic and the tragic. The issues at stake would extend to complex, universal truths as well as the trivial or commonplace. Examples include birth and life contrasted with death; the unheroic/heroic; quotidian/cosmic; existential/purposeful.

COMPLICATION

The complications might be similar to those in any traditional comedy, but their pace toward the end would not speed out of control in a silly way. Rather, more dignity and depth would generate the plot and its ending.

TONE AND VOICE

Tone and voice extend from gentle to sarcastic; from pathetic to serious.

ENDING

The ending would be either bittersweet or tragic.

Where's the tragedy in Alan Haft's short story below? Where's the comedy? What does Camelot have to do with all this?

The Museum

ALAN HAFT

Today the class took a trip to the museum. It was fun, but Mom forgot the twinkie. So I stole Jeremy's brownie and Mrs. Greenspam, that lizard, yelled at me. I pinched Dana's tit on the bus and she told Mrs. Greenspam. So I had to sit next to the lizard all the way. But I got her back with an unplanned odor of mine.

In the museum, I got all the cool guys, except for Jack, to come with me. Jack sucks, that's why he wasn't allowed with us. I took them to a picture of a naked lady. We laughed and had fun. Danny dared Fred to pull down his pants. He said Fred's moon looked like the lady in the picture's. Fred did and Mrs. Greenspam, that lizard, saw. Fred said he was dared by Danny but we blamed it on Cheerio. Cheerio denied the whole thing and began to cry. We all started making fun of him and he cried more. Cheerio grabbed the thing Mom puts flowers in and pretended to throw it at Fred. Mrs. Greenspam, that lizard, told Cheerio to put it down at once. She said it was old and an antkike, or somethin'. Cheerio placed it back on the stand, but just like last week when he spilled the sauce on Gator, the thing fell. Luckily it didn't break. Mrs. Greenspam, that lizard, told Cheerio to stay with her the rest of the time. We said goodbye to Cheerio and he cried.

We asked the tour guide why the painting with only a red stripe was so famous. She began telling us that it had to do with war or somethin'. But Chewie and I had better things to do. We flung snot at Mrs. Greenspam. Mine wasn't as sticky as Chewie's was. He always has sticky.

Alexandria was getting in the way. So Chewie pushed her and she fell into the tour guide. Jack told that it was Chewie. I told Jack he's gonna be dead. He told me that my mother eats crabs' balls so, as my Dad says, I smoked 'im in the face. Danny grabbed Fred and threw him on Jack. Wilbur looked like he was going to be sick. Probably because of all the Yodels he told us he ate for breakfast. Mrs. Greenspam yelled and the kids started laughing because they saw the snot. Cheech took out his chocolate pudding and threw it on Sue's white pants by her ass. Gator yelled, "Sue made in her pants! Sue made!" And the kids laughed. Mrs. Greenspam had no control. The tour guide didn't know what to do. So Cheerio began to cry again. We thought it was for nothing but later on Vinny said he squeezed his balls.

Finally everything stopped and Mrs. Greenspam had us all sit down and be quiet for five minutes in order to restore ourselves.

The tour guide spoke of all the dumb paintings in front of us. Who painted them and what they meant. I did nothing but stare at Carolyn sitting by Jamie and dream of holding her hand while buying some Chocolate Nutty Buncher for us down at Ed's. I always thought of asking her to go, but never got the guts up. I looked at her for the rest of the time until Mrs. Greenspam told us we'd be going home.

On the way out Chewie snotted Mrs. Greenspam again. Cheerio cried because Fred and Danny sandwiched him while Cheech regretted throwing his pudding at Sue. He was still hungry. And me, I found the knight in shining armor. I stared at it more intensely than I did at Carolyn. Maybe one day I can put it on and ride a horse covered in silk down a path heading for the castle Camelot. I would be meeting Carolyn and we would play together for hours and hours. I'd have all the whipped cream in the world because of my armor. And I'd have, in a separate room, all the video games I can imagine. I'd have my men specially arrange each game so that I could play with as many turns needed to reach the end. I'd have two Space Invader machines in my room and a parrot with brilliant colors dazzling the room. He would be trained to say anything I wanted. And his name would be Henry. Henry the Parrot. And he would ride on my shoulder all day, even while I'm on the horse. That armor in the glass case would one day be mine and I would be the best.

Chewie wanted me to smoke Jack again, but I was too caught up in my dream to do it. During my dreaming, I learned that Wilbur threw up Yodels on Marvin. But nobody really cared. The walk to the bus was very quiet for me an' everyone asked me what was wrong. I didn't speak back. Mrs. Greenspam was the most happiest.

But when we got back on the bus I decided to return to earth. Mrs. Greenspam was the most unhappiest. I spitballed Cheerio and he cried. I called Wilbur names and told Sue she made in her pants. I told Cheech he sucks monkey piss. I asked Marvin if he had anything to eat and kissed Marcia on the lips. She freaked and then cried. I made Cheerio cry once more when I told him he's not playing Kill the Guy with us anymore. But I know he will be allowed. I just like to make him cry.

And I dreamed of Carolyn riding on my horse while I shone in bright armor towards Camelot.

SUGGESTIONS FOR WRITING

Stuck for an idea? How about these? The characters could be you, if you're writing a personal essay, or an imagined character, if you're writing fiction.

Love or Sex
Write about a moment of revelation or self-awareness:
- a moment where you (your character) first realized the complexities of love
- a love affair you're having with a celebrity or fantasy figure: a television star; television character; movie star; rock star (I'm in love with Batman . . .)
- coming together and coming apart

Other Kinds of Trouble
Write about a moment you (your character) realized a weakness or strength.
- a time you got arrested
- a time you pulled a prank
- a time you defied authority (teacher, coach, parent)
- a time you spoke up to your boss (or didn't)
- a time of rule and anti-rule

Triumphs and Defeats
Write about an event that taught you (your character) strong emotions like embarrassment, joy, pleasure, the bittersweet.
- a moment you beat all odds
- a moment you got a one-upmanship
- a moment of triumph in a sport like football or checkers
- a moment of terrible, embarrassing defeat
- the most fair/unfair punishment you ever received

Emotions
Write about an experience with an emotion that taught you (your character) something about yourself you didn't know before.
- a moment someone hurt your feelings
- a moment you got caught doing something you weren't supposed to do
- a moment you got caught seeing something you weren't supposed to see
- a moment you first learned some truth about another person (a wonderful discovery; a sad discovery)
- a moment you first learned some truth about yourself (a wonderful discovery; a sad discovery)
- a time you were insulted
- a single, precise instance when you experienced a strong emotion—a look, a glance

REMEMBERING PLACES

Write about a place that captures some special meaning for you (your character).
- a place that entices you to clown around
- a place that causes you to dress in a weird way
- a country fair, rock concert, picnic, dance, locker room, lunch hour, Saturday night, the mall, a video arcade

THE CLOWN

Write about a turning point in your life (your character's life) where you learned something about your comic self you didn't know before.
- a time you felt ridiculous
- a time you acted silly or made a fool of yourself
- a time you stood up for what you believed in—maybe too foolishly
- a time you realized you were a clown
- a time you realized you were a fool
- yourself as a cartoon figure
- yourself as a one-line joke
- a time you first learned your comic place in society: social class, race, sex
- a time you came to understand your comic physical "limitations" or "flaws"
- a time you came to understand your comic intellectual or spiritual "limitations" or "flaws"
- the time you first learned your comic place in the universe: religious, universal, or existential
- a time you hid behind a comic mask

VALUES AND BELIEFS

Write about a moment where you (your character) learned some truth about the values or beliefs you hold.
- a time you had to confront your basic attitudes, values, morals
- a time you realized the whole world was crazy
- a time you were "saved"
- a time you were "damned"
- a time you realized how fragile we all are
- a time you were outside the wall
- a time you experienced moral remorse

- a time you faced the measure of death
- a time you confronted the road we travel
- write about honor, and the brave or the weak

The quality of your work should be founded on strong narrative, so when you get a full draft, check for the following.

CHARACTERIZATION

Is the main character flat (having only one trait) or round (having many traits, some contradictory)? If he or she is flat, can you give him/her some conflicting characteristics? If that isn't possible given the nature of your intentions, do you have good reasons for creating a flat character?

DIALOGUE

Are you creating complexity in your characters by having them talk? Are you using direct dialogue? Is the dialogue succinct, appropriate to the speaker, and meaningful? Does your dialogue characterize as well as accelerate the narrative?

MINOR CHARACTERS

Check the minor characters. Can you make them round so they become more complex? Can you add any description or actions?

POINT OF VIEW AND VOICE

Check the point of view. Who's speaking? Are you using a first- or third-person point of view? Is it consistent? What voice and tone do you use? Are they consistent?

PLOT

What structure is taking shape? Is it classical (three scenes) or a variation? If classical, does it have a beginning, a well-developed middle, and a strong end? If it's shaped at random, is it unified in some way the reader can understand?

SETTING

If setting matters at all in your comedy, have you described it enough and are the details well developed? Does it have a special identity? At the very least, make sure we know where you are.

Grammar

Use your spell checker.

Humor

Check for humor. Have you incorporated surprising imagery and vivid details? Are the incongruities clever?

The Catch

"Yeah," you say, "this is all pretty easy. So what's the catch?"

"Well, you're right," says the prof. "There's always a catch. If you want to create a brilliant comedy, you have to have a theme."

Theme

A theme is the underlying significance of it all: the meaning; the purpose; the terrific insight you give us into life that startles, delights, and shocks us and changes our perception forever. It's the *internal* action of the story that parallels the *external*.

Think about your comedy as literature and whether you can develop it beyond an anecdote or simple narrative.

To strengthen theme, ask yourself: what point am I trying to make? Is it significant? What did you (or your character) learn about yourself from the experience? What does it all mean? Has it enhanced or decreased your (your character's) understanding of life? Is the comedy about relationships? If so, what are you saying about them? Is the theme threaded throughout the narrative? If you're writing a personal essay, these ideas should be what drives the narrative. If you're writing a short story (or some other crazy made-up genre), the theme could be stated outright, embedded in the narrative, or sprinkled over the story like a gentle mist.

"And," says the prof, "because life is cruel, here comes the second catch."

A point or theme wrapped in a plain brown wrapper won't do. A theme that is obvious, contrived, dull, standard, stereotyped, clichéd, or immature won't rate a Nobel Prize (all other things being brilliant). You've got to address some complexity that moves your comedy from a sketch or a "nice little work" into "literature." "Thus I learned true love" isn't enough. "Thus I learned that my father can't cut the ice" isn't enough. "Thus I learned true love can only be viewed through a prism, and that prism changes colors constantly" is better. "Thus I learned that my father can't cut the ice, but I worship him for that" is better. The theme should be a twin; it should have two sides. The theme doesn't have to be stated as a moral at the end in your work. Best if it's implied. But as effervescent as it might be, it's got to be there.

Drawing a plotline of both the *external* and *internal* action may help you see your theme. By envisioning the structure, you'll picture the shape of your story and its strengths and weaknesses. When a story doesn't work, it's often because these two lines aren't extended and intertwined. Sketch them for yourself. It's important. Really. Do this.

Your Final Draft

The final draft fuses your earlier drafts into a coherent whole. Everything should fit together to effect your theme or point. The final draft is honed much more consciously than the earlier versions, and some of the rewriting might drag for you. Accept the inevitable. That's just the way writing happens. If you get stymied, brainstorm some more, focusing on the areas or sections you think need more work. Or conjure up something very different to see if that might trigger insights or relevancy to the whole. In these final stages, you'll write two, three, four drafts, scratching out, adding to, sliding around sections in a cut-and-paste maneuver until your work best expresses your intentions and summons the emotions you want from your audience.

Finally, look closely at the language. Go word by word. Yes, that's right, word by word, line by line, inch by inch. Do you have enough concrete details? Are the paragraphs developed enough? Test the sounds and rhythms. Try your work out on some friends and note their responses. If they like it, good news; if they don't, don't get discouraged. Figure out why and learn from it. Put aside any weak writing (but don't throw it away since you might use it in a different form later) and move on to your next work.

Remember that writing is like training for a marathon. You'll have good days and bad days. You're in this for the long haul.

Slapstick

Tweaking the nose; sticky gum; toothaches; buzzing flies; loose floorboards; falling pants; collapsing houses; sliding on banana peels; flatulence (for example, Mel Brooks's *Blazing Saddles* bean-eating campfire scene); and the classic, ever popular, pie in the face: no question about it, we love slapstick. Maybe it has to do with our armchair safety; maybe it's the cleverness of our favorite comedian in overcoming these embarrassments and tribulations; maybe it's our noble acceptance of life's terrible but comic wrath. Whatever. But slapstick's appeal overlaps generations from ancient times to the present, and it's only the stodgy among us who harrumph in disapproval.

Slapstick is any exaggerated physical humor. Named after a two-slatted wooden paddle that cracks loudly when harmlessly slapped across a person's bottom, slapstick comedy claims the stage rather than the page as its traditional home since it's highly visual, but it can be found in any literary form that takes to heart its boisterous kicks, shoves, punches, slaps, spills, falls, chases, or other madcap antics. Weak slapstick repeats the obvious and ends with the obvious; good slapstick, visual or written, can be brilliant when it's varied and tumbles up in joke toppers. Read James Thurber's classic story below. How does Thurber use slapstick to reveal each character? What does the slapstick tell us about the social fabric of the family?

The Night the Bed Fell

James Thurber

I suppose that the high-water mark of my youth in Columbus, Ohio, was the night the bed fell on my father. It makes a better recitation (unless, as some friends of mine have said, one has heard it five or six times) than it does a piece of writing, for it is almost necessary to throw furniture around, shake doors, and bark like a dog, to lend the proper atmosphere and verisimilitude to what is admittedly a somewhat incredible tale. Still, it did take place.

It happened, then, that my father had decided to sleep in the attic one night, to be away where he could think. My mother opposed the notion strongly because, she said, the old wooden bed up there was unsafe, it was wobbly and the heavy head-board would crash down on father's head in case the bed fell, and kill him. There was no dissuading him, however, and at a quarter past ten he closed the attic door behind him and went up the narrow twisting stairs. We later heard ominous creakings as he crawled into bed. Grandfather, who usually slept in the attic bed when he was with us, had disappeared some days before. (On these occasions he was usually gone six or eight days and returned growling and out of temper, with the news that the federal Union was run by a passel of blockheads and that the Army of the Potomac didn't have any more chance than a fiddler's bitch.)

We had visiting us at this time a nervous first cousin of mine named Briggs Beall, who believed that he was likely to cease breathing when he was asleep. It was his feeling that if he were not awakened every hour during the night, he might die of suffocation. He had been accustomed to setting an alarm clock to ring at intervals until morning, but I persuaded him to abandon this. He slept in my room and I told him that I was such a light sleeper that if anybody quit breathing in the same room with me, I would wake instantly. He tested me the first night—which I had suspected he would—by holding his breath after my regular breathing had convinced him I was asleep. I was not asleep, however, and called to him. This seemed to allay his fears a little, but he took the precaution of putting a glass of spirits of camphor on a little table at the head of his bed. In case I didn't arouse him until he was almost gone, he said, he would sniff the camphor, a powerful reviver. Briggs was not the only member of his family who had his crotchets. Old Aunt Melissa Beall (who could whistle like a man, with two fingers in her mouth) suffered under the premonition that she was destined to die on South High Street, because she had been born on South High Street and married on South High Street. Then there was Aunt Sarah Shoaf, who never went to bed at night without the fear that a burglar was going to get in and blow chloroform under her floor through a tube. To avert this calamity—for she was in greater dread of anesthetics than of losing her household goods—she always piled her money, silverware, and other valuables in a neat stack just outside her bedroom with a note reading: "This is all I have. Please take it and do not use your chloroform, as this is all I have." Aunt Gracie Shoaf also had a burglar phobia, but she met it with more fortitude. She was confident that burglars had been getting into her house every night for forty years. The fact that she never missed anything was to her no proof to the contrary. She always claimed that she scared them off before they could take anything, by throwing shoes down the hallway. When she went to bed she piled, where she could get at them handily, all the shoes there were about her house. Five minutes after she had turned off the light, she would sit up in bed and say "Hark!" Her husband, who had learned to ignore the whole situation as long ago as 1903, would either be sound asleep or pretend to be sound asleep. In either case he would not respond to her tugging and pulling, so that presently she would arise, tiptoe to the door, open it slightly and heave a shoe down the hall in one direction, and its mate down the hall in the other direction. Some nights she threw them all, some nights only a couple of pair.

But I am straying from the remarkable incidents that took place during the night that the bed fell on father. By midnight we were all in bed. The layout of the rooms and the disposition of their occupants is important to an understanding of what later occurred. In the front room upstairs (just under father's attic bedroom) were my mother and my brother Herman, who sometimes sang in his sleep, usually "Marching Through Georgia" or "Onward, Christian Soldiers." Briggs Beall and myself were in a room adjoining this one. My brother Roy was in a room across the hall from ours. Our bull terrier, Rex, slept in the hall.

My bed was an army cot, one of those affairs which are made wide enough to sleep on comfortably only by putting up, flat with the middle section, the two sides which ordinarily hang down like the sideboards of a drop-leaf table. When these sides are up, it is perilous to roll too far toward the edge, for then the cot is likely to tip completely over, bringing the whole bed down on top of one, with a tremendous banging crash. This, in fact, is precisely what happened, about two o'clock in the morning. (It was my mother who, in recalling the scene later, first referred to it as "the night the bed fell on your father.")

Always a deep sleeper, slow to arouse (I had lied to Briggs), I was at first unconscious of what had happened when the iron cot rolled me onto the floor and toppled over on me. It left me still warmly bundled up and unhurt, for the bed rested above me like a canopy. Hence I did not wake up, only reached the edge of consciousness and went back. The racket, however, instantly awakened my mother, in the next room, who came to the immediate conclusion that her worst dread was realized: the big wooden bed upstairs had fallen on father. She therefore screamed, "Let's go to your poor father!" It was this shout, rather than the noise of my cot falling, that awakened Herman, in the same room with her.

He thought that mother had become, for no apparent reason, hysterical. "You're all right, Mamma!" he shouted, trying to calm her. They exchanged shout for shout for perhaps ten seconds: "Let's go to your poor father!" and "You're all right!" That woke up Briggs. By this time I was conscious of what was going on, in a vague way, but did not yet realize that I was under my bed instead of on it. Briggs, awakening in the midst of loud shouts of fear and apprehension, came to the quick conclusion that he was suffocating and that we were all trying to "bring him out." With a low moan, he grasped the glass of camphor at the head of his bed and instead of sniffing it poured it over himself. The room reeked of camphor. "Ugf, ahfg," choked Briggs, like a drowning man, for he had almost succeeded in stopping his breath under the deluge of pungent spirits. He leaped out of bed and groped toward the open window, but he came up against one that was closed. With his hand, he beat out the glass, and I could hear it crash and tinkle on the alleyway below. It was at this juncture that I, in trying to get up, had the uncanny sensation of feeling my bed above me! Foggy with sleep, I now suspected, in my turn, that the whole uproar was being made in a frantic endeavor to extricate me from what must be an unheard-of and perilous situation. "Get me out of this!" I bawled. "Get me out!" I think I had the nightmarish belief that I was entombed in a mine. "Gugh," gasped Briggs, floundering in his camphor.

By this time my mother, still shouting, pursued by Herman, still shouting, was trying to open the door to the attic, in order to go up and get my father's body out of the wreckage. The door was stuck, however, and wouldn't yield. Her frantic pulls on it only added to the general banging and confusion. Roy and the dog were now up, the one shouting questions, the other barking.

Father, farthest away and soundest sleeper of all, had by this time been awakened by the battering on the attic door. He decided that the house was on fire. "I'm coming, I'm coming!" he wailed in a slow, sleepy voice—it took him many minutes to regain full consciousness. My mother, still believing he was caught under the bed, detected in his "I'm coming!" the mournful, resigned note of one who is preparing to meet his Maker. "He's dying!" she shouted.

"I'm all right!" Briggs yelled to reassure her. "I'm all right!" He still believed that it was his own closeness to death that was worrying mother. I found at last the light switch in my room, unlocked the door, and Briggs and I joined the others at the attic door. The dog, who never did like Briggs, jumped for him—assuming that he was the culprit in whatever was going on—and Roy had to throw Rex and hold him. We could hear father crawling out of bed upstairs. Roy pulled the attic door open, with a mighty jerk, and father came down the stairs, sleepy and irritable but safe and sound. My mother began to weep when she saw him. Rex began to howl. "What in the name of God is going on here?" asked father.

The situation was finally put together like a gigantic jig-saw puzzle. Father caught a cold from prowling around in his bare feet but there were no other bad results. "I'm glad," said mother, who always looked on the bright side of things, "that your grandfather wasn't here."

SUGGESTION FOR WRITING

Write about a moment with a group of people—family, friends, field hockey fans—where some chaotic misunderstanding results in quirky, slapstick behavior. Who's the zaniest? Why?

ASK A FRIEND

READER'S WORKSHEET — COMEDY

1. Did the opening grab your attention? Does it make you want to read on? Any suggestions for spicing it up?
2. How would you best characterize the plot complications? What chaos occurs? Maybe nothing happens at all?
3. List three crises (emotional tension points) in the plot. Are they well placed? Do they increase in intensity?
4. Analyze the main character. Is he/she simple or complex? Give two suggestions for making the character more complex.
5. Does the character learn something about him- or herself at the end that increases self-awareness and changes internal understanding so strongly that the character will never again be the same? If there's no self-awareness, is that in keeping with the character's experience?
6. Analyze a minor character. Is he/she simple or complex? Give two suggestions for more complexity.
7. What thematic point does the writer make? What internal conflict is at stake? If you can't identify the internal conflict, can you suggest possibilities for it?
8. List three places where the humor works well. Where does it come from: characters? action? dialogue? other?
9. List three places where humor could be improved, if any.
10. Other comments?

8

Stuck? Writer's Block?

Mouth dry and your mind blank? Not an idea in sight? Do you wring your hands and sigh? Instead of brilliant comic characters, are you thinking of cigarettes and chocolate? Don't. Many writers, even the most accomplished ones, experience writer's block, where the brain's circuitry disconnects words, and ideas stick inside the subconscious. Don't worry; help's on the way. Writers have techniques to disentangle themselves from this blockage. If you freeze each time you begin, jumpstart your writing by extensive *brainstorming*. To brainstorm, do this: daydream about your topic as a kind of creative self-hypnosis; make lists of details from your daydreaming as quickly as they pop into your mind; cluster the lists into common areas; focus in on a specific area then brainstorm that topic. Then write from these details—fast.

Brainstorming, a prewriting exercise, stimulates your subconscious and gets you to move physically, pen to paper, loosening up your hand and arm. Think of this as the warm-up for a two-mile run. Like runners, most writers get momentum once they get their hands moving. Try it.

To Begin, Daydream and Make Lists

Let's say that you want to describe yourself, or a fictional version of yourself, at a job. Imagine yourself at age ten . . . fifteen . . . twenty, each time doing some kind of work. What did you look like? How did you act? What was your boss like? The other workers? The customers? How did all of you relate to each other? What traits about each person were funny? Describe them.

Cluster Common Areas

After you've daydreamed about your topic and written down random lists of details, focus your ideas by circling the ones that fit a single point, scene, or character. Envision yourself or your character selling pastries, painting a wall, or just pretending to work as the boss watches.

117

Focused Brainstorming

Focus on a specific part of the scene, listing details as fast as you can, almost without thinking. Let your imagination spin and roam. Don't worry if ideas are irrelevant. Don't stop to evaluate. Take risks with your imagination. Go for broke. Since writing itself is an act of discovery, sometimes you don't know what you want to write until you've written it. This is "focused brainstorming." Later you'll cross out details you don't want.

Write the First Draft

After you've clustered a list, quickly capture the scene in your mind and write as fast as you can. Don't censor yourself, but write a paragraph with some order to it. From your list, mix and match whatever comes to mind. At this stage, don't worry about spelling, punctuation, or grammar. You can redo those later. Don't worry about whether you're right or wrong, neat or sloppy; just get words down.

Think about one moment at one job: a customer throws gum in your hair; the blinds on the windows shimmer in the dark; cement steps crumble as you walk on them; the acrid smell of tar from a neighboring roof makes you drop the hammer; jacking up the car dislocates your shoulder; and so on. Write at a comfortable but fast pace.

If you're nervous, it's best to have a goal, like writing for five minutes or filling one page. If you divide your writing into small components, the project contains itself in workable segments and you won't feel that you're entering a tunnel without end. So get that pencil, pen, computer, or crayon moving.

A Model for the Exercise

Here are examples from my own writing-in-progress, "Samson's Shoestore," to show you how I followed the exercise, but your individual approach might be very different and, if so, that's OK. Do whatever works for you. As for myself, first, I brainstormed descriptions of my characters.

Description

FIRST DRAFT—PERSON DESCRIPTION

> Betty Lou . . . mean manager. Patsy crazy. How crazy? Wore different shoes from the shoestore without buying them. Got them

dirty. Patsy did dumb things like wear a 666, with straps all the way up to the knees or the clogs or the plastic ankle boot. Climbed wall really fast. Jumping between the shoeboxes and then yelling. "Ta daaaaaaa."

Second Draft—Person Description

But even if Patsy was different from Betty Lou, she did what she did, and she broke up the day by doing dumb things. Her favorite routine was to put on some goofy shoe like a 666, with straps all the way up to the knees, or the clog heel chevvy or the plastic see-through ankle boot with the tractor tire ridges, and walk around the store. Also, she had the best trick of being able to climb practically to the top of the wall real fast by sticking her bare toes between the shoeboxes and the shelf and give a yell, then pretend that she was hanging there, eating her sandwich.

"Ta daaaaaaaaa—"

She'd just be walking along past the chairs like nothing was going on when she'd kick off her shoes, give a whoop, then climb right up practically to the top of the shelves, sticking her toes in between the shoeboxes.

If you sense that your characterization is flat, boring, or "stuck," it may be that you're envisioning only one technique for description. Review the list below, which offers different angles for describing a character and which might energize your characterization by adding complexities or different points of view.

Ways to Describe a Person

- clothes, hair, face, stature
- what they say and how they say it
- what others say about them
- how they act toward others
- how others act toward them
- mannerisms, quirks, or uniqueness
- moods and emotions
- habits
- thoughts
- beliefs
- goals
- values (materialistic or philosophic)
- religion (or lack of one)
- objects they use

- background and past
- education
- social class
- sex, race, ethnicity, heritage, family
- setting (place they live or frequent)
- space they inhabit: near to far; far to near
- place in history
- myths/legends
- dreams
- symbols
- figurative language
- sights, sounds, tastes, touch, smells
- stories or anecdotes about them
- stories or anecdotes they tell

FIRST DRAFT—PLACE DESCRIPTION

My first draft of place description sets the atmosphere of Samson's store:

> Samson's Shoe Store, next to Jay's, was a low price ladies store, where every shoe was in window. Pick out just by pointing to it. Inside the store, center of the main room . . . turntable with all the shoes on it. Customers point to the shoes they wanted. Don't have to second guess them.

SECOND DRAFT—PLACE DESCRIPTION

In the second draft I polished the sentence structure and added conflict and speech.

> Samson's Shoe Store on First Avenue, next to Jay's Jewelers, was a low price ladies store, one where you could get a pair of heels right from the racks and give the salesgirl the number. Every type of shoe they had was crowded together in the window and sometimes at the front by the door like a 5 and 10 cent counter display, and with the number system and the customers' just pointing to the shoe they liked, the salesgirls didn't have to second guess what the customers wanted. The customers liked this, they said, because that way they weren't missing out on anything, and Samson's liked it because they wanted to get you to buy as fast as they could.
>
> Inside the store, the blue chairs were nice enough. But there were no stools to put your feet on, and Patsy and the other girls had to bend over and rest the customer's foot on their upper legs

to push the shoe, or in the case of Betty Lou, the manager, she just let the customers put on their own shoes and stamp them to fit against the floor.

"477–477 . . . 5 No Charlies, 4 Bennys, 1 Alfie, . . . 5 1/2 No Charlies, 3 Bennys, 1 Alfie, 6 No Charlies, 1, 2, 3, 4, 5, . . . 21 . . . no, I mean, 22 Bennys, 10 Alfies . . ."

Patsy was singing out the inventory sizes, her feet propped on the seat of a chair, snuggled in a pair of flip flops, when Betty Lou came in that Saturday, that day before Christmas. Betty Lou walked fast through the store.

Narration

Narration orders events in time; these time sequences organize and shape the story. Some ways to narrate follow.

CHRONOLOGICAL

First, second, third, fourth, etc.

FLASHBACK

Return to earlier events in the story or in memory, that is, second, third, *first*, fourth, etc.

FLASH AHEAD

An advance ahead in time, as in science fiction or memory, for example, first, second, *fourth*, third, etc.

EPISODIC

Each sequence has its own chronology only loosely related to the next: [one, two, three, four]; [one, two, three, four.]

IN MEDIAS RES

Opening with a highly dramatic event—even though it happened late in the story: *four*, one, two, three, five, etc.

STREAM OF CONSCIOUSNESS

Events occur in random order, as in a dream or as completely unrelated events: two, five, three, one, four, etc.

FRAME

Story within a story: *one*—one, two, three, four—one.

Most Important to Least Important

This has more to do with emphasis or logic than with time.

In the event your story requires transition passages, just briefly summarize events, as in the following example.

> At 9:00 sharp Betty Lou pulled back the chain and snapped open the double lock, using her "customer" grin at the door. Then they came. That day there would be eight salesgirls to meet them—Betty Lou and Patsy, regulars, and six other girls—temporaries—all of these who were put on special for the Christmas rush, including the floater from the Pittsburgh office who was just polish and accessories plus cash. . . .
>
> So the day went, with Betty Lou yelling "Front, front!" anytime anybody stayed in the back shelves too long, and it was almost 4:00 before things slowed down enough for Betty Lou to say they could scatter their one-half hours for supper.

Revision

Revise the first draft by layering it with details. Touch it up here and there as though you were dabbing paint on a canvas. Review the list of techniques given above and write a little more from those suggestions. Ask yourself: who, what, when, where, why, how.

Check it for humor. If the writing isn't funny to you, rework words so that they're concrete—and incongruous. Step back and reread what you wrote. Where does the humor appear? In the plot? The character? The words? Is it what you've intended? If not, reshape.

Do Whatever Works for You

If what you've written carries importance for you, you might want to develop it into something larger. If you've exhausted the topic, put it aside and rest for a day. Whatever amount of time you spend writing, eventually take a break. This is important to energize yourself for the next revision. The next day reread your writing and decide whether it's important enough to revise. If so, cycle through the brainstorming, then rewrite. Remember that you can omit steps of the writing process, add to them, or change the way you tackle a topic.

9

Oh Lord, Oh Lord, Not Again, Not Again

Yes, it's true. Failure. Negative velocity. Moon walking. All for nothing. Again.

Well, so what?

Don't let yourself freeze because your writing hasn't met your high standards, and don't become compulsive about trying to make something perfect when it's just not working out. When your writing isn't so hot, think of it as a training run. If it's really bad, throw it out or put it away until next year. Or study those failures and learn from them. But the real trick is to *immediately* write something else. Write a little the very next day, like for thirty seconds or so; this will make you feel virtuous, and the pain and frustration will dissipate. Jotting down notes in a journal counts as writing, even if they're scribbles on a gum wrapper, my favorite way to write. And the better your training, the better your performance. As always, after you've written, reward yourself.

Also, forgive yourself when you don't live up to your daily writing expectations. Don't look back. Everyone has "lost weeks." Think of those wanton, frivolous days when you didn't write as potential material for a comedy. Even if you didn't write to schedule, you were doing something important—like fixing the car, taking the cat to the vet, or living. Whatever you did can be material for humor. Remember that comedy forgives. But once you've pardoned yourself, get back on schedule. Don't fall into the phony reasoning that once-I've-lapsed-into-sin-I'm-going-to-Hell-for-sure.

Sometimes sad things will happen in your life that won't allow you to write humor. That's OK. Take time out to deal with the problem and recover. If you can heal by writing humor, so much the better. But it's OK not to write when you're sad or upset. And it's OK to lose your sense of humor during these times.

123

"Yeah, but still," you ask, "what if I think my writing is funny but my audience doesn't?"

If you worry about your audience too much, you won't write because you'll spend more energy on pleasing it than on the significance of your work. You shouldn't write exclusively to conform to an audience's tastes because this often produces dull, unoriginal, prepackaged work. Results of this emerge in canned television programs, where one show after the other duplicates itself with only the names and places changed. Do this and you won't feel fulfilled. Better to write because you have something significant to say. (Could be trivial, but it's significant *to you*.) If an interesting character says important things in a funny way, the audience will listen. And those "absolutely nothing is funny" critics exhibit idiosyncrasies you won't change. Ignore them.

As you rethink your efforts, rethink your priorities. Your first obligation as a writer should be to yourself. What do *you* want to write about; how do *you* want to say it; what do *you* think is funny? Your second obligation is to your character or topic. How would your character say this? What does your character think about X? Your third obligation is to the work as a whole. Do all the parts fit appropriately? Is this the right ending or have you artificially tacked it onto the story? Are the images appropriate for the tone you've set up?

And, yes, it's true, ultimately you'll have to be accountable to an audience. At some point during your last revision, you need to ask yourself if the humor will work for other people. Survey the makeup of your audience: Who is it? A large, general audience? A small in-group? Ask whether your work will offend some people and if so, do you want the risk? Think about these questions, then revise accordingly. But for now, concentrate on yourself and everything that's important to your character. You'll read more about audience in chapter 20.

Also . . . Do Your Homework!

Don't kid yourself. Anyone who's successful has done homework. If you want to write terrific humor, you'll have to work hard. Very hard. So, educate yourself.

Read! Read! Read! Good humorous writers are well read. Read at least two newspapers a day, good ones. Read magazines and books, including difficult ones. You don't have to understand everything you read but by studying, you'll educate yourself. You don't have to have a college degree, although that helps, but you'll need to inform yourself by reading critically and thinking carefully. Go to films, lectures, and other cultural events that you don't usually attend, even if you drop in on a museum, art show, or dog show for an hour. Be a people-watcher. All this can be potential material for your writing. A highly observant, super-reflective life spawns great writers, humorous and otherwise.

Script Writing

First, a Little Business

Before you begin writing your script, let's talk business. It'll keep you from going into shock later on. Each dramatic form—film, teleplays (television), and plays (theater)—has its own specific characteristics and idiosyncrasies, and these are determined by the "business" of the profession: how much performance time is practical; how much money the producer can offer; what technology is required; how many actors are necessary; and so forth. All these choices hold their own flexibility and their own constraints, both economic and artistic. Whatever dramatic genre you choose, producing a script costs money and, therefore, the more expensive and complex the enterprise, the less control you'll have over the final project. Be prepared for this frustration.

You'll also want to think about any extended life your script might have. Are you proposing a pilot for a new weekly TV show? A script on spec for an established show? An adaptation from a short story or novel? A script for an original, once-only performance? A trilogy? And which is it: television? film? theater? You'll have to consider your genre as you brainstorm the ideas for your script, since how it'll be produced becomes a function of its form. This is not to discourage you, however, since performance writers need some common sense about their art, and one day seeing your script come alive is worth some compromise.

The Agent

If you want to sell your manuscript, you'll have to catch the eye of an agent by providing an overview of your story. The film industry, for example, requires a *treatment* of your script, which is a long summary of the plot that includes descriptions of the characters and some dialogue, usually about 12–45 pages long, double spaced. You may also be asked to present an *outline* of the script, usually about 7–12 pages long, and a *synop-*

sis, a condensed summary, about one page. Consider the size of the final script, too. This industry only accepts manuscripts that are approximately 100–120 pages in length, double spaced, since this story length best fits the usual film length of one and one half to two hours. Teleplays also should be accompanied by a treatment, outline, and synopsis if the production company requires them, although their lengths would be adjusted to variable television time frames such as one-half hour, one hour, or two hours. Playwrights have more flexibility with length and play structure than film and television writers, although the parameters of the physical stage are factors in production design. For more information about the business of selling a script, contact the Writers Guild of America, which provides excellent advice (see "A Few More Questions,"Appendix A at the end of the book for address).

When submitting your script for consideration, be sure to follow the properly typed format exactly. You can find examples of film scripts, teleplays, and plays in your library or on the Web. See also the "How to Write" books in any bookstore. The script included in this book can be a guide, too. Scripts not professionally and appropriately presented could be tossed overboard. Producers are finicky, and they might even reject Shakespeare if he didn't type his plays appropriately. Ultimately, mastering the correct typed format is trivial and, for now, you should concentrate your energy on writing a terrific script.

'Nuff said about business. Let's get back to you, the writer, your dynamic artistic visions, and the original comedy you want to create.

The Plot

Drama means what it says: it's dramatic. That is, the audience feels emotional tension and the subsequent release as it experiences conflicts in the story. In other words, you're showing, not telling. You should design a strong energetic plot with both internal and external action, although the dramatic drive doesn't have to be pure physical action, as psychological action generates good comedy, too. As always, there are zillions of plots for a story, and an exceptional comedy writer will break traditional rules in surprising and unheard-of ways. For starters, however, let's stay with Aristotle's *Poetics* (varied for our purposes) and, as in any comic narrative, proceed with the same plot structure described in chapter 6 on comedy: introduction, complication, conflict, crises, climax, conclusion.

Scribbling Rough Notes

A great dramatic comedy explodes with great characters, ones who are vivid, vibrant, and vivacious. Your characters should radiate comic power through their appearance, actions, hopes, and dreams. Start writing by brainstorming characters. Jot down their physical appearance, background, behavior, thoughts, values, and yearnings. Which characters exude energy and charisma? Which ones contrast sharply with your main character and, therefore, make good sidekicks? Which one rubs the action?

Zero in on the character that most interests you. Now, what does your character want (*introduction*), how does he plan to get it (*complication*), and what's stopping him (*conflict*)? To ignite this tension, think about cause and effect so that events in one scene propel events in the next. This interweaving will lend your story its drama (*more complications and crises*). How does the highest emotional crisis reach its peak (*climax*)? How do all the loose ends come together (*conclusion*)?

Scribble notes with rough outlines of scenes and their crises. Write down everything that comes to mind, even if later you toss out most of it. After you've scrawled notes for your script, take some time to think about the professional films, teleplays, or plays you find really funny. Jot down their names, then zero in on one. Why do you like it? What are the characters like? What's comic about the plot? Make a rough sketch of its structure and study its main features.

You might study further the dramatic structures of the films described here. I've labeled the plot elements in these films for you, but you might label them differently, because plot components in the richest comedies reverberate at many points.

One of my favorites films for zany plotting is Neil Simon's *Murder by Death* (directed by Robert Moore), a parody of the detective genre and a devilish play on logic. What better opening can a mystery lover get than a dinner invitation from Lionel Twain (Truman Capote) to five guests that reads: "You are cordially invited to Dinner and a Murder Sat evening 8 P.M." Great start.

Twain, a rich eccentric, invites the five greatest living detectives in the world, none of whom has ever had an unsolved case, for the weekend to his country mansion to solve a murder.

He's determined to prove that he, not they, is the world's #1 detective (*introduction*). Each detective parodies a popular fictional detective—Dick and Dora Charleston, Sidney Wang, Milo Perrier, Sam Diamond, and Jessica Marbles, respectively parodying Nick and Nora Charles, Charlie Chan, Monsieur Hercule Poirot, Sam Spade, and Miss Marple. Entangling the plot further are Butler Bensonmum, who is blind, and Maid Yetta, who is deaf and mute. The *complication* occurs upon the guests' arrival when all the doors deadbolt shut.

The *conflict*, one of many, erupts with Twain's egotistic belief that he possesses the greatest logical mind in the world, which he'll prove by his puzzle that someone at the table will be murdered by someone at the table. The murderer, of course, can't be Twain, because that would easily solve the mystery. So how can Twain trick one of the invited detectives to commit a murder—and who will then solve it?? Whoever wins the game will be awarded one million tax-free dollars and, of course, paperback and film rights.

Add more *complications* of secret doors, trick mirrors, failing lights, fierce lightning, banging shutters, sliding panels, and disappearing rooms—and you've got a fun-packed, breathless run of comedy—but Simon doesn't let the audience off so easily. Just as we think we've solved the crime and the film will end, Twain spins us off again into more puzzles. Who Done It?

Study this film for its superb plotting and parody.

Another outstanding film for study is Preston Sturges's *Hail the Conquering Hero*, starring Eddie Bracken. The *complication* is that, unbeknownst to everyone in his hometown, Woodrow Truesmith sat out World War II stateside because the Marines, as well as every other branch of service, rejected him due to his hay fever. He concealed his shame by having letters mailed to his mother by soldiers bound for Europe. To make matters worse, his father had won the Congressional Medal of Honor in World War I, dying in action the day Woodrow was born, and Woodrow has had to live with the legacy of being the son of the town's most famous hero.

Now that the war has ended, Woodrow must return home (*conflict*). One misunderstanding leads to another, and when he arrives on the train, the whole town, banners flying and band playing, comes out to greet him as the Great Returning Hero (*crisis #1*). How does he face up to this moral dilemma?

Sturges's wit pinches everyone, and this ranks among the best comic American films. Study it for its poignant characterization and social satire.

In *Harold and Maude,* written by Colin Higgins and directed by Hal Ashby, black humor assaults us instantly as Harold (Bud Cort) methodically sets up a noose for his own hanging. Harold fakes grotesque and witty suicides to shock his materialistic, unprincipled mother into moral awareness (*introduction*). The theme becomes obvious immediately: he's seeking spiritual fulfillment, a need his wealthy mother doesn't understand (*conflict*).

"What do you do for fun?" asks his shrink.

Harold responds quietly, "I go to funerals."

Attending yet another funeral for a person he doesn't know, Harold meets the irrepressible Maude (Ruth Gordon), an octogenarian who oozes sexuality and joie de vivre, a woman who "greet(s) the dawn with a breath of fire." *Complications* ensue as she steals his car—a hearse—then invites him along for a high-speed, careening drive back to her place, unperturbed by her theft. As she later points out, "It's best not to be too moral; you cheat yourself out of life."

What happens next? What do Harold's fake suicides have to do with Maude? Can a boy age eighteen and a woman age eighty fall in love, passionately and sexually? You bet.

A major tragicomedy from the early 1970s deserving close analysis by every writer is Milos Forman's *One Flew over the Cuckoo's Nest* (screenplay by Lawrence Hauben and Bo Goldman, novel by Ken Kesey). The film begins with the arrival of Randel Patrick McMurphy (Jack Nicholson), thirty-eight years old, at the Home for the Mentally Disturbed (*introduction*). Vivacious, impish, brimming with life, he has been committed to determine if he's faking mental illness to escape work detail during his prison term at a work farm. He's in jail for statutory rape, although he claims innocence. Whether he's really insane or just a mischievous but harmless scamp remains to be seen, but he says he's been sent to the mental institution because he fights and loves too much (*complication*). The *conflict* begins immediately and ominously when he's put under the care of Miss Ratched (Louise Fletcher), the ward's fascist nurse. More *complications and crises* ensue from his comic exuberance and her horrifying iron will, conflicts that increasingly choke the life out of the inmates. Early in the film, McMurphy wants to watch the World Series (*complication*) and Nurse Ratched is determined not to allow it. When she asks for a vote to change the work schedule and the majority votes in favor, she changes the rules for the ballot. She will not permit them to watch the Series. Defying Nurse Ratched, Mc-Murphy brings the game to life through his creative and zesty play-by-play description of an imaginary game, full of spirit and baseball lingo, with the other patients joining in with great delight (*crisis*). Nurse Ratched calmly accepts her temporary defeat but we chillingly sense that McMurphy hasn't heard the last of the word "obedience."

McMurphy's comic spirit fights all odds, however insane he might be for rebelling against such brutal authority, and you'll want to study his optimism, rich intelligence, common sense, and relish for life. His character evokes the universal comic spirit.

More Writing—the Plotline

After studying one or two of your favorite scripts, return to your rough notes. Think about what you've learned from the professionals, then map your ideas into a plotline or an outline, whatever works best for you. Scriptwriters outline an act by subdividing its scenes on 3 x 5 cards so they can shuffle them at will. You can also use computer programs for this, which display the appropriate formats. Label each act and scene with a brief phrase and a sentence or two describing its action, such as:

> EXT: TUESDAY, 3:00 P.M.
>> CEMETERY ON A HILL IN RIDGE VIEW.
>> Joe, Yancy, and the gravedigger stare at the ground where a grave has been freshly dug.
>> OR
>> INT: LATE AFTERNOON-HOSPITAL ROOM
>> UNCLE PERK LIES IN A HOSPITAL BED. AUNT KATE SITS ON A CHAIR NEAR HIM
>> Members of the family have just left the room after visiting with Uncle Perk. He has recently learned that he'll have his leg amputated, and he's dealing with the shock. Aunt Kate awkwardly tries to comfort him.

Writing a Scene

When you get a rough sense of the overall structure of your story, write out a scene. Sketch a moment between two opposing characters: roofer/cement mixer; pizza-dough maker/pizza pepperoni cutter; hairdresser/model. Imagine it visually as you write, but remember that in scripts it's all talk.

It's Not Just Talk; It Says Something

Great comedy requires great characters, and good dialogue is central to character. What's being said should reveal what the character wants, her underlying motives, her mood, and her self-awareness (or lack of it). Good dialogue interacts with another character, and it includes silences. It also hints at what's not being said and it should, at the highest dramatic moments, reveal the heart of the character, for better or worse, and the urgency of the conflict. Dialogue isn't just "talk." It ignites the character, conflict, and plot.

Study this dramatized scene adapted from short story "Uncle Perk's Leg," where Perk and Kate are discussing, according to the Church's teachings, whether or not they should have a funeral for his amputated leg. Perk is lying in his hospital bed. Which version of dialogue works best?

Too Little?

INT. HOSPITAL

UNCLE PERK
   I ain't goin' to do it.

AUNT KATE
   You have to have respect.

UNCLE PERK
   This didn't happen when Lizzy Zablonski had her operation.

AUNT KATE
   Perk, that operation was small.

Too Much?

UNCLE PERK
   I ain't goin,' I don't want to go, and I've told you that once if I've told you a thousand times. I don't want to go. I ain't goin' to my own leg's funeral.

AUNT KATE
   Perk, that's the most ridiculous thing I've ever heard. You can't look at it that way. You have to think about it religiously and spiritually. You have to look at it like our priest Father

O'Donovan. He's investigated its tradition. You have to have respect for the sanctity of the body and what it represents. *She pulls at the sheets Uncle Perk has wrinkled.* You just can't always have your own way and do what you want to, like some unruly, unprincipled kid.

UNCLE PERK

When Lizzy Zablonski was operated on last month and Dr. Wilson took off her goiter in an emergency operation, the hospital didn't bury it.

AUNT KATE

Perk, you know the size of goiters and that the size of the body part determines its spirituality. That goiter was small and therefore is considered lesser by the Church. A leg is big. It goes by size.

TOO DULL (NO CONFLICT)

UNCLE PERK

I don't think I want to do it.

AUNT KATE

Maybe you should.

UNCLE PERK

When people have certain operations, they don't have to account for them.

AUNT KATE

I think it depends on the size of those operations.

TOO FLASHY (TOO MUCH CONFLICT)

UNCLE PERK

Damn it, I ain't goin' to any no-good, useless funeral where the priest is going to pray over rotting flesh that's rotting in a grave eaten by worms.

AUNT KATE

You always want your way, thinking that you're special compared to the rest of suffering mankind, that you're the only one who counts and who can always be an exception.

UNCLE PERK

Think about Lizzy Zablonski and them ripping out her goiter and then you know what your yapping is doin' to me. Now shut up about it.

AUNT KATE
I should throw your leg at you, you slob. You don't know anything about blood and guts. I should show you what they really
mean, I should tear off your other leg.

BEST?

UNCLE PERK
I ain't goin' to my own leg's funeral.

AUNT KATE
Perk, you can't look at it that way. You have to look at it like
Father O'Donovan. You have to have respect.
She pulls at the sheets Perk has wrinkled.
You just can't always do what you want.

UNCLE PERK
(raising his voice)
When Lizzy Zablonski had her goiter taken off, they didn't bury
it.

AUNT KATE
Perk, that goiter was small. A leg is big. It goes by size.

Theme

Don't worry about the theme until you get a strong draft of your
script, but at some point, as in any good comedy, you'll want some
internal action that'll drive the character's intent. What motives
and values does the main character hold? What does he want?
How will he try to get it? What does he learn about himself at
the end? What revelation about human nature does he come to
understand?

Embroidery (Visuals, Light, Sound, Music)

Directors claim ownership over the show; they don't want writers
to direct. That's both good and bad. It's too bad that the creator
of the work isn't allowed to visualize it, and this premise holds
because of the huge investment companies make to produce a
film or a play. It's good in that the writer can concentrate on the
characters and the plot.

Even if the director doesn't want you to think beyond the
script itself, embroider it anyway as you write, with visuals, light,
sound, music—for yourself. This visualization can help you "see"

the dialogue. How do you picture the surrounding visual "stuff": the way the sky clouds up; the clothing worn by the sidekick; the bumping, bumbling crowd as it arches to see the parade, all wearing red t-shirts that say "Come to the Firemen's Balls"; the mustard truck that matches HER hair.

Embroider it however you want—stuffing in as many scene directions as will help you write it—and later you can take them out if you need to please some producer's ego (or common sense, because sometimes they're right and you're not). Write down what you're seeing between the dialogue or on another sheet of paper, labeling it by scenes and acts.

Annex sound effects and lighting if you want to. Can you establish a joke by dancing some lighting on a character's face? What kinds of sounds break up a character's dignity? How does music or silence create humor? Mark them in a column on the right-hand side of the page or on a separate sheet of paper.

Among the best of the best, the television series *M*A*S*H* provides an ensemble of outstanding characters, great wit, and complex themes. Study the script that follows to learn how they achieve these.

*M*A*S*H*

Written by Gene Reynolds, Don Reo, Allan Katz, and Jay Folb, in the first scene of this *M*A*S*H* script, "Movie Tonight," the characters banter with jokes that arrive pretty much on schedule, each the caboose of a gag line. Does this traditional way of setting up jokes dull the humor? If not, what generates the spark? What do you learn about each character? How do a few lines of dialogue establish that person's personality and his/her relationship to all the others? How does the humor extend to the larger dynamics of the war?

"MOVIE TONIGHT"

ACT ONE
FADE IN

INT. O.R.

GI party is in progress. HOT LIPS and NURSES are checking instrument packs. Klinger, in house dress, and IGOR are on knees scrubbing floor. HAWKEYE and B.J. are checking anesthesia tanks. ABLE and BAKER assist.

KLINGER
(singing and scrubbing)
'Nobody knows the trouble I've seen.'

HAWKEYE
I know.

KLINGER
(singing)
'Somebody knows the trouble I've seen.'

HAWKEYE
(re tanks)
This thing has knocked out more guys than Joe Louis.

B.J.
(holds up mask from machine)
The winner and still champion.

KLINGER
(to Hawkeye)
Captain, may I be excused from this detail? My nylons are bagging around the knees?

HAWKEYE
Get bigger knees.

HOT LIPS
(approaching Klinger)
Corporal, you'll have to do a better job than that. I want this floor clean enough to eat off.

KLINGER
That's easy, it's already cleaner than the tables in the mess.

HOT LIPS
Keep scrubbing.
(She returns to checking instruments.)

B.J.
What a festive mood people get in at a GI party.
FRANK ENTERS and walks over to Hop Lips and the Nurses.

FRANK
Major Houlihan, I hope you and your nurses are doing a good job.

HOT LIPS
We can hold up our end. Why don't you go hold up yours?

FRANK
Very well.

(walks over to Hawkeye and B.J.)
When you're finished checking that machine, check it again!

B.J.

Frank, how long are you going to be here?

FRANK

About ten minutes.

B.J.

(to Hawkeye)
Wake me when he's gone.
He puts mask over his nose, takes a deep breath and slumps over table.

FRANK

Those tanks aren't even connected.

B.J.

(lifts his head; to Hawkeye)
I told you this was a tankless job.

HAWKEYE

(to B.J.)
You crazy guy. Frank, make yourself useful.

FRANK

I'm the supervisor. I don't have to be useful.

HAWKEYE

Then you're doing a good job.

FRANK

Oh, go stuff a goose.
He walks over to Klinger who is now mopping the floor.

FRANK

Put a little more elbow grease into that, Corporal.

KLINGER

I'm all out of elbow grease.

FRANK

Don't talk back to me.

KLINGER

(comes to attention)
Yes, sir.
He raises mop to set over his shoulder. He turns and hits Frank on the side of the head with the wet mop.

FRANK
> *(yelling)*
> You did that on purpose! You Lebanese lout!
> POTTER ENTERS *while Frank is yelling.*

POTTER
> Hold it! What's going on here.

HAWKEYE
> I saw the whole thing. Frank tried to eat Klinger's mop.

POTTER
> Burns, I put you in charge of this clean-up detail.

B.J.
> He's doing a fine job. He's already washed his face and his shirt.

HAWKEYE
> At the same time.

POTTER
> Why is it taking so long?

FRANK
> Nobody's following orders and they're all grumpy.

B.J.
> Not true. I'm grumpy.
> *He points to Hawkeye.*

HAWKEYE
> He's sneezy.
> *He points to Klinger.*

B.J.
> He's bashful.
> *He points to Hot Lips.*

HAWKEYE
> She's dopey.

HOT LIPS
> Watch your mouth.

POTTER
> Okey, just get the job done. Let's all try to get along.

HOMEWORK

1. Study a television, film, or theater production you think is especially good. If possible, rent a videotape of it so you can view it over and over. Map its structure. Analyze the characters and

how they evolve. Block out the wit and joking. How often does humor appear? Where? How is it woven into the story? How does it enrich the theme? Do you find the theme significant in some way? If the theme is trivial, does the comedy have any other artistic value?

2. Locate the script of a popular movie, play, or television comedy. You can get them at the library, in bookstores, or from production companies, then get the video. How does the performance differ from the script?

3. Watch a film or television production you haven't seen before to the halfway point, then plot out the rest of it yourself. Compare your version to the original one. Did you easily guess what would happen in the original? If so, what does that teach you about clichés and formulas? In what ways was your version better? Is what ways was theirs better?

4. Study your favorite TV show over several weeks. What remains the same each week? What changes? Plot the jokes. What forms the humor: situation, character, wit, or slapstick? What do you find original about the show? What do you find formulaic?

5. Review an ancient Greek comedy, like one written by Aristophanes. In what ways does it make you laugh even though it was written centuries ago?

6. Analyze classic comic theater, like the eighteenth-century plays of Molière or Ben Jonson or the brilliant *Henry IV, Part One,* by Shakespeare, with Prince Hal's sidekick, the glorious cad Falstaff. Work through the language even if it stymies you at first. It'll be worth it. Why is Falstaff among the greatest comic characters of all time?

7. Study film, television, and theater comedies from each decade of the twentieth century to get some historical perspective. See the bibliography at the end of this book for possibilities.

Now write your script from beginning to end, adding and subtracting as your characters and plot develop. Examine the way the dialogue flows. Ask some friends to act it out for you, so you see how it might be performed.

Collaborative Writing

The enormous costs of film/television/theater production demand that scriptwriters work collaboratively, and you might try this, too. Although collaborative writing means you'll relinquish total control of the script, group work might result in a more creative production. Besides, even if you make the big time in Hollywood or New York, you'll have to collaborate with writers, producers, and actors at jam sessions. So go for it, for the experience, even if you're highly independent.

Group collaboration requires some goof-up friends with imagination who'll write a joint script with you. Usually no one is in charge and no one has a specific job, although individual talents might emerge as the gag sessions get underway. The idea is to bounce ideas off one another as you write together. Someone might start with a scene, another shouts out a character, another polishes some dialogue, and another writes it out as more ideas are shuffled to create a script. Everyone contributes spontaneously, spreading as many ideas and jokes on the floor as possible. Once the group decides on a general theme and the characters, it can continue as a group or each person can retire to a corner of the room to write by him-/herself for a while, reuniting for more shouting, adding, subtracting, acting out, and revising. Eventually, someone will have to smooth out the script so it hangs together logically. Early in the collaboration, decide how each person shares in the millions of dollars you'll make when you sell your work to the great producers.

Satire

The trouble with political jokes is that they usually get elected to office.

Crime wouldn't pay if the government ran it.

Whatever it is, I'm against it.

GROUCHO MARX, SONG IN THE FILM *HORSE FEATHERS*

Satire: The criticizing of society in a humorous way. Its main purpose is to reform society; the writer's intention is to expose stupidity, excess, incompetency, or evil.

Satire isn't a specific genre. It assumes any shape and structure: sketch, poem, short story, novel, play, film, sitcom, monologue, process, cartoon (see cartoon 2), editorial, or argument. It can appear as a part or a whole. A *whole* play, story, narrative, monologue, etc., could be satiric, or a *single word or sentence* within a play, story, or other genre could be satiric.

Thus some confusion. Since satire assumes many genres, and since definitions in humor are so haphazard, the word "satire" carries two meanings. *First, it refers to an author's attitude toward a subject, where the author criticizes something in a humorous way; second, it refers to a whole genre itself, when that genre is a formal argument.*

When a whole piece of writing is shaped like an academic argument (the structure is designed as thesis and supporting evidence) and its logic dominates more than the story and emotions do, it's called a *formal* satire (also referred to as "Aristotelian" or "direct" satire). If you're running down the street and you shout at someone, "I just wrote a satire," that person will think that you just wrote a critical argument ("direct," "formal," or "Aristotelian" satire), which in this case would be an argument that's humorous. That person will not think you wrote a story, a poem, or a monologue. If you wrote a satire in story form (also referred

"I don't pretend to be great. I merely know myself to be very, very good."

Cartoon 2. © The New Yorker Collection 1976, Robert Weber from cartoonbank.com. All rights reserved.

to as *indirect* or *informal* satire) and you wanted to be understood precisely, then you would have to run down the street shouting, "I just wrote a satiric story."

Writing a satire differs in several ways from writing a "pure" or non-satiric comedy, which is determined by the writer's attitude toward the material. When writing a "pure" comedy, the author likes, sympathizes with, or identifies with the character(s): *When writing a satire, the author dislikes or disapproves of the behavior/values of a character(s)—or the behavior/values of society.* In a pure comedy, the author holds him-/herself equal to the audience and asks for its emotional understanding. In a satire, the author hovers *over* the audience as an expert, advisor, or teacher; its main purpose is not to draw out emotions from the audience but to reform or educate it. In comedy, the artistic intention focuses on individuals; in satire, the message is usually directed at human behavior or society at large.

Background

Humans have expressed themselves satirically since the beginnings of recorded history. Prehistoric satiric hieroglyphs have been discovered on the walls of caves, such as one found in ancient Egypt where an animal figure carries a staff and drives forward its human master; animal activists thrived even then. Our English word "satire," however, originates from the Greek *satyr* and his ridiculing antics. While informal satire appeared in Greek drama, the Romans created more formal argumentative satires in the work of Horace (65–8 B.C.) and Juvenal (60?–140? A.D.).

The Great Age of Satire in English literature began in the seventeenth century with the playwright Ben Jonson and accelerated in Restoration and eighteenth-century English literature in the works of Alexander Pope, John Dryden, Jonathan Swift, and Henry Fielding. In France, François Rabelais, Molière, and Voltaire challenged the follies of their societies. Not to be outdone, early American journalists seized their opportunity to make political statements using satire. On May 9, 1754, the grandfather of Benjamin Franklin published in the *Philadelphia Gazette* the first American political cartoon.

The nineteenth century, laughing in embarrassment, watched itself mirrored in the satiric plays of George Bernard Shaw and the musical operettas of Gilbert and Sullivan. By the early twentieth century, the satiric British magazine *Punch* captured an appreciative public, and in America the *New Yorker* magazine was born, heralding an urban wit. Satire remains popular, in television with *Saturday Night Live* and the stand-up routines of comedians Jay Leno and David Letterman, and in the print journalism of Russell Baker and Art Buchwald.

Using satire rather than direct criticism proves advantageous for two reasons: people accept criticism more readily when it's humorous; and it's safer politically, both in Roman times and now, since a satirist can hide behind the humor if any government official decides to take offense. With satire, you're less likely to get sued. Or get your head chopped off.

This chapter follows satire through several genres: narrative, process (how to do something), argument (formal satire), contrast-comparison, and analogy. You've also seen examples of it in the comedy chapter, like Brett Ross's "I Was a Fat Child."

Satiric Narrative

In this satiric narrative, the character discovers a new, skeptical philosophy. What's Steven Hartman satirizing? What audience would best appreciate this? How does he top the joke?

The Philosopher

STEVEN HARTMAN

Excitement hung in the air as the university's brightest students and faculty gathered in the lecture hall to hear the legendary philosopher. The members of this impressive assembly chatted idly with one another in a smattering of small groups until it was time to take their seats for the lecture. Existentialists spoke with Neo-Platonists. Atheists mixed with theists. Here and there lone nihilists stood, saying nothing, mixing with no one, just being skeptical. Most of the scholars tried to disguise their excitement by discussing commonplace subjects: the weather, sports, Kierkegaard's radical fideist challenge to nineteenth century rationalists.

One senior professor, Alan Wittenberg, was winding his way to the punch line of a rather involved joke. "And so Socrates says—get this—'Hey Euthyphro, if I don't discover the nature of true piety in the next week, you better come in after me!'" A chorus of hearty chuckles erupted over this knee-slapper. Nearby, three adjuncts were arguing over whether Aristotle wore open or close-faced sandals, while the university's sole Confucian stood quietly to the side, nibbling on a fortune cookie. A group of young graduate students seemed to be the only ones who weren't trying to hide their excitement over the speaker. I was one of these. Although I said nothing, I listened with keen interest to what some of the better-informed students had to say about our distinguished guest.

"Why does he always wear the sailor's outfit?" asked a new student.

Warren Holborn, a fourth-year grad student, was more than happy to enlighten us all. "Well, it's an ingenious way of making a statement, if you think about it. On one hand, the sailor's uniform is symbolic of man being forced out alone at sea—in this case, the sea of thought. But it's also emblematic of society's rigid militarization—an ironic affront to the establishment."

"Wow," squeaked a second-year student, "I've never heard of a philosopher so willing to literally embody his intellectual enterprise."

"What about the name?" asked another first-year student. "Why the pseudonym 'Popeye'? What does it stand for?"

Holborn, an absolute apostle of the man, dazzled us again with his superior knowledge. "Well, the name is undoubtedly an admixture of two roots: the Latin 'populus,' for people, and the Modern English 'eye,' after the Middle English 'eie,' from the Old English 'eage,' akin to the Old High German 'ouga'—or 'eye.' So you see, even his name—'eye of the people'—conveys a subtle message. He is saying, in effect: 'Let me be the means through which you view existence.' If I may, let me quote the intrepid—"

Holborn's words were cut short. The chair of the Philosophy Department, Professor White, had approached the podium to inform us that Mr. Popeye would begin in a few minutes. We all scrambled to our seats. As luck would have it, I ended up right between Holborn and another dedicated Popeyite, Terrance VanBrou, both of whom kept leaning across me, discussing everything their minds could summon up about this monumental thinker.

I was already a little self-conscious about my provisional standing as a grad student, so I can't say it bolstered my confidence to be sandwiched in between the two rising stars of the Philosophy Department. What's more, I knew almost nothing about Mr. Popeye's philosophy. I couldn't read any of his works because he didn't have any. He was illiterate. VanBrou explained to me that this was yet another of the man's many masterstrokes—a symbolic gesture that amounted to a scathing indictment of our educational system.

"Print is dead," Holborn added. "And no one knows this better than Popeye, for whom it was never alive to begin with. Oration is his medium. You might even call him the Demosthenes of our age, raging against wave after ignorant wave on the shore of a decadent sea."

Anyway, Mr. Popeye travelled from university to university giving these lectures, and his following was growing every day, along with his reputation. Tonight's talk would be my first real introduction to his work.

At last, Mr. Popeye himself walked out on stage. He didn't look anything like I'd expected. Except for a single squiggly hair that stood up on the top of his skull, he was entirely bald. He had a large, almost grotesquely cleft chin, and for some reason he only held one eye open at a time. He was wearing his trademark sailor's suit, of course, and on each of his enormous forearms was a tattoo of an anchor. Hanging from his mouth, as if glued to his bottom lip, was a corn-cob pipe. When Mr. Popeye approached the podium, applause resounded throughout the lecture hall.

It didn't end until he held up one hand. Then he let out the strangest giggle I have ever heard and his pipe spun around all by itself, sounding two short, high-pitched "toots."

"I yam what I yam and dat's all what I yam!"

Holborn leaned over me and whispered to VanBrou. "A sly nod to Sartre and the other French existentialists."

"Without question," replied VanBrou. "Not to mention an echo of Yahweh's words to Moses in Chapter III of Genesis."

The giggling philosopher continued. "Now, remembers—I wants ya alls to eats yer spinachk. . . ."

"I like how he emphasizes the sustaining power of nature," whispered VanBrou. "It's very Thoreauvian."

"Yes," remarked Holborn. "With some definite Zen over-tones."

" . . . cause ifs ya doesn't eats yer spinachk, you'll never be ables to fights off da Brutus's of dis woild."

Van Brou turned to Holborn. "Brutus?"

"Obviously an allusion to the assassination of Caesar," said Holborn. "A subtle condemnation of Machiavellian opportun-ism."

"When I comes home from da seven seas," Mr. Popeye contin-ued, "I loves to smooches with me Olive Oyl. But nevers in front of little Swee' Pea. I don't wants to sets no bad examplees . . . g-g-g-g-g-g-g-g-g!!!"

Both my neighbors were quiet for a moment. Then Holborn closed his eyes and shook his head in amazement. "It will take me years of study to master his rhetoric. That one went right over my head."

And so it went for another forty minutes. Over and over again, Holborn and VanBrou noted the extraordinary range of diverse philosophies Mr. Popeye weaved into his own. Almost every statement he made seemed to draw upon the best of Marx or Hegel, Spinoza or Derrida, not to mention dozens of other great philosophers. At the end of his talk, Mr. Popeye received a fifteen-minute standing ovation.

But I didn't stick around for the wine and cheese reception af-terwards. I was too depressed. You see, after that lecture I came to a sad and sober realization. I was no scholar, and I probably never would be. I just didn't have the necessary powers of infer-ence. Or maybe I simply lacked the philosopher's innate ability to perceive beyond the surface of things to their real essence. While my teachers and peers found one ingenious insight after another in Mr. Popeye's lecture, I couldn't help feeling that I was listening to the demented babblings of some over-the-hill, punch-drunk sailor. That's when I knew for sure I could never be a true intellectual.

SUGGESTION FOR WRITING

Write a scene where your character reflects disapprovingly on a philosophical or artistic idea. Who's speaking? What point is the character making? What does he/she want changed?

The "How to Do Something" or "Process" Satire

and any variation thereof . . .

How Muffy Aspero and the Ukrainian Cossacks Saved Europe
A Short History of Catsup
How to Cheat at Lying
How to Reset Your Vertebrae in Three Easy Steps

Among the easiest satires to write is the process or "how to do something." As in other satires, you can make your process as close to reality or as convoluted as you want, but whatever approach you adopt, don't lose sight of its underlying logical structure, because satire always appeals to reason. The process satire assumes the structure of a recipe, lab report, or manual. You usually have the following components:

Title
Purpose
Materials needed (or ingredients)
Cautions
Definitions of special terms
Procedure
    1.
    2.
    3.
    Etc. . . .
Conclusion

To create a process satire, walk us through the procedure. You can number these 1, 2, and 3 or imply the order of the steps with words like "next," "and then," "still another requirement," etc. To sustain its logic, place points in some order, such as chronologically, spatially, least important to most important, or most important to least important. You can also label section headings for added clarity—optional, of course.

As in any good process writing, give reasons for the steps involved and clarify cautions. Repeat the cautions listed in your outline if you think they need to be stressed; if you haven't set them in a separate category, include them where necessary within the procedures. Emphasize what's very important and what's not. Negative directions emphasize the cautions. Give complete details, including background information, if necessary. By all means, feel free to use sketches or pictures to enhance your explanations.

You might not need a conclusion, but for a finishing touch to your process satire you can restate the main point, review briefly the major steps, summarize the results, create an anecdote that satirizes the process itself, explain the topic's significance, place the topic within a broader context, or end on a witty remark.

As you write, select any point of view—first, second, or third—although in genres that give directions, second person is most common. Of course, to create the satire, you'll layer it with incongruous humor.

Brett Ross's "Cool Guy" sets up a chillingly funny indictment of sexism in dating. He elects to bypass the more rigid structure of process, but it underlies the scene. What's the narrator like? What is Ross saying about society's values?

How to Be a Cool Guy in a Bar
Brett Ross

This procedure is universally accepted in collegetown type bars and, once mastered, will enable any guy to be cool.

First of all, always carry cigarettes. Don't smoke them, they'll kill you, just carry them. Some wild looking girls get their kicks off bumming cigarettes, and all of them smoke Marlboro Lights, so they're the ones to carry.

Walk into the bar with a cigarette, lit, dangling from your mouth. Once inside, stop, squint, and slowly look around bar. Do not focus on anything. Look bored. Take a drag off cigarette and drop it to the floor. Don't put it out with your foot; fires are the management's problem. Get bartender's eye. Raise one finger in air and call out your beer's nickname, i.e., Bud! Mic! Heiny dark! O.V.! etc.

When you get your beer, place your free hand in pants pocket, and slowly raise bottle to your mouth. (Cool guys don't use glasses.) Look around bar as you slowly drink. As you swallow, pull lips back from teeth and release an "ahhh" sound. Act as if you haven't had a drink in years. Act as if beer burns on way down and feels good.

Look bored. Peel label off the bottle, drop pieces to floor. Tap foot lightly to beat of music, mouth words, play bottle like guitar. By this time, everyone has noticed you and is impressed. Now it's time to find a girl.

Cool guys don't want relationships, so look for wild girls. Set your sights on one. Smirk and stare with heavy eyes. Wild girls think heavy eyes are cool. Finish your beer, making sure she's watching, and set the bottle on the bar. Approach the girl slowly. Remember, heavy eyes. When you get to her end of the bar, order another beer, using the method discussed earlier. While you're waiting, make a comment to her about the bar, like,

"This place is packed, huh?"

or

"This place is beat, huh?"

Once you've got her, fill up the rest of the evening with superficial small talk in the Hi-how-are-you-where-you-from-where-do-you-go-to-school-what's-your-major vein. Wild girls like to do shots, which are cheaper than most mixed drinks, so keep 'em coming.

When the girl is really messed, it's time to take her home. Slap high five with every guy you know on the way out of the bar, while mugging and rolling your eyes in answer to their knowing smiles.

To be really cool, the next time you see her in the bar, act like you don't know her, but if any guys ask you about her, tell them she's wild and a tramp.

SUGGESTIONS FOR WRITING

Write a satiric process outlining the steps for a behavior you dislike: for example, how to corrupt society with lottery tickets; how to make professional wrestling more violent (or colorful); or how to make computer programs indecipherable.

Formal Satire

a.k.a. . . . the Aristotelian argument

a.k.a. . . . the essay

The formal satire, the essay, is a brief prose composition that argues an issue. While the topics can vary from less serious like "Foul Air in Dormitory Restrooms" to more serious like "Nuclear Waste in Your Own Backyard," the formal satire is distinguished from the informal by structure. Informal satires absorb loose constructions like narrative and dialogue, but *the formal satire (Aristotelian argument or essay) begins with a thesis and progresses in logical steps with supporting evidence.* A thesis, usually a single sentence, contains a topic and a claim, and the claim is the position you're arguing. For example, "the U.S. needs more football" is a thesis that includes the topic "football" and the claim "needs." In the thesis, "the American deficit defines an invalid capitalism," the topic is "the American deficit" and the claim is "defines an invalid capitalism."

The body of the formal satire advances the claim through a series of reasons for the writer's beliefs (also known in high school English classes as "topic sentences," "subclaims," or "subpoints") supported by detailed evidence, and in satire, through humorous examples or facts. The standard number of sections within the body of the essay is three or four, and you can embellish a point with background material. Also, you can include an "opposition" section, where you refute or concede the argument to your opponents. If you prefer, and if your topic warrants it, you can thread this counteropposition throughout the satire. If you cluster the opposition in a single section, this usually appears early in the essay or right before the conclusion.

The structure of formal satire is shown in Figure 7. Although most writers don't restrict themselves to this specific design (and below you'll find some argumentative satires that stray from it), most satirists don't veer too far from a logical structure because logical thought keynotes the satire. Whether you include narratives, anecdotes, or examples as your evidence, an underlying thread of reason for your position should weave through the satire so that the audience sees a convincing advancement of the claim. Although you can opt for a structural base of least important to most important, most important to least important, chronological, spatial, cause-effect, or contrast-comparison, a formal satire must be structured rationally if it is to persuade us.

Since a satire directs criticism at society, you should consider the following:

- The criticism must be valid and fundamentally factual. You can't attack irresponsibly.
- The behavior you're satirizing must be able to be changed: gluttony, yes; obesity as an illness, no.
- The intention must be to persuade us to reform.
- The organizational structure must have a clear focus, either covertly or overtly.

Argument (Formal)

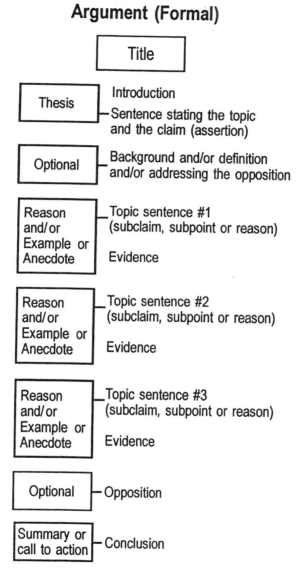

Figure 7. Argument (formal structure)

- The satire must advance a series of claims, either covertly or overtly.
- The criticism must cover all major points; you can't ignore essential points, so know your stuff.
- The topic could be trivial or significant, but significance will have a higher literary value.

Study this editorial for its formal satire properties. In it, Art Buchwald narrates his trials and tribulations when searching for a public washroom. How does the structure fulfill conditions of a formal satire? Look at the beginning and the end. What are the topic and claim in the thesis? The evidence progresses as a series of examples. How do these examples persuade us to believe that this is a serious problem that needs a solution? What humorous effect comes from the "call for action"? What's so funny about placing the issue in a larger context replete with "high value"?

Brother, Can You Spare a John?

ART BUCHWALD

Something is happening in America, and I think you should all know about it. There is a conspiracy underfoot to prevent a majority of people in this country from emptying their bladders. Don't go away—I'm dead serious.

The power elite in this country are locking their washrooms, putting "keep out" signs on their water closets and warning people that only those favored by the management have bathroom privileges.

I know what I'm talking about. As a member of the Kidney Foundation, and a person who has to tinkle more often than the norm, I have discovered it is getting harder and harder to find public accommodations where the welcome mat is out.

A national lockout: The public washroom, as we have known it, is disappearing from the face of the land.

While great strides have been made in this country to help the handicapped, the government has turned its back on people who must go to the john.

Get Lost: Any non-customer who asks a restaurant owner or gas-station attendant if he can use the bathroom is told to get lost. Department stores, catering to thousands of people a day, hide their washrooms in inaccessible corners of the building where only stock clerks can find them. Sports arenas holding 16,000 people have men's and women's rooms that will handle no more than five at a time. Offices lock their washrooms tighter than they do their safes. Hotels have lavabos that are reserved for the use of "registered" guests.

In a society where

everyone is guaranteed equal rights, there is no such thing as a free tinkle.

On a recent trip to New York, I discovered how difficult it was to go to the bathroom.

I was walking down the Avenue of the Americas when I got the urge. I looked around desperately for some place I could make a pit stop. A large black building loomed up in front of me. I rushed in and took the elevator to the fifth floor where an attractive receptionist smiled and asked if she could help me.

"Yes, you can," I told her. "Could I please have the key to the washroom?"

Her expression immediately changed and she said coldly, "I'm very sorry. I'm not permitted to give the key to strangers."

"But this is an emergency," I begged. "I promise I won't even use the paper towels."

"I don't have the authority to make exceptions," she said. "Why don't you go to the subway?"

"I haven't time to make it to the subway."

She would not be moved. I took the elevator down, rushed out into the street and looked around frantically. I saw a bookstore and went in. "May I use your men's room?" I asked the man behind the counter.

"We don't have one," he snarled.

"Where do the employees go?" I cried.

"That's none of your damn business," he said.

I didn't have time to argue, so it was back on the sidewalk. There was a class hotel on the corner. I went in looking as nonchalant as I possible could, under the circumstances. My eyes spotted a sign "Barber Shop." Experience has taught me that a hotel always places the men's room next to the barber shop—presumably to attract shoe-shine business. I pounded down the steps. There it was in all its tiled splendor. I made a dash for it, but was stopped at the entrance by the house detective.

"May I help you, sir?"

"Not really. I'm on my way in there."

"Are you a guest of the hotel?" he wanted to know.

"No, but I have a friend staying here."

"That's what everyone says. Now get out of here before I nab you for trespassing."

I ran two blocks down the avenue until I found a bar advertising the "Happy Hour." I went in and said to the bartender. "Give me a drink."

"What kind of a drink?"

"Who cares?" I said. "Where's the men's room?"

"That will be three dollars," he said.

"Why do I have to pay now? Why can't I pay after I've finished my drink?"

"You're not the first guy who walked in here and wanted to use the men's room."

The incident I describe is not unusual as anyone who works in New York City will testify.

But it's not just New York. The lockout is sweeping the country. The public washroom, as we have known it, is disappearing from the face of the land. It is now easier to get an artificial kidney than to use the one you've got.

What's even more frightening is that architects, in order to save space, are cutting down on washroom facilities in everything they design.

It's even worse for women than it is for men. Anyone who has gone to a theater knows the agony and defeat of waiting in line for twenty minutes during intermission to get near a stall.

Crisis: The airlines are putting fewer bathrooms on planes so they'll have moreroom for passenger seats. The designers of concert halls, football stadiums and movie houses couldn't care less about the physical needs of people who go there.

The United States, which leads the world in modern plumbing, now heaps scorn and abuse on those who want to use it.

No politician in this country will face up to this crisis.

No President of the United States will take a stand on it. Editorial writers ignore it. Even Mike Wallace is afraid to investigate it.

Yet it affectsevery single person in the country.

The right to tinkle is a God-given one, so basic to every man, woman and child that unless it is acknowledged as such, citizens will soon take the law into their own hands. A person who has to go in a hurry considers jail a small price to pay for civil disobedience.

The time has come for the people to raise their voices in protest. It is imperative to remember that each time a washroom door is slammed in anyone's face, something in all of us dies.

SUGGESTION FOR WRITING

Write a formal satire about something you dislike and support it with a series of evidentiary examples either researched or taken from your experience. Include a thesis with its topic and claim. Topic: sports figures (or team owners, doctors, lawyers, media stars, computer whizzes). Claim: they make too much money.

Contrast and Comparison

Suzanne Britt topples example after example in this satiric essay by enumerating the differences between fat and thin people and arguing that fat people are nicer. This essay first appeared in *Newsweek* and was later included in her book *Skinny People Are Dull and Crunchy Like Carrots* (1982). Study it to see how she structures contrast and comparison. What does Britt say about how fat people view themselves? In what ways does she break stereotypes about fat and thin people? What does she say about personality that goes beyond "size"? Why is it funny?

That Lean and Hungry Look

SUZANNE BRITT

Caesar was right. Thin people need watching. I've been watching them for most of my adult life, and I don't like what I see. When these narrow fellows spring at me, I quiver to my toes. Thin people come in all personalities, most of them menacing. You've got your "together" thin person, your mechanical thin person, your condescending thin person, your tsk-tsk thin person, your efficiency-expert thin person. All of them are dangerous.

In the first place, thin people aren't fun. They don't know how to goof off, at least in the best, fat sense of the word. They've always got to be adoing. Give them a coffee break, and they'll jog around the block. Supply them with a quiet evening at home, and they'll fix the screen door and lick S&H green stamps. They say things like "there aren't enough hours in the day." Fat people never say that. Fat people think the day is too damn long already.

Thin people make me tired. They've got speedy little metabolisms that cause them to bustle briskly. They're forever rubbing their bony hands together and eyeing new problems to "tackle." I like to surround myself with sluggish, inert, easy going fat people, the kind who believe that if you clean it up today, it'll just get dirty again tomorrow.

Some people say the business about the jolly fat person is a myth, that all of us chubbies are neurotic, sick, sad people. I disagree. Fat people may not be chortling all day long, but they're a hell of a lot *nicer* than the wizened and shriveled. Thin people turn surly, mean, and hard at a young age because they never learn the value of a hot-fudge sundae for easing tension. Thin people don't like gooey soft things because they themselves are neither gooey nor soft. They are crunchy and dull, like carrots. They go straight to the heart of the matter while fat people let things stay all blurry and hazy and vague, the way things actually are. Thin people want to face the truth. Fat people know there is no truth. One of my thin friends is always staring at complex, unsolvable problems and saying, "The key thing is . . ." Fat people never say that. They know there isn't any such thing as the key thing about anything.

Thin people believe in logic. Fat people see all sides. The sides fat people see are rounded blobs, usually gray, always nebulous and truly not worth worrying about. But the thin person persists. "If you consume more calories than you burn," says one of my thin friends, "you will gain weight. It's that simple." Fat people always grin when they hear statements like that. They know better.

Fat people realize that life is illogical and unfair. They know very well that God is not in his heaven and all is not right with the world. If God was up there, fat people could have two doughnuts and a big orange drink anytime they wanted it.

Thin people have a long list of logical things they are always spouting off to me. They hold up one finger at a time as they reel off these things, so I won't lose track. They speak slowly as if to a young child. The list is long and full of holes. It contains tidbits like "get a grip on yourself," "cigarettes kill," "cholesterol clogs," "fit as a fiddle," "ducks in a row," "organize," and "sound fiscal management." Phrases like that.

They think these 2,000-point plans lead to happiness. Fat people know happiness is elusive at best and even if they could get the kind thin people talk about, they wouldn't want it. Wisely fat people see that such programs are too dull, too hard, too off the mark. They are never better than a whole cheesecake.

Fat people know all about the mystery of life. They are the ones acquainted with the night, with luck, with fate, with playing it by ear. One thin person I know once suggested that we arrange all the parts of a jigsaw puzzle into groups according to size, shape, and color. He figured this would cut the time needed to complete the puzzle by at least 50 percent. I said I wouldn't do it. One, I like to muddle through. Two, what good would it do to finish early? Three, the jigsaw puzzle isn't the important thing. The important thing is the fun of four people (one thin person included) sitting around a card table, working a jigsaw puzzle. My thin friend had no use for my list. Instead of joining us, he went outside and mulched the boxwoods. The three remaining fat people finished the puzzle and made chocolate, double-fudged brownies to celebrate.

The main problem with thin people is they oppress. Their good intentions, bony torsos, tight ships, neat corners, cerebral machinations, and pat solutions loom like dark clouds over the loose, comfortable, spreadout, soft world of the fat. Long after fat people have removed their coats and shoes and put their feet up on the coffee table, thin people are still sitting on the edge of the sofa, looking neat as a pin, discussing rutabagas. Fat people are heavily into fits of laughter, slapping their thighs and whooping it up, while thin people are still politely waiting for the punch line.

Thin people are downers. They like math and morality and reasoned evaluation of the limitations of human beings. They have their skinny little acts together. They expound, prognose, probe, and prick.

Fat people are convivial. They will like you even if you're irregular and have acne. They will come up with a good reason why you never wrote the great American novel. They will cry in your beer with you. They will put your name in the pot. They will let you off the hook. Fat people will gab, giggle, guffaw, gallumph, gyrate, and gossip. They are generous, giving, and gallant. They are gluttonous and goodly and great. What you want when you're down is soft and jiggly, not muscled and stable. Fat people know this. Fat people have plenty of room. Fat people will take you in.

SUGGESTIONS FOR WRITING

Write an argumentative satire, with a thesis and examples, which compares or contrasts two things: high fashion/low fashion; playing football/watching football; sports cars/trucks; Midwest/coast; House of Representatives/Senate. Which side are you on? What do you want to reform or change? What can you suggest about society's dumb, silly, or irrational attitudes toward one or the other group?

Analogies

You can create a satire using an analogy, where you compare the subject you want to criticize with something ridiculously different. This works if you can get a comparison that holds our attention and if you draw the analogy at enough points for us to see some logic in the connection, as ridiculous as it might be. Try an analogy with a thesis like the following:

Standing in line at motor vehicle registration is like swallowing an aardvark.

Getting into that exclusive restaurant (name it) is like mud wrestling a giraffe.

Paying the IRS is like having a face peel.

ASK A FRIEND

READER'S WORKSHEET—SATIRE

1. Is the situation being satirized sufficiently complicated, ridiculous, annoying, unfair, or unjust—and, therefore, truly deserving of criticism?
2. Can the behavior really be reformed? Is the writer attacking

the relevant issues or has the author inadvertently—or maybe even intentionally—introduced a hit "below the belt"?

3. Has the writer taken responsibility as a satirist? Is the issue valid (true)?

4. Is the evidence full and appropriate? Has the writer committed himself to research, if necessary?

5. Has the writer covered all important points so that the satire convincingly persuades? Are there enough points to sufficiently advance the thesis?

6. Who's speaking and why? Has the voice developed a strong personality? What tone is being used?

7. What overall structure does the satire have? Is it the best one to represent the topic? If it's a narrative, is each scene dramatized fully? If it's a process or argument, are the examples adequately developed? Do clear transitions connect the logic?

8. Is the satire exaggerated enough so that we know it's humor? Any place where the humor falls flat? Where does the humor work well?

12

Irony and Wit

Irony sets up tension between opposites: the ideal and real; dreams and reality; what is said and what is meant; the intended and achieved; expectations and results. In the *Simpsons*, the highly sensitive and brilliant Lisa is born into a dysfunctional and unappreciative family. When she finds a soul mate in a fellow jazz saxophonist, he dies. That's irony. In *Arsenic and Old Lace*, inside a quiet, innocent clapboard New England cottage, two kind but pathological little old ladies graciously offer their hospitality to a half dozen or more gentleman visitors, then "hospitably" murder them and bury them in the basement. Illusion clashes with reality. More irony.

Irony resides in appearances, actions, language, situations; thoughts, settings, or values: the teenager, who plays his heart out in the championship game, catches a pass for the winning touchdown, except that he then runs in the wrong direction; the kidnappers who snatch a kid for ransom, and the kid kicks up such a racket that they beg the parents to take him back; the author of this book who climbs bravely and agonizingly to the summit of New Hampshire's Mount Washington—only to find it topped by a hamburger stand.

What irony is not: irony isn't necessarily humorous; it can be funny, grim, or tragic. More subtle than sarcasm and a component of wit, but not wit itself, irony pulls at opposites. If you study all night and get an F on a test and then you study all night and get an A on a test, that's not irony, that's an "opposite." If you study all night and get an F on a test and your roommate never studied at all and gets an A, that's irony. The word "irony" derives from the Greek *eiron*, a character in ancient plays who foils the braggart Alazon with sly, sarcastic remarks and who wins the conflict by cunning ingenuity. Because irony appeals to the intellect, it flashes a keen observant eye to the audience.

To make sure we grasp the irony in your humor, you need to

scatter clues. For example, you can understate, overstate, contrast styles, employ double negatives, or say the opposite of what you mean.

Understatement ("meiosis"): As we described in an earlier chapter, when you understate, you indicate that something is much less important than it really is, and you can do this by using words that suggest your attitude toward the topic is less concerned than the situation merits:

"Jonathan Swift—Last week I saw a woman flayed, and you will hardly believe how much it altered her person for the worse."

"Irish remark—Is he dead? Well, I don't know if he's dead but somebody took the liberty of burying him."

Overstatement ("hyperbole"): For overstatement, reclassify something unimportant as important:

"Going to the junior prom with Monica Seblecci, Jerry thought, would establish him as a major Kebblestone Academy stud."

"Finding the seven dollars, Janet believed, would be the onset of a lifetime of financial success, a steppingstone to someday meeting Donald Trump himself."

Opposite styles: To create this manner of irony, begin on an even keel then jump into an exaggeration with an image that contrasts with the previous tone or language. Flip styles from formal to informal, or the reverse:

"Lawyers can represent the finest principles of our constitutions and many do this in our courts of law every day by their careful logic and reasoned evidence, but some lawyers—ya gotta watch out for, cause they'll sneak anything under the table."

Use negatives to make a positive statement about something negative ("litotes"):

"Scrubbing that floor is not too terrific an experience."

"It was not a trivial act when you shot me."

Verbal Irony

Most irony will emerge in your writing by naturally flowing from character and situation; however, you might want to write some direct irony, an easy way to create satire. The principle is simple: say the opposite of what you mean. Look at the three examples below to see the tonal distinctions: literal (not ironic), exaggerated satire (not ironic), and satiric verbal irony.

Literal (Not Ironic)

The following passage says exactly what the writer means, assuming he really doesn't like boring classes:

"I *really hate* boring classes. They're a main reason I *hate* to go to school. Nothing *dulls* my mind more than an hour and fifteen minutes of *meaningless* talk."

Satire Using Exaggeration (Not Verbal Irony)

In this passage the satire is produced by *exaggeration* through heightened examples. Since the author doesn't like boring classes and he says he doesn't like them, this satire isn't direct verbal irony; the viewpoints of the author and the narrator are identical. Using exaggeration without verbal irony is, of course, a perfectly good way to write satire, if this is what you want:

> I really *hate* boring classes. They're a main reason I *hate* to go to school. *Nothing dulls my mind more* than an hour and fifteen minutes of the grumbling and sneezes of a professor who spits on the first row of kids as he asks: "What is the significance of paralysis in Joyce's *Dubliners?*" First of all, it takes a minute of silence before the class realizes the teacher has asked a question and when this happens, *everyone buries their heads in their books, concerned with finding the answer.* Then the prof *tries to stimulate* his students by posing another question. "How might this paralysis erupt in Joyce's linguistic underpinnings?" Again, no one answers. I *doze* off in the back, *dreaming of the bell and Dante's hell.*

Satire Using Verbal Irony

To write verbal irony, reverse your meaning. If you dislike something, tell us how much you like it. Say one thing, but mean the opposite. Of course, all other principles of writing humor still apply, like exaggeration, which will signal the audience that the passage should be read as humorously ironic. Once you decide to write verbal irony, don't switch back and forth between straight and ironic clues, as that will confuse your audience. Note how Alan Miller signals the irony.

Boring Classes
ALAN MILLER

Some people don't like boring classes, but I *do*. Boring classes are *the only reason I attend school. I couldn't imagine* what

I would do in a class if it wasn't repetitively boring. Nothing *stimulates my mind* as much as an hour and fifteen minutes of dull silence.

I guess if I'm going to speak of my *passion* for boring classes, I must begin by mentioning the professor. I always ENJOY a boring class when I have a *really great downbeat boring* professor, and I find his *cool saliva refreshing* whenever he spits on me as he speaks. I really get a *big kick* out of the *meaningful silence* that follows a *brilliant* question posed by a boring prof: "What is the significance of paralysis in Joyce's *Dubliners*?" Usually it takes a full minute of silence before the class realizes the teacher has asked a question and when this happens, *intellectual fireworks burst* as everyone buries their heads in their books, *so overcome are they by the question's significance. To intensify the intellectual moment* the prof tries to *stimulate* the students even further by posing another *intriguing* question: "How might this paralysis that erupts in Joyce's writing be relevant to our own lives?" Again, *stunned by its philosophical implications*, no one answers. The prof glances around the room and when his eyes meet my blank eyes I sense he's thinking, "That bastard of a student, he never says anything, what an idiot he is." *But I know a professor would never think such a thing about one of his or her students.*

Alan Miller draws an extra dimension of irony here at the end with the second question, because who's boring whom?

Another example of verbal irony is introduced through the lovable dog Boz.

Boz

I *love* my dog Boz. He's an *interior decorator*. Not a single day will pass without Boz making some subtle, *innovative* changes in the appearance of our home. Whether it be the *ambience* of tattered toilet paper strewn *geometrically* about the house, or *impressionist* chew marks on my mom's eight-dollar lamp shade, Boz's *creative decorative genius* continues to be the *dominant force in the trend-setting look* of our house. When my mom becomes tired of the decor of a certain room, she needs only to leave the door to it opened as she goes out to shop, and Boz does the rest. My dad *especially likes the rusticated look* of the chewed legs of the dining room furniture. . . .

I love my dog Boz. He is the single *greatest* financial responsibility I've ever had. We *get along well* because we both have a preoccupation with fecal matter; he *creates* it, and I dispose of it. I *love* Boz because anything he does is a *direct reflection* of me, his *proud* owner. If he shits on someone's rug then I must have taught him that. If he shoves his cold wet nose under my neighbor's skirt, she glares at me as if I had done it myself. *Yes, sir, I love my dog Boz.*

AUTHOR UNKNOWN (SNIFF)

Like-to-Dislike Irony

Another form of verbal irony would start with a premise of liking something and then switching to achieve an ironic "dislike." You would use this reversal for comic roasts and teases, but it results not in satire but friendly ribbing. Lucille Ball was teased at her roast by Phyllis Diller, who said: "Lucille wants to change her hair to its original color, but she can't remember what it was."

Still Not Sure about Irony? Maybe This Exercise Will Help

Here are some examples of types of irony. Study them and then in the sentences that follow, identity the kind of irony that best describes each situation. Because irony appears in both comedy and tragedy, the list below includes both.

1. *situational irony*—where an incongruity appears between what might be expected and what actually occurs. Ex: Buster Keaton expects the anchor to sink and it floats.

2. *irony of intention*—where a character does not understand his own intentions and does something against his will. Ex: The clown tries to lock the lion in the cage and instead lets the animal out.

3. *dramatic irony or tragic irony*—where a dramatic effect is achieved by leading the audience to know one thing while the characters in the play think another. Most often associated with tragedy, we see it when King Lear rejects his most devoted daughter, Cordelia, for not loving him. Ex: The audience may know that Bugsy is going to blow himself up if he lights the cigar, but he continues to flick the lighter, unaware of the danger.

4. *cosmic irony or irony of fate*—where we know that the odds are always against perfect happiness because we're human. Ex: Joey falls in love but will never be loved in return.

5. *verbal irony*—where a person says the opposite of what she/he means. Ex: "Dieting is fun," said Ollie, as he eyed the apple pie.

1. You throw a fast ball and it accidentally hits a lamppost, ricochets, and bops you in the head.
2. The famous composer Beethoven goes deaf.
3. "No, I don't mind that you just totaled my car."
4. We all work hard to create a valued life but in the end we will all die and be "nothing."
5. You vomit over the side of the boat and the wind blows it back in your face.
6. "How could I sit with Aunt Martha, Mom? I didn't even know she was at the party."
7. Gritface, who plans to murder Detective Simon by throwing him down the elevator shaft, falls into it himself.
8. Macbeth doesn't know that the predictions of the three witches reflect his ambition and downfall, but the audience knows.
9. The tsarina's intense belief in God and mysticism causes her to ignore the pleas of the Russian people for reform and thus causes the downfall of the great Russian dynasty.
10. You go to an expensive hairdresser and he cuts your hair in the shape of a salad bowl leaf.

SUGGESTED ANSWERS

(some questions overlap types):
(1) 2; (2) 4; (3) 5; (4) 4; (5) 2; (6) 5; (7) 2; (8) 3; (9) 2; (10) 1

SUGGESTIONS FOR WRITING

Write a verbal irony on violations of our First Amendment, violations of the Clean Air Act, or violations of privacy. As you write, consider the following:
1. What do you disapprove of? Can it be changed? Research this, if necessary.
2. Select 3–5 specific examples or anecdotes from the list that would best illustrate the practice as unjust, illogical, or inefficient.
3. After sketching a draft, arrange the examples or anecdotes in the most natural order for your purpose: narrative, process, comparison/contrast, reasons, least important to most important, or most important to least important. Check to see that the design is clearly structured and the paragraphs sufficiently developed.

4. Either sketch the satire straight (not ironic) then go back and flip it into verbal irony or write it ironically from the start, whichever is easier for you.
5. Exaggerate so your reader recognizes the satire.
6. Check to see that the irony is sustained throughout. If it is not, where does the language go "straight" and how should it be changed?
7. Remember that your ultimate goal is to effect change as you make us laugh. As a satirist, have you assumed a serious commitment to right wrongs?
8. Try it out on some friends. Revise as necessary.

Wit

> A cynic is a man who, when he smells flowers, looks around for a coffin.
> H. L. MENCKEN

> Nothing is impossible until it is sent to a committee.
> JAMES H. BOREN

> Military intelligence is a contradiction in terms.
> GROUCHO MARX

Wit refers to an ingenious, deft, satiric phrase. Compressed and stylish, wit deserves special mention because it's highly prized among sophisticates as the most clever and pointed criticism. In wit, word play figures as prominently as critical purpose, and its humor converges simultaneously to attack the opponent and to show off the brilliance of the satirist's surprising turn of phrase. Wit combines agile language with a critical comment about a person or society, and although the tone can range from genial to biting, it's always ironic because it draws tension between intelligence and ignorance.

Joseph Addison, the eighteenth-century critic and essayist, distinguishes between true wit and false wit. He says that true wit associates words and ideas; false wit associates only words. False wit occurs in puzzle word games; true wit addresses issues and behavior. We laugh at the unfortunate truth of sharp wit. In the three witticisms that open this chapter, H. L. Mencken sarcastically ribs the cynic for his distorted view of reality; James H. Boren twists a paradox into a stab at bureaucracy; and Groucho Marx clarifies the oxymoron of an "intelligent military."

U.S. presidents have used wit to parry a difficult or embarrassing situation—or to charm the people. Responding to Stephen Douglas's rude remark that Abraham Lincoln had once been a bartender, Lincoln, famous for his wit, said: "I have long since quit my side of the bar, while Mr. Douglas clings to his as tenaciously as ever." John F. Kennedy, honoring Nobel Prize winners at a White House dinner, joked: "I think this is the most extraordinary collection of talent, of human knowledge, that has ever been gathered together at the White House—with the possible exception of when Thomas Jefferson dined alone." Lyndon Johnson expressed his down-home, teasing wit in a 1964 speech in East Chicago, Indiana, to warm up the audience: "I want to thank you for that wonderful introduction. I think it was the best introduction I have ever had in my political life, except one. One time down in Texas the fellow that was supposed to show up didn't get there and I had to introduce myself." And Ronald Reagan, upon entering the operating room after being wounded by an assassin's bullet, quipped, in spite of his pain, "I hope my surgeon is a Republican."

Literary historians have compiled a long etymology for the word "wit" in drama and literature. In the Middle Ages the word meant "sense," and in the Renaissance, "wisdom." Seventeenth-century writers, who admired it greatly, defined wit as agility of imagination and language. The Restoration plays of that century parlayed their drama on many witty repartees between two cynical lovers, as in the marriage-contract scene in William Congreve's *The Way of the World.* In the eighteenth century, Alexander Pope used the word with several different meanings, including this oft-quoted phrase: "True wit is nature to advantage dressed / what oft was thought, but ne'er so well expressed." By the nineteenth century, wit referred to any humorous comment and now it means an ingenious, deft, satiric phrase.

Another term we use for this humor is "dry wit." Though "wet wit" doesn't exist as the corollary, "dry wit" commonly refers to a highly intellectual and icily disapproving comment. The speaker, often supercilious and smug, regales in his superior knowledge.

Fusing an intellectual incongruity with a sparkling phrase, wit compacts its meaning through paradox or opposites, imagery, understatement, overstatement, sounds, or puns. Wit is often formed through a balanced sentence, where part two reverses the elements of part one, also known as antithesis or chiasmas. Read the following remarks. How is wit established in each? Can you imitate the witticisms by substituting your own satiric barb but employing the same syntax and principles of word play?

1. It's what you learn after you know it all that counts. —John Wooden
2. Politicians are the same all over. They promise to build a bridge even where there is no river.—Nikita Khrushchev
3. If you look like your passport photo, you're too ill to travel. —Will Kommen
4. The rooster makes more racket than the hen that lays the egg. —Joel Chandler Harris
5. Hanging is the worst use man can be put to.—Henry Wotton
6. A specialist is one who knows everything about something and nothing about anything else.—Author unknown
7. Lawyers are the people who get us out of all the trouble we never would have gotten into if it hadn't been for lawyers. —Author unknown
8. People who have half an hour to spare usually spend it with someone who hasn't.—Author unknown
9. Death is nature's way of telling us to slow down. —Author unknown
10. Avenge yourself. Live long enough to be a problem to your children.—Author unknown

SUGGESTED RESPONSES

1. paradox; 2. imagery; 3. imagery; 4. reversal; 5. understatement; 6. reversal; 7. paradox; 8. reversal; 9. understatement; 10. reversal

SUGGESTIONS FOR WRITING

Creating wit can be difficult, so you might have to polish and condense your phrasing many times. Try mental spins to create paradoxes; free associate for clever similes or metaphors. Not every sentence in your sketch, however, needs to be witty; in fact, too many could make it contrived and boring, although three or four witty phrases could spiff up a scene. Read Oscar Wilde's play *The Importance of Being Earnest*, which is jam-packed with wit, for an excellent exception to this rule.

1. Write a sketch with at least one witty character. Create a con- versation where the characters talk about the government, the medical profession, or Wall Street. Have one character belong

to the establishment that the witty character puts down. Let the wit casually point out flaws in the establishment with comments about that profession.
2. Write a conversation between an artist and a critic of art. You decide which one should be witty.
3. Write a conversation between a witty young kid and an arrogant, pompous teenager. Let them argue over who's better at something.

Snap'N Crackle . . . a.k.a. "Tone"

While satire depicts a playfully critical attitude that the author holds toward a subject, *the degree of that disapproval—the tone—* can vary from genial and friendly to caustic and bitter; as tone edges toward the caustic, satire loses its humor. We can place satiric tones along a continuum (see Figure 8).

We signal tone, manifested either subtly or outright, through clues in the language, as the imagery below illustrates.

- *genial, gentle:* Your haircut reminds me of a strawberry sundae.
- *clownish:* Your haircut reminds me of Groucho Marx with a perm.
- *amused, bemused:* Your haircut looks like a faded rose petal.
- *intellectual, witty:* Your haircut could bring down an Aristotelian argument.
- *ironic, wry:* Your haystack haircut isn't exactly clever.
- *dark, grotesque:* Your haircut looks like a six-car pileup in the Lincoln Tunnel.
- *sarcastic, biting, coarse:* Looks like your cosmetic surgeon yanked up your facelift and knotted it at the top of your head.
- *caustic, cruel, vicious:* Your haircut looks like the shit of a tsetse fly.

Sarcasm

Sarcasm, from the Greek word meaning "to tear flesh," refers to a crude, sneering, direct assault, and while its tone could be ironic, its intention is meaner and therefore rarely, if ever, humorous. Sometimes humorists confuse sarcasm with satire: sarcasm hurts and insults the victim; satire humors as it corrects. Avoid sarcasm if you want to get a laugh since it scares and alienates an audience. Some stand-up comedians use mock sarcasm

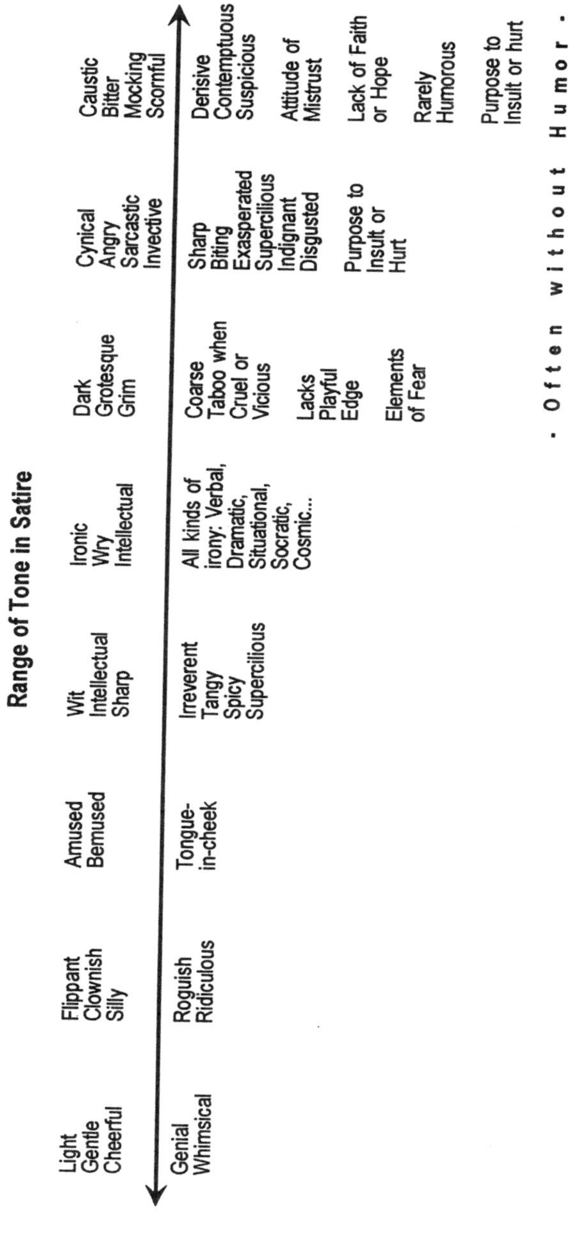

Range of Tone in Satire

Light Gentle Cheerful	Flippant Clownish Silly	Amused Bemused	Wit Intellectual Sharp	Ironic Wry Intellectual	Dark Grotesque Grim	Cynical Angry Sarcastic Invective	Caustic Bitter Mocking Scornful
Genial Whimsical	Roguish Ridiculous	Tongue-in-cheek	Irreverent Tangy Spicy Supercilious	All kinds of irony: Verbal, Dramatic, Situational, Socratic, Cosmic...	Coarse Taboo when Cruel or Vicious	Sharp Biting Exasperated Supercilious Indignant Disgusted	Derisive Contemptuous Suspicious
					Lacks Playful Edge		Attitude of Mistrust
					Elements of Fear	Purpose to Insult or Hurt	Lack of Faith or Hope
							Rarely Humorous
							Purpose to Insult or hurt

• Often without Humor •

Figure 8. Range of tone in satire

as counterculture statements, but this isn't the same as real sarcasm. "You're so stupid you don't know your head from your ass" might get laughs if the context is safe, but isolated from humorous clues, this speaker insults and attacks the person receiving the sarcasm. Writers famous for their sarcasm include George Bernard Shaw and Truman Capote; comedians include Don Rickles and Joan Rivers.

   Read the examples below and identify the tone in each. What clues do the writers plant to define their tone?

1. It was a widely known fact that the Try Harder Bakeoff would be held in Liverpool next month, and that country cooks all over town were warming up to the competition, especially my ten-year-old brother, who believed as blind faith that his special peanut butter and jelly sandwich could sweep out all other entries. The secret, he told me, was glucose.

2. ITHACA—The meteorological world was turned upside down yesterday when a strange and bizarre weather pattern developed near the ordinarily unnewsworthy city of Ithaca, New York. Despite the region's unfortunate location and biological chemistry, which have combined to produce some of the worst weather trends ever recorded, New York's Southern Tier, also known as "The Grey Belt," experienced its very first sunny day in more than two years.—John Sangimino, Jr.

3. Jim Beechman was used to having things fall on him. Since childhood, objects in the sky seemed to be attracted to his head. At his First Communion, Jesus in the form of a plaster statue had dived off the wall and split open Jim's eyebrow. While it did earn him the respect of the nuns at his elementary school, he was left with a scar that always caused people to ask, "Why did you shave a line through your eyebrow?" . . . So it was no surprise to Jim when, walking down Elm Street that day in March, a dog fell from above and landed in his arms. A Chihuahua, to be precise, weighing no more than five pounds, and Jim's first thought concerned the irony of the event, seeing as the word "Chihuahua" literally means "little dog who fell from the sky."—Laura Klink

4. Zeus had puked all over the solar system and Buddha had managed to crush a number of larger planets into smaller planets while trying to slam dance his way out of a black hole. As God was washing down his Divine Strength Tylenol, Buddha and Zeus rose from their graves and surveyed the damage. —John Duff

5. Let me tell you, I don't give a damn what the government says, I love my gun and I'm not going to let anyone take it away from me except over my cold, dead body. We're Americans, right? The government has to learn that a real gun owner acts on what he says. When I talk, I shoot. So what if there are accidents. So what if I splatter someone's guts. That's the cost of living. Let any government shoot off its mouth to me about my gun and it'll have to re-learn to swallow. Besides, the Constitution and God are on my side. When the Bible says the shepherd should carry his staff, that means a gun. Our real motto should be: "In guns we trust."

Possible Answers

1. genial; 2. lightly ironic; 3. bemused; 4. sophisticated, irreverent; 5. sarcastic, sour, angry

13

Grotesque (Black), Sick, and Absurd Humor

Eat right; stay fit; die anyway.

Grotesque Humor (Black Humor)

When the cartoonist Charles Addams got married, the ceremony was held—where else?—in his favorite cemetery. And the bride wore black. All in keeping with his *New Yorker* cartoons of the Addams Family, a loveable, ghoulish Frankensteinian family that slogs and slithers through a creaky, cobwebbed Victorian mansion as it acts out grotesque happenings in a perfectly normal way. Another cartoonist, John Callahan, a quadriplegic and recovering alcoholic, author of *Don't Worry, He Won't Get Far on Foot*, comes to terms with his disabilities by using them as the subject for his humor. One of his well-known cartoons shows an aerobics class for quads with the instructor saying, "OK, let's get those eyeballs moving." Among his many honors is the Free Expression Award, given to him by the ACLU of Oregon for his artistic courage. Both Addams and Callahan use grotesquerie to define their worlds.

Grotesque humor, also known as black humor, makes us laugh at the same time it repulses and shocks. By combining bizarre imagery with chilling topics like war, death, or disease, it has two purposes: to make fun of sentimental, prejudiced, and conformist thought; and to voice a moral hopelessness for our meaningless, irrational life.

Grotesque humor has a long history, stretching from ancient Greek and Roman satires through the mystery plays of medieval Europe to eighteenth-century English pamphleteers to current political stand-up. In fact, the word "grotesque" comes from the bizarre underground paintings (*grotte*) found in ancient Roman ruins. Throughout literary history, some of the world's most honored writers have used the grotesque in their work. Edgar Allan

172

Poe, for example, merges comic irony with horror in his short story "The Cask of Amontillado"; Joseph Heller, in his novel *Catch-22*, deplores senseless war through the book's tragicomic protagonist, Yossarian. Other writers of the grotesque include Nicolai Gogol, Isaac Babel, Charles Dickens, Flannery O'Connor, Franz Kafka, Eugene Ionesco, and Samuel Beckett.

Look at the following satire by Phil Cormier. Do you think the grotesque imagery is valid for what he's trying to say? Why or why not?

Go Cook Yourself

PHIL CORMIER

Toasting a human body is much like toasting a bagel. The ideal bagel begins with a generous application of butter to prevent drying and shriveling. The two halves are then exposed to a 275 degree heating source for about 2 1/2 minutes, or until golden brown.

A human body, however, differs in a few ways. If you plan to toast yourself, prepare your skin with butter or cocoa butter, but expose it to the sun for about 2 1/2 hours, with the air preheated to 85 degrees. Unlike the bagel, your body must be flipped for browning on the underside as well. For this I often bring to the beach a standard kitchen timer and an aluminum snow shovel, which works quite well as a spatula, although the edges tend to become jagged and I take great care not to pierce the meat.

If you're cooking yourself without supervision, please understand that not everyone is intended to be well done. In fact, the majority of all avid beach-goers are in the medium-rare to medium-well range and, consequently, it's not a bad idea to bring along a serrated carving knife to make sure you don't overcook. A nice place to test yourself for doneness is right above either knee cap. Cut into the fleshy crust of the thigh about 2 inches down. If you still look pinkish, you're safe for another hour or so.

If you're bored with the same old crusty brown glossy skin outcome, here's an interesting twist. When you're good and moist with perspiration, very quickly and thoroughly slap your body around in the sand as if you were a piece of veal. Bake for 2 hours (one hour each side) at 88 degrees. You'll love the breaded texture of your skin and the way people can light matches on you at parties. Whether you're cooking out in the open air or inside a microwave booth, your main concern should be to brown evenly because nobody likes rippled crisp skin except shedding snakes.

So best wishes and good cooking, and tune in next week when I'll return with some tips on freezing.

With grotesque satire, a writer criticizes society, using shock to discomfort the audience in order to reform it. It's like any satire, except that the author's tone is flip, exasperated, ironic, or angry, and the approach to the subject repulses us as it makes us laugh. Shock for shock's sake, however, yields little satiric value. To create good grotesque satire, take a responsible position so that you reform us, not repulse us per se. If this humor has satiric integrity, it rises in artistic value; therefore, ask yourself what value it has beyond the grotesque.

What repulses us in this satire? Why would we laugh? Does the work have literary merit? Why or why not?

The Remains of Scople Library

At 1:30 P.M. on Friday of this week the brain of Andy Acular imploded then exploded from mental exhaustion. He was a resident of the McKlintock Dormitory. Collapsing on the protruding front steps of the Scople Library, Acular promptly died. The neural bundles from the pre-frontal lobes of his brain burst above his left ear, and he reposed in a pool of coagulated blood.

Although the change of 2:00 classes occurred shortly thereafter, his body was virtually ignored by students anxious to go elsewhere. One Environmental Science major, however, paused briefly to complain about the destruction to the campus environment when Acular's brain oozed over into the freshly mowed grass, and one Political Science major stated loudly that this death was clearly a media event contrived by the Democrats to get more funding for educational research. Debbie Swawze, director of Visual Panning Operations in TV/Film, wandered upon the scene eating an ice cream cone, double chocolate. She stated, and we quote: "I averted my eyes so that I wouldn't get indigestion from the blood wedgie which extended from Acular's skull. Acular clearly had studied too much."

Eventually, the Security Police were notified that the body must be cleared from the sidewalk as it was attracting fleas, the Nile virus and the President's dog. In an informal eulogy on the library steps, Bouser McDonald, president of the college, stated that Acular's mental sacrifice symbolized far beyond words the peace and contentment that comes from a good college education.

The next day, the campus television station announced that some deconstructionists doubted Acular really died, but the humanists reported that they felt his pain. The station suggested that any CD's left on the body should be distributed among the poor.

Is this the best means to make a satiric point? Why or why not? In what ways does it indict our apathetic society?

HOMEWORK

Analyze a grotesque joke, anecdote, play, film, or sitcom you've recently encountered. What do you think were the writer's intentions? Whose sensibilities are embarrassed, insulted, or harmed? Does the work have artistic value? Why or why not?

SUGGESTIONS FOR WRITING

Have your character rap about some annoyance or sadness that has larger cosmic implications, such as traffic jams that make us wait so long that time stops; a prayer from a clown that's never heard; a prayer from a clown that God answers, much to the clown's dismay; guns that go off by themselves. What's your artistic intent? What reaction do you want from your audience?

Sick Humor

"Understand you buried your wife last week."
"Had to. Dead, you know."

Bad joke? Maybe.

While style and intention overlap, we'll distinguish between *grotesque* and *sick humor* to demonstrate their different effects on audience. Both use shock images to create humor, but grotesque humor is satire and sick humor is not. Grotesque humor demands social reform and a strong awareness of our humanity. *Sick humor, on the other hand, refuses any moral purpose* by deliberately violating taboos for the sake of the violation and directly challenging proper conventions of what we're allowed to think and feel. Grotesque humor says that we really shouldn't enjoy blood and guts; sick humor give us permission to savor them. The sick humorist revels in violating all we hold sacred.

Like grotesque humor, sick humor can often be identified by its subjects—death, blood, disease, deformity, and suffering—but the writer of sick humor relishes the breaking of taboos. Why would a writer do this? Critics argue that sick humor plays to the lowest instincts of human nature and we should shun it; its proponents say it provides a valuable emotional outlet by exposing cultural demons and giving permission for absolute freedom of thought. Psychologists offer some theories for its value. Sick humor, they say, allows us to express hatred and anger without punishment, not unlike the shaman in some cultures who exorcises evil and purifies guilt. They also hypothesize that sick humor comes out of a mass reaction as the means to eventual acceptance of a tragic event. Life gives us no choice but to accept tragedy or to break down psychologically. By laughing, these psychologists say, we choose life, the healthiest way to cope.

We see this, for example, in disaster jokes. After the Mexico City earthquake, people joked publicly about it: "How do you make a Mexican sandwich? With one Mexican and two slices of concrete."

Sick humor surfaces in jokes about death, as in the "Mommy, Mommy" campus craze back in the 1950s, just as GIs returned from the war:

"'Mommy, Mommy, Daddy's been hit by a car!'

'Don't make me laugh, Sheldon. You know my lips are chapped.'"

"Mommy, Mommy, where are the marshmallows? Sheldon's on fire."

Why would an audience laugh at Michael Alan Miller's "Gourmet Pet Recipes"? Would you read it as sick humor, satire, or just plain fun? Explain.

Gourmet Pet Recipes

MICHAEL ALAN MILLER

Chihuahua Con Carne

Clean and skin 2 medium size Chihuahuas. Arrange in baking pan, and smother with beans, onions, tomato sauce, and chili powder. Bake at 305 degrees until they stop barking.

Hamster and Cheese Melt

Clean and boil hamster for 20 minutes. Allow to cool. When cool, slice hamster thinly and arrange slices on rye bread. Top with cheese and mustard. Toast.

Milk Snake

In blender, combine 12 oz milk, 2 tablespoons chocolate sauce, and 1 or 2 snakes. Blend at high speed until creamy or eyes separate and float to surface.

Fried Fish
Place 1 dozen tropical fish (goldfish are excellent) in bowl of
flour. Allow fish to wiggle and flip about freely until they are
well covered. Deep fry immediately.
Cat-kabobs
Skin cat. Stop! Cat is moving around too much. Cut its throat.
Finish skinning cat. Clean and dismember. Separate ears, eyes,
nose, tongue, paws, tail, and set aside. Cut meat into 1 1/2 inch
cubes. Arrange on skewers, alternating meat, features, and an
occasionally cherry tomato. Broil for 15 minutes, turning once.
Serve with warm milk.

When sick humor is intended as pure shock, it fills the psychological purpose of assuaging fear, anger, or anxiety, but it contains
a troublesome violent and scatological edge that can offend audiences. As always, we writers must insist on total freedom of
speech, but if you plan to use sick humor in your work, think
about why you write and what you hope to achieve.

HOMEWORK

Think about a sick joke, cartoon, or anecdote you've recently encountered. What do you think the writer's intentions are? Think
about the audience it addresses. What sensibilities are insulted?
Who might take offense?

Absurd Humor

The word "absurd" originally meant out of harmony, illogical, or
ridiculous. In *Theatre of the Absurd,* drama critic Martin Esslin
coined it as human existence that is purposeless, hopeless, or futile, and now that's how this term is generally used. Absurdists
see life as having no spiritual purpose and death as nothingness;
although much absurd literature isn't funny, twentieth-century
humor writers have found the absurd voice well suited to express
their own comic despair. *Absurd humor intermingles humor with
disillusionment and cynicism.* Grotesque works are sometimes
overlaid with absurdity, as in Joseph Heller's *Catch-22,* but absurd humor, unlike grotesque and sick humor, doesn't usually
rely on repulsive imagery to make its point. More intellectual and
much more philosophical, it generates humor through a grotesque
logic—or an amusing absence of logic. Literature that seeks to
dramatize the absurd eschews traditional plot structure, employing sets of images as the vehicles for the story. Among the most

famous absurdist plays is Samuel Beckett's *Waiting for Godot*, where the tramp desperately wants to hang himself but can't because the only available rope is holding up his pants.

In this monologue by Michael Alan Miller, the speaker fights an absurd battle with annoying flies as he raises questions about human and insect existence. In what ways is the absurdity existential and, therefore, funny?

Flies

MICHAEL ALAN MILLER

My theory is that flies appear via spontaneous existence, and my theory is as follows:

Go to any farm and pick a sunny spot in the pasture where you have real good visibility. Notice something. You don't see any flies. Sure, there are butterflies and moths and even caterpillars crawling on the daisies, but no flies. Now have Eugene the farmhand walk that old grey mare, Betsy, over to your area and induce the horse to dispose of its previous solid meal onto the flyless ground. (I usually spur on this incident by placing my Sony Walkman on the horse and playing, at a moderate level, Dolly Parton's single "Nine to Five.")

Once the specimen is secured on the spot, and Betsy has been taken away for her daily dancing lesson, watch the pile of . . . well, ah . . . we'll call it protein. After about one minute a fly should appear. It doesn't crawl out from under the pile or fly over from a nearby lily pad. It just appears. In three to five minutes, Bango!!, you've got at least half a dozen of the little critters. And you can't make them go away. Don't even waste your breath trying. Once they're there, they're there.

Flies irritate us because they have an attitude problem. They don't care about building nests, raising families, or quibbling over the Genome Project. They don't spin webs, build colonies, hunt, or even relax. Flies are very rude. They will land on your ice cream cone and rub stuff off their back legs onto your food right in front of your face. You can't see the stuff, but you know it's there, and you eat your ice cream with a grudge. Even worse, on those really tough nights when you've finally stopped tossing and turning after five hours of restless awkwardness, a fly will inevitably buzz by your ear, land on your face, and check out if you have a vacancy in your right nostril.

A fly's purpose in life? To fly. No more, just to fly. They fly from your hair to the garbage can to the toilet to your food and eventually back to your hair. They don't care about anything. They just fly.

To cope with flies, we humans have attempted psychological

analysis of the insect and the results of our long study show that the unrelenting fly appears to have no other motive in life than to bother us as much as they can. We shoo them away once, twice, and again and again, and yet they still return. Our diagnosis? Flies have suicidal tendencies with delusions of grandeur. Even the fly can see that we are much bigger than they are and that our physical capabilities are more advanced, with the exception of being able to fly. And yet they not only fly around our heads (at which point they're blatantly challenging our defense mechanisms), but they then proceed to buzz around our heads three more times and laugh in our ears. So we kill them.

Yet in the ancient Jungian ritual between man and fly, these little neurotic newts return again and again, to harass us—to torture us—to tickle us—and to demonstrate their power and its prickly, beastly force.

You'd think they'd learn.

SUGGESTIONS FOR WRITING

Let your character ruminate on some small element in life and its cosmic significance: a child's jump rope that becomes a universal umbilical cord; a taxi driver's horn that becomes a cosmic voice; a strawberry milkshake that symbolizes life's sweetness.

Nonsense

Sign in shopping mall in New York: "Ears Pierced Free—While You Wait!"

College Bookstore: "Please Deposit 25 Cents for Use of Free Locker."

Oldie but goodie: What's grey, has four legs and a trunk? A mouse on vacation.

Definition, History, Purpose

Whatever humor's more serious purpose, sexual and aggressive relief notwithstanding, *nonsense* is one of life's great pleasures because it *respects the smallness of absurdities as it celebrates life's greatest inductive leaps.* Nonsense lets us see as we've never seen before, yoking together our subconscious visions, then flashing them before us in ways that defy evaluation or reply. Releasing us from the constrictions of logic, it unleashes our fantasies and imagination. Protecting us from disapproval, since its context is understood to be safely nonsensical, it's the ultimate freedom. Nonsense twists, turns, and flips images and chronology; it dips into our nether life. Sometimes it overlaps as satire, for it outrageously criticizes dullness, joylessness, stolidity, and the ultimate taboo, lack of creativity. Standing by itself, it's a genre in and of itself.

Nonsense differs from gibberish because nonsense contains a logic of its own. Premised on absurd syllogisms in its own context, it makes sense. Gibberish confuses an audience, who would be puzzled by it, not pleased, and even possibly uncomfortable. For nonsense to work, there has to be an inductive leap into another "logical" plane, which itself violates some logical principle.

Although considered a minor genre by most critics, nonsense shares a long history with more respected literatures: Shakespeare couples it with serious themes in his plays; and in nineteenth-century England, "nonsense" is classified as "major" literature in Lewis Carroll's *Alice in Wonderland* (1865) and *Through the Looking-Glass* (1872), beloved by children and adults alike. Other writers who have written nonsense include Rabelais (*Gargantua and Pantagruel*), G. K. Chesterton, Edith Sitwell, Gertrude Stein, James Thurber, William Saroyan, and J. D. Salinger. James Joyce's *Finnegan's Wake,* a masterful novel of word play, puns, and neologisms, gets much of its genius from nonsense.

Nonsense has influenced philosophers, artists, and writers alike. Symbolist and surrealist painters like Marc Chagall have created free-associative landscapes depicting dreams and wishes, as have dramatists in the Theater of the Absurd like Samuel Beckett with his games, wit, and puns in *Waiting for Godot.* Existential philosophers speculate that we create nonsense to nullify an unemotional universe, irrational pain, and ultimately our death, and nonsense has influenced black humor in the existential questioning, "Is there life before death?" Of course, Jack Handey might retort, "I don't understand people who say life is a mystery, because what is it they want to know?"

Sounds and Rhythms

Do you remember the tickling along your neck as your grandma whispered in your ear, "Fuzzy Wuzzy was a Bear"?

> Fuzzy Wuzzy waz a bear,
> Fuzzy Wuzzy had no hair,
> Fuzzy Wuzzy wazn't fuzzy,
> was he?

Your grandma taught you the music of the letter "z" by appealing to more than one sense—sound and touch—doubling your opportunity to learn words.

Nonsensical sounds and rhythms appeal especially to children, and many psychologists believe that a child's normal linguistic development originates from enjoyment of this component of language. We learn merged sounds by reciting, "How much wood can a woodchuck chuck if a woodchuck could chuck wood?" And counting rhymes help us remember numbers as they coordinate our jump rope skills. "One, two, buckle my shoe; three, four, close the door; five, six, pick up sticks," which we follow with preadolescent games, puzzles, and riddles. Big favorites, of course, are those tongue twisters where we impishly wait to hear somebody make a profane slip: "The sixth sick sheik's sixth sheep's sick."

You can write nonsense by playing on *sounds and rhythms*, but you'll want to think about audience. Although playful sounds can't be sustained for a long time without boring an adult listener, short bursts can be funny and, combined with other genres like parody or satire, they can intensify the humor.

Jennifer Lynne Miller combines sounds with a clearly organized, logical, persuasive argument. Her letter "p" tap-dances across the page, yet we're also reading a parody of an editorial that exhorts us to community action. In what ways does this move beyond nonsense? Any satire here? Read it aloud for an extra tickle. Imagine it being performed.

Editorial

JENNIFER LYNNE MILLER

The Pittsburgh Independent, as part of its public awareness project, has been reporting upon various propositions and policies which will be presented for passage in the upcoming election next week.

In view of some particularly important issues, the publishers of this paper would like to make public their support of "Proposition Penguin." Ms. Pamela Penelope Putnam, a member of the People's Party, has been the prime developer of this proposition. Pamela, in addressing one of the perplexing problems in Pennsylvania, has proposed to promote the proliferation of penguins in the public parks of Pittsburgh. These particular penguins, for which Pamela has pleaded her case, have been placed under the protection of the Society for the Prevention of Poaching of Penguins, otherwise known as the SPPP.

The problem of increasing poaching has apparently been due in part to the newly opened chain of Tuxedo Junction stores within the perimeters of Pittsburgh. Under present penal codes, penguin poachers are fined only a few pennies per penguin pelt possessed. However, now that the proprietors of the Tuxedo Junction stores are paying a premium price for pelts to be used in publicity and window displays, the population of Pittsburgh penguins is plummeting.

Ms. Pamela Penelope Putnam, who was a past president of the National SPPP, is now pleading the case against the penguin poachers of Pittsburgh. The primary part of "Proposition Penguin" proclaims that all Pennsylvania penguins will become part of public property. People caught poaching penguins, whether they, the penguins, be from the Pittsburgh Zoo or private penguin producers, will be subject to prosecution and penalties, which might possibly lead to their placement in Pennsylvania Penitentiaries.

In view of all the positive prospects possible with the promotion of penguin proliferation and obliteration of solicitations of penguin pelts for profit, the *Pittsburgh Independent* proudly pronounces its support of Ms. Pamela Penelope Putnam's proposed "Proposition Penguin." We strongly suggest that you vote "Yes" on item number three in column "B." Vote "Yes," Pittsburghians, and put a penguin in your park.

Besides the play on sounds, Miller infuses satire with logic; she pleads for humane treatment of animals through a formal, Aristotelian argument. The first paragraph announces the background for the argument, and the first sentence in the second paragraph boldly states the thesis: "the publishers of this paper would like to make public their support of 'Proposition Penguin.'" The third paragraph outlines the cause of the decreasing penguin population in Pittsburgh and the fourth proposes a solution to the problem: that Pennsylvania penguins become part of public property. The last paragraph restates the thesis as the *Pittsburgh Independent* entreats all of us to support its position.

Bob Elliott and Ray Goulding, of early radio and television fame, slide through a whole routine, one of their most famous, by laughing at language rhythms.

Slow Talkers of America

BOB ELLIOTT AND RAY GOULDING

Ray: It's surprise time for me now, because I haven't had the opportunity to meet and talk to my next guest. . . . Sit down, sir. Would you tell us your name and where you're from?

Whitcomb: Harlowe . . . P . . . Whitcomb . . .

Ray: Where are you from?

Whitcomb: . . . from . . . Glens . . . Falls . . .

Ray: New York?

Whitcomb: New . . . York.

Ray: What do you do?

Whitcomb: I . . . am the . . . president . . . and recording . . .

Ray: Secretary? . . . Recording secretary?

Whitcomb: . . . secretary . . . of . . . the S . . . T . . . O . . . A . . .

Ray: What does that stand for?

Whitcomb: The . . . Slow . . . Talkers . . . of . . .

Ray: America.

Whitcomb: America. . . . We believe . . . in speaking slowly . . .
Ray: So that you'll never be misunderstood!
Whitcomb: . . . so that our ideas . . . our thoughts . . .
Ray: Words!
Whitcomb: . . . and opinions . . .
Ray: Will never be misunderstood.
Whitcomb: Will always . . . be . . .
Ray: Understood!
Whitcomb: Understood. We . . . are . . . here . . .
Ray: In New York City.
Whitcomb: . . . in New York . . . City . . . for our . . . annual . . .
Ray: Convention.
Whitcomb: . . . membership . . .
Ray: Convention.
Whitcomb: Convention. All . . . two hundred . . .
Ray: Members.
Whitcomb: . . . and fifty . . .
Ray: Members!
Whitcomb: . . . seven . . . members . . . speaking . . .
Ray: Slowly!!
Whitcomb: . . . slowly. As opposed . . . to the members . . . of the . . . F . . .
Ray: T.O.A.!
Whitcomb: T . . .
Ray: O.A.!!
Whitcomb: O . . .
Ray: A!!!!
Whitcomb: A. The Fast . . .
Ray: Talkers of America!
Whitcomb: Talkers . . .
Ray: of America! You're making me a nervous wreck, sir!
Whitcomb: of . . .
Ray: Cut to a commercial . . . PLEASE!!!
Whitcomb: America. We have a credo. . . .

SUGGESTIONS FOR WRITING

1. Create an editorial where the speaker, using playful sounds, tries to convince the audience that it should vote to cancel the construction of a local cemetery to make room for a shopping mall.

2. Play with sounds and rhythms in a dialogue between two characters in which they discuss the ways people go through a revolving door.

Spin a Word or an Image

Nonsense thrives on the minuscule and quotidian, and while elephants thunder overhead, we're smiling at the daisy at our feet. Read the following sketches, then try some yourself. Think small by spinning on a word or an image.

Super Balls

SUSAN ARONSON

Do you remember "Super Balls"? What a terrific bounce! You used to throw them on the ground with all your might, and they would bounce up high into the air, dropping back down to earth months later. My brother Harvey once gave two-hundred arm winds to a super ball and slammed it to the ground at full force only to find that seconds later it had skyrocketed into his left nostril. He couldn't breathe out of his nose for six years! What saved him, though, was a huge sneeze at a Mets game. The super ball belted out of his nose straight into the stadium, where the bases were loaded, and nailed the batter who automatically advanced to first, which won the game, the series and free season tickets for next year.

How does Anne Marie Dinardo create narrative unity in this nonsensical sketch?

Unsolved Sandal Mysteries

ANNE MARIE DINARDO

Do you ever wonder why sandals are left in the middle of the road? I do. One day I was driving my red Delorian and almost ran over a lone sandal. . . . It was one of those yellow, beach-thong sandals made from the same synthetic styrofoam material as McDonalds hamburger containers, looked almost new and had a lot of mileage left in it. Then I started wondering. What the hell is that sandal doing in the middle of the road?

Why is it just one sandal? Where is the other sandal? I have offered the following analysis and theory to The Institute of Unsolved Shoe Mysteries for investigation.

First I asked myself: Did some guy actually walk in the middle of the road and decide he really didn't need two sandals and left the other behind? Was he thinking there must be someone who needs one sandal? "I'll just leave it here for anyone who is lucky enough to come by," he says. Or maybe this sandal belongs to someone who is simply clueless. This is the same guy who walks down the middle of the street for the hell of it. Cars beep in back while trailing him and finally pass by breaking the double yellow line rule. The motorists wonder if they missed the sign for SLOW CHILDREN. Through this chaos, the sandal slips off.

But maybe the sandal didn't belong to a pedestrian. No, maybe it belonged to a motorist with a hatred for sandals. Kind of like sandalphobia: the fear of revealing one's toes to the world. At first the motorist suffering from this strange affliction drives down the road rather calmly listening to a Barry Manilow tape. The song "Mandy" explodes out of prehistoric eight track speakers. The motorist glances at her foot as she presses on the gas pedal. Her toes strike her as being a little bit odder then they usually appear, and Barry's voice becomes a little bit more annoying then he usually sounds. Oh Mandy. Oh Mandy. Oh Mandy. Then the motorist loses it. Suddenly the car swerves to the side. She grabs her left sandal and hurls it like a football out the open window in a fit of fury. As she reaches for her right sandal, Barry's crooning subsides. She regains her composure and fearfully scans the roads for a witness. Too embarrassed to retrieve the exiled sandal, she proceeds to drive over the sandal as she continues on her course for destruction. . . .

But to be fair, I must describe the behavior of the recipient of the sandal. Who would pick up a sandal in the middle of the highway? Who would risk getting plastered onto the highway like the remains of a caterpillar flattened by a dirty cleat? Will someone actually think of finding a match later on? I can almost see a renegade motorist spy that spiffy yellow sandal in the rear view window. He'd say, "Hey what a spiffy sandal. I'll just add it to my collection of lost highway shoes and maybe, just maybe I'll someday find a match."

SUGGESTIONS FOR WRITING

Spin on an object, issue, idea, action, habit, or mannerism, like root beer, pigeons, spitting, doorknobs, or butter. Ponder the uses of a body part, like how to grow ear wax for fun and profit. Think about eyelashes, lips, the elbow, or earlobes. Analyze all the uses for paper clips, a jump rope, shoelaces. As you revise, ask yourself: Are you writing nonsense for nonsense's sake or does your sketch have a larger purpose? If you want a larger purpose, think about a theme or unifying factor and, if necessary, rearrange the sketch accordingly. What could be its social/political/philosophical meaning?

The Logical and Illogical

To write logical and illogical nonsense, spin on the literal, obvious, paradoxical, or nonsequitur.

Literal or Obvious

The law requires that we use explanatory signs indicating danger ahead, but in cartoon 3 Stan Hunt jabs at the absurdity of this logic by satirizing our lack of faith in simple common sense. *Literal or obvious nonsense occurs when the writer interprets meaning as denotative—it is exactly what it says it is—even though the context actually requires a more figurative meaning.*

Paradox

A paradox is meaning that conveys two contradictory truths. While appearing absurd, it shadows an underlying logic. Usually the conclusion in this reasoning contradicts the premise, although the premise is logical. To create paradoxes, use contrasting terms

Cartoon 3. © The New Yorker Collection 1981, Stan Hunt from cartoonbank.com. All rights reserved.

Cartoon 4. FRANK & ERNEST reprinted by permission of Newspaper Enterprise Association, Inc.

(oxymorons) as the basis for the humor, such as ignorance/expert; lies/truth; peace/war. See cartoon 4.

> What ruins mankind is the *ignorance* of the *expert.*
>
> G. K. Chesterton

> When two politicians accuse each other of *lying*, both of them are telling the *truth.*
>
> Logicians' joke

In his famous war novel *Catch-22*, Joseph Heller creates profound social commentary through the paradox of *peace and war*, sanity and insanity. In this scene, Yossarian desperately tries to excuse himself from dangerous flight missions, but whenever he asks to be grounded for reasons of insanity, Doc Daneeka refuses to declare him crazy since, according to military logic, only a sane man would be afraid to fly—and if you're sane, you have to fly.

Catch-22

Joseph Heller

It was a horrible joke, but Doc Daneeka didn't laugh until Yossarian came to him one mission later and pleaded again, without any real expectation of success, to be grounded. Doc Daneeka snickered once and was soon immersed in problems of his own, which included Chief White Halfoat, who had been challenging him all that morning to Indian wrestle, and Yossarian, who decided right then and there to go crazy.

"You're wasting your time," Doc Daneeka was forced to tell him.

"Can't you ground someone who's crazy?"

"Oh, sure. I have to. There's a rule saying I have to ground anyone who's crazy."

"Then why don't you ground me? I'm crazy. Ask Clevinger."

"Clevinger? Where *is* Clevinger? You find Clevinger and I'll ask him."

"Then ask any of the others. They'll tell you how crazy I am."

"They're crazy."

"Then why don't you ground them?"

"Why don't they ask me to ground them?"

"Because they're crazy, that's why."

"Of course they're crazy," Doc Daneeka replied. "I just told you they're crazy, didn't I? And you can't let crazy people decide whether you're crazy or not, can you?"

Yossarian looked at him soberly and tried another approach. "Is Orr crazy?"

"He sure is," Doc Daneeka said.

"Can you ground him?"

"I sure can. But first he has to ask me to. That's part of the rule."

"Then why doesn't he ask you to?"

"Because he's crazy," Doc Daneeka said. "He has to be crazy to keep flying combat missions after all the close calls he's had. Sure, I can ground Orr. But first he has to ask me to."

"That's all he has to do to be grounded?"

"That's all. Let him ask me."

"And then you can ground him?" Yossarian asked.

"No. Then I can't ground him."

"You mean there's a catch?"

"Sure there's a catch," Doc Daneeka replied. "Catch-22. Anyone who wants to get out of combat duty isn't really crazy."

There was only one catch and that was Catch-22, which specified that a concern for one's own safety in the face of dangers that were real and immediate was the process of a rational mind. Orr was crazy and could be grounded. All he had to do was ask; and as soon as he did, he would no longer be crazy and would have to fly more missions. Orr would be crazy to fly more missions and sane if he didn't, but if he was sane he had to fly them. If he flew them he was crazy and didn't have to; but if he didn't want to he was sane and had to. Yossarian was moved very deeply by the absolute simplicity of this clause of Catch-22 and let out a respectful whistle.

"That's some catch, that Catch-22," he observed.

"It's the best there is," Doc Daneeka agreed.

Nonsequiturs

Nonsequitur means "it does not follow," that is, a word, image, situation, or idea doesn't logically extend what proceeds it. Nonsequiturs are easier to create than paradoxes, which require intuition, since to form a nonsequitur all you need to do is jump outside the meaning of any sentence or context. You'll want to be careful in your judgment of the distance of that jump and its frequency, however. Nonsequiturs should fit appropriately with the intention of the whole piece. Any mechanical application of this—setup, nonsequitur; setup, nonsequitur; setup, nonsequitur—will wear thin fast. Too far a jump gets confusing or plain silly. But nonsequiturs are the heart of nonsense, and if cleverly done, most readers can take a lot of them.

What might make a reader laugh in the following sketch? What's nonsensical about the character's thoughts as he's falling? How do the nonsequiturs evolve from this absurd, existential situation? Where does the obvious logic occur? Any paradoxes? Other illogical reasoning?

Zooming Past One Hundred Bikers on the Way to Baltimore

Tucker zoomed out of the hundred-biker starting line, skimming the right-hand lane at Central and Main, aka Woolworth's Square, south of York, PA, near the roadside stand where the Dutch Pantry was selling blueberry pies. He passed two University of Pennsylvania experimental pigeons, who were nesting on the window ledge of the Chemical Life Insurance Company, both birds munching on an overripe sour cherry. Tucker had always delighted in many things, but none so much as his current full body press against the wind as he descended down Deadbird Hill, slowly at first, then more rapidly, in absolute accord with the multiplying exponents of the law of gravity. The first big question he asked himself was whether he might be able to see what was playing at the Triangle Theatre, a view available to him if he angled his body seven degrees to the left. His curiosity puzzled him, however, since he hated show tunes, and neon gave him migraines. He also wondered if winning the race would put him on the front page of the York Gazette or if he would be relegated to the lesser sports news posted behind the stock quotes in the business section. Democrat that he was, he didn't like any association with rich capitalists, and this possibility worried him.

The third question he asked himself he promptly forgot, but the disconnect of his neural channels led him to ponder chocolate ice cream. With pecans. And also the significance of literary theory. He wondered: Did Nietzsche really influence Derrida? Can deconstruction be equally applied to gun control and butter? Is butter a text or a poem? And will the possible crack of his brain against these philosophical premises signify death?

Tucker continued his descent across Seventh Street, across Sixth, across Fifth, and past the dusty writing on a dirty window that read "Miss Fraum." Was this a true spelling of the heroine in Hitchcock's *The Lady Vanishes,* he asked himself, or just a subconscious associative pun on his own image as loser. He wasn't sure.

As you write, of course, you'll let the nonsense rise spontaneously from your subconscious creativity and from the context of your work. As you revise, if you're not satisfied with the richness of the texture, you can layer it with more consciously applied non-sequiturs.

Nonsense as Parody and Satire

Besides pure fun, nonsense can spark more "serious" purpose through comedic and satiric characters, situations, or values. In this work, the nonsensical language tacks on a natural effect arising out of the premise of Digger, his famous career, and his death. What is Chris Regan satirizing? What's being parodied?

Digger, The Wonder-Hound

CHRIS REGAN

(AP HOLLYWOOD)—Hollywood mourns the passing of one of its all time greats, Digger, the Wonder-Hound. The famous canine, who starred in over forty films, died last night in his Beverly Hills home. He was fifty-six for you and me. Digger had been complaining of chest pains all morning when he showed up at the studio for a taping of the Oprah Winfrey show, where he was to discuss his recent triumph over drugs and alcohol. Digger did the interview and decided to relax by chasing a few cars with long-time friend, Benji. At around 3 P.M., while chasing a Supra, he collapsed and at 3:20 was pronounced dead on arrival at Compassion Heights Doggie Heaven.

Digger is fondly remembered for his many film roles. He sprung to prominence with his portrayal of Heathcliff, the passion consumed Dachshund, in "Wuthering Heats." After that, a variety of brilliant portrayals followed, including "The Maltese Schnauzer," "To Have and Hydrant," "Dr. Spaniel; or How I Learned to Stop Worrying and Love the Flea Bath," and "Hannah and Her Litter."

Digger's career suffered many setbacks, mostly notably at the hands of the McCarthy witch hunts in the early fifties. Digger was accused of not only being a Communist party member but a sympathizer of Pit Bulls for Peace. He found himself on a blacklist and supported himself doing dog food commercials and playing the Catskills.

He found a new career for himself in the early sixties on television. He showed an interesting flair for physical comedy in "My Mother the Dog," and for hard hitting journalism in "This Week with Digger." No one realized the suffering that was going on beneath the collar, as he wrote in his autobiography, "Woof," where he revealed that he was an alcoholic and drug user, along with pal actor Dennis Hopper. Many people believe that it was Digger's influence that was the brilliance of "Easy Rider."

Digger leaves behind no wives but many children.

Dan Amrich merges nonsense with satire, parody, and burlesque to jab at society's hilarious fascination with superstars and the media. What satiric points does he make?

Jesus Concert Hotter Than Hell

DAN AMRICH

NEW YORK—Over 60,000 fans turned out to see Jesus Christ perform in His only tri-state appearance on His "Second Coming 2000" tour at Madison Square Garden last night. Shrouded in mystery and hype since its announcement, the show was not a disappointment. Instead, it was the triumphant return of a man who's been away from the public eye far too long.

Jesus' last public appearance was in Jerusalem in 33 A.D., where he rose from the dead after having been crucified three days earlier. Some were worried that Jesus would not be able to wow the people like He used to in today's age of rigorous touring schedules, high ticket prices, and pyrotechnics, but His marketing tour managers kept The Son of God right up to date with all the latest in modern concert miracles.

The Grateful Dead opened the show and played for a solid hour. The lights dimmed and Jesus took the stage as only the Messiah could. Christ, dressed in his trademark white robes and neatly trimmed beard, hovered above the audience for a few minutes to thunderous applause, then he grabbed his guitar and opened the show with his recent hit "I Told You (I'd Be Back)." His backing band, the Holy Rollers, featuring St. Michael the Archangel on lead guitar, were in rare form throughout the evening, pumping high energy rock and roll number after number. A special mention goes to the horn section of Matthew,

Mark, Luke, and John, who put on an incredible musical performance for four guys known mainly for their writing.

Many of the production numbers required numerous special effects, which usually leaves lots of room for potential error. But the changing of water into wine during "It's a Wedding (Let's Party)," the multiplying loaves and fishes in the middle of "Hungry?" and the miraculous guest appearance of the Eternal Fires of Hell during "H-E-Double Hockey Sticks" were all accomplished with split-second timing and perfection.

Jesus came up with a few musical surprises as well, performing such favorites as "Just Hanging Around (The Crucifixion Song)" and "My Dad's Bigger Than Your Dad," and even the Chuck Berry classic "Johnny B. Goode." The show lasted a full two and a half hours, with His Holiness inviting on stage special guests Eric "God" Clapton and Jesus lookalike Ted Nugent for a few numbers. A concert movie is slated for a Christmas release, which will give all non-believers a chance to glimpse history, as Jesus sadly announced that He will not be touring again for quite some time. He did not give any indication to how long "quite some time" might be. "I'm real busy," Jesus said in a recent interview. Jesus' latest album, "Life at the Top," has already gone quadruple platinum.

In his current performances, Jesus shows that He still has what it takes to not only be the leader of one of the world's largest religions, but also to really rock when the Spirit moves Him.

Amrich's parody-burlesque of an art review and satire of rock musicians and religion spins off the first premise, that Jesus is a rock star. Once Amrich conceives that premise, everything else falls smoothly in place. How many different elements of nonsense can you find?

SUGGESTIONS FOR WRITING

1. Ask a serious question. Answer it in a ridiculous or nonsensical way. Or ask a nonsensical question. Answer it in a serious way.
2. Pose a serious "problem" and find a nonsensical "solution." Or pose a nonsensical "problem" and find a serious "solution."
3. Write about dry mouth; beards; tofu; artichokes; dachshunds; a broom handle; your computer mouse.
4. Write a story about the shape of something: your knee; jazz; "hello."

5. Write a sketch about a character who meets a cartoon or comic-strip character. What happens?
6. Write a story where your main character is an animal. Put him/her in a human situation.
7. Write about something that puzzles you, like the nonsensical elements of nuclear physics.
8. Write about the relationship between garbage and religion.

AND EVEN MORE IDEAS

Write a monologue. Give your character a strong personality (drum major, roofer, line skater) with a strong voice and a "cause." Let that character observe things about society by jabbing at war, the president, education, the press, big business. Don't worry about structure. Just let the character talk. As you revise, check for the "sense" of it. What "logical" purpose might it have? Are the nonsensical references appropriate for the kind of speaker you want to create?

To write great nonsense (the literary kind) you need some exceptionally clever imagery or highly original perspective on your topic.

"And . . . ," says the prof.

"OK, go ahead, hit me with it," you say.

"Theme or purpose or unity or some semblance of sense. On some level, surface or gut, the nonsense has to make sense." So . . .

Although your details might fly in all directions, keep a thread (main idea) throughout. Maybe this thread arrives at the end and ties everything together—a statement about the value of the topic, its valuelessness, how it fits into life, how it's used, how it most affects you, how it will change life for the better. Maybe you just want to end with some brilliant image. Or clever remark. That's OK.

However you choose to do it, the work should have direction or a playfulness that forms its intention.

We can validate writing nonsense intellectually (in case you're wondering if your money for this book has been well spent), for it allows you to explore the far galaxies of your imagination by breaking free from the gravity of logic. Arthur Koestler, in his famous and highly respected work, *The Act of Creation*, argues that people who are able to look at everyday things in unusual, zany, or weird ways are better able to problem solve, and that all great artists and scientists have this ability. Standing on your head, looking backward into a mirror, or wearing your jacket inside out are preparatory acts for creativity. Don't be embarrassed to try them.

> Famous maxim: Outside of a dog, a book is man's best friend; inside of a dog, it's too dark to read.
>
> Groucho Marx

Light Verse

Shake and shake the catsup bottle.
None will come, and then a lot'll.

RICHARD ARMOUR

I never had a piece of toast
Particularly long and wide,
But fell upon the dirty floor,
And always on the buttered side.

JAMES PAYN

Light verse fashions nonsense through situation, word play, rhymes, or rhythms. Brief and epigrammatical, light verse might have a satiric purpose, but just as often it hovers on nothing more substantial than childlike playfulness. Common characteristics are coaxed word play, including altered orthography to extend meaning and humor; rhymes and rhythms that stretch, jump, or clog along; and splintering turns of wit. Some light verse conforms to fit the theme of the poem: a poem about a tree branches out like a tree; a poem about stairs staggers like stairs.

Many serious writers have written light verse: John Milton, Goethe, Alexander Pope, W. H. Auden, and Morris Bishop. Light verse hides in subsets of other genres like the song lyrics of Cole Porter. Nonsense verse has been particularly associated with Victorian England, its popularity attributed to a linguistic rebellion of that era's social strictures, and to the talents of two major proponents, Edward Lear and Lewis Carroll. In this century, the acknowledged master of light verse is Ogden Nash, known for rhyming the unrhymable.

EXAMPLES

Model some poems from these gems by Ogden Nash, either using a similar rhyme and rhythm or a variation on the topic.

196

Taboo to Boot

One bliss for which
There is no match
Is, when you itch,
To up and scratch.

The Termite

Some primal termite knocked on wood
And tasted it, and found it good,
And that it why your Cousin May
Fell through the parlor floor today.

The Fly

God in His wisdom made the fly,
And then forgot to tell us why.

Study the following poem as a model for one of your own. Try to imitate it. Select an uncommon animal or insect, and list its attributes using repeated rhythms and an a, a, b, b rhyme scheme. As always, vary it wherever your instincts take you and break a rule if that works better.

The Goldfish

Consider the Goldfish as a household pet,
you have nothing to do—but keep him wet.
His bearing is mild, his manners are neat,
his face is clean, his breath is sweet.
He doesn't bark, he doesn't sing,
he doesn't bite, or scratch, or sting.
He doesn't shed feathers, or fur, or hairs,
all over the sofa, and carpet, and chairs.
You never find him underfoot;
you put him someplace, and he stays put.
He asks but little here below,
just food to eat, and room to grow.
If either of these is long denied,
when you look for him, he has quietly died.

ANONYMOUS

In the much anthologized poem, "Hazel Tells Laverne," by Katharyn Howd Machan, Hazel screeches her cynical disbelief in fairy tales. Why classify it as "nonsense"? In what ways does it stand as a serious, "literary" poem? After you've studied it, write a poem using a narrator who speaks in a voice very different from yours and who, after observing some trivial phenomenon, comes to a new awareness.

Hazel Tells Laverne

last night
im cleanin out my
howard johnsons ladies room
when all of a sudden
up pops this frog
musta come from the sewer
swimmin aroun an tryin ta
climb up the sida the bowl
so i goes ta flushm down
but sohelpmegod he starts talkin
bout a golden ball
an how i can be a princess
me a princess
well my mouth drops
all the way to the floor
an he says
kiss me just kiss me
once on the nose
well i screams
ya little green pervert
an i hitsm with my mop
an has ta flush
the toilet down three times
me
a princess

Limericks

Limericks, a popular form of light verse, come from obscure origins. One theory is that they were named after the Irish town of

Limerick, where they first appeared in about 1700 among soldiers returning from war. By 1765 they were popular enough to be published in *Mother Goose's Melody,* a collection of nursery rhymes, although they circulated through the oral tradition as well, reaching their height of popularity in England during the Victorian era with the publication of Edward Lear's *Book of Nonsense* in 1846. James Joyce and W. H. Auden, among other major writers, have written limericks.

A limerick is a short poem with specific conventions:
Lines 1, 2, and 5 rhyme
Lines 3 and 4 rhyme
Lines 1, 2, and 5 have 8–10 syllables, usually in an anapestic
    rhythm (one heavy beat and two light beats)
Lines 3 and 4 have 5–7 syllables, also anapestic
The limerick usually describes some action, and a good limerick contains ingenious rhyme and a witty, clever last line. If an occasional limerick contains four lines, the third line will rhyme both internally and at the end, and really scans as though it were both lines 3 and 4. Perhaps because of their military origin, many limericks are bawdy. While some limericks satirize social behavior, most delight in nothing more than the peculiarities of people or nonsensical wit.

There once was a sculptor named Phidias,
Who had a distaste for the hideous,
So he sculpted Aphrodite
Without any nightie,
And shocked all the ultra-fastidious.

    ANONYMOUS

There was a young lady of Keighley
Whose principal charm in her teeth lay;
When they fell on her plate,
She called out, "I hate
Mithhapth of thith kind; they are beathly."

    ANONYMOUS

There was a young lady named Bright,
Who could travel much faster than light.
She started one day

In a relative way,
And came back the previous night.

A. H. R. BULLER

SUGGESTIONS FOR WRITING

Write a first line. Think about words that rhyme with its last word to see if that sets off a story for you. Or start with a terrific last line and work backward.

To write a people-in-action limerick, write a first line introducing a person, then describe that person in action, using the conventions of the limerick. Or write a first line introducing a person, then tell a brief story about that person, again using conventions of the limerick.

To shape the wit, try puns, alliteration, word play, vivid description, or a zany behavior. Read your limerick aloud. Does it have unity? Wit? Content? Originality? Do you do clever things with rhythm or rhyme?

ASK A FRIEND

READER'S WORKSHEET — NONSENSE

1. Is the verse pure nonsense? Satire? Parody? A mix?
2. Does the work have unity? However elemental, does it make sense?
3. What nonsensical techniques does the writer use? Rhythm? Rhyme? Wit? Nonsequiturs? How successful are those techniques?
4. Does the humor work? If so, where? If not, any suggestions?
5. Does the nonsense reach for a higher literary value? If not, what nonsensical value does it have?

Parody and Burlesque

Parody

"What's parody?" you ask. Do you remember how you entertained your fifth-grade class when your teacher left the room? You stood front and center by the chalkboard, chalk and pointer in hand, imitating his quivering voice. That's parody. You were the class clown then, because of all the students only you could break a word at the right syllable exactly as your teacher did—"Now, class-s-s , settle down"—sputtering (and spitting) over the kids in the front row, and recreating his totally ineffectual discipline. No one in the class ever listened to your teacher. Everyone in the class listened to you. And your friends loved you for it.

Our enjoyment of parody comes from our delight in imitation, an intellectual pride in knowing an original source so well that we can brilliantly reimagine it in new ways that mirror the original. And the good news is that it's easy to write. First, a definition.

A parody is a humorous imitation of a specific artistic work, person, idea, or historical period.

Like the word "humor," the word "parody" carries its meaning loosely, and we use it indiscriminately to refer to any humorous imitation. In this book, we'll make a distinction between parody (an imitation of a specific work) and burlesque (an imitation of more general concepts), although you'll see that in complex works this distinction quickly fades. Being aware of the difference, however, is important for the writer.

When writing a parody, you imitate a *specific* work in a humorous way: a poem, story, novel, television show, painting, film, speech, newspaper article, dance, opera, and so forth. You could also parody another person's individual style, such as facial expression, mannerisms, speech, tone, dress, or walk. In a broader interpretation of the definition, you could imitate a specific idea or a specific historical period. A parody could be serious or humorous, but most are humorous.

I remember well my sensation as we first entered
the house. I knew instantly that something was
very wrong. I realized that my father's chair had
been sat in, as well as my mother's and my own.
The porridge we had left on the table to cool had
been partially eaten. None of this, however, prepared me for what we were about to discover upstairs. . . .

Cartoon 5. © The New Yorker Collection 1979, Whitney Darrow from
cartoonbank.com. All rights reserved.

"Why write parodies?" you ask?

- Because you really like the specific work you're imitating and
  you "make fun" of it out of respect. You "parody" yourself
  for your feeble attempts to achieve the greatness of the original.
- Because you dislike the specific work you're imitating, and you
  make fun of it as a means of criticism. This parody overlaps
  with satire.
- Because you want to use an existing art form or an established,
  recognizable genre as a vehicle for your own original ideas.

History of Parody

As with most humorous genres, enjoyment of parody can be traced to ancient times. The Egyptians parody politicians in their stone drawings of anthropomorphic figures. Aristophanes parodies the tragedians Aeschylus and Euripides in his play *The Frogs*, and in eighteenth-century England, Henry Fielding's novel *Shamela* (1741) parodies Samuel Richardson's earlier novel *Pamela*. In the 1920s and 1930s, the witty and sophisticated *New Yorker* magazine rose to a golden age of parody with writers like Robert Benchley, E. B. White, and S. J. Perelman, paralleling the success of England's long-running humor magazine *Punch*. The *New Yorker* extends the tradition today with stories and cartoons by some of the best-known parodists in the United States, like Woody Allen and Ian Frazier. Washingtonian Mark Russell croons political parodies on his television show, culled from current news events, much to the delight of anti-establishment audiences.

In popular culture, *MAD* magazine, founded in 1952 with its Alfred E. Newman caricature, has popularized parody with comic strips and no-holds-barred articles. *Monty Python*, a British television import, frequently parodies politicians, royalty, and sports events, and in 1970 the *National Lampoon* magazine burst on the scene with satiric parody, impishly nipped at the heels by the television show *Saturday Night Live.*

How to Write a Parody

Parodies are easy to write because you already have structure and language in place; since the shape of the work is prefabricated, you just have to fill in the blanks, although, of course, this filler should be clever and wonderful.

To Write a Parody, Do One of Three Things

1. Keep the *content* of the original work the *same* and *change the language or style.*
2. Keep the *style* of the original work the *same* and *change the content.*
3. *Stir, weave, mix* elements from *one or more* original sources into an entirely different work of your own. You could take substantial liberties with your interpretations of these sources.

Let's look at each of these in turn.

Content Is the Same; Change the Language or Style

These two versions of a stylistic parody of *Ecclesiastes* demonstrate how this works.

ORIGINAL ECCLESIASTES

I returned and saw under the sun, that the race is not to the swift, nor the battle to the strong, neither yet bread to the wise, nor yet riches to men of understanding, nor yet favour to men of skill; but time and chance happeneth to them all.

SLANG

So I come back on my heels and spot under the Dome that the track ain't just for Kentucky fillies, and the fight ain't just for Brawny Jake, and the donuts ain't just for Cookin' with Charlie, and the bucks ain't just for the IRS, but if ya live long enough, even us losers get to slot a quarter in Vegas.

DASHIELL HAMMETT'S HARD-BOILED DETECTIVE STYLE

Tough Talk

As I stood there and watched the hot ball of sun burn the valley below, baking the endless rows of houses that marked the end of the city, I realized that the fastest horse don't always cross the line first; the biggest guy can always be taken out by a swift kick in the groin; smarts won't feed you unless you got a job in a library; nice guys finish last; and a hand of three aces is no good unless you're dealt the fourth; but on the big crap table of life, you can toss the dice and call your bet.

PAUL DUNSCOMB

In the above examples, while the voice, imagery, and diction have changed, both the meaning and the sentence structure sufficiently resemble the original for us to recognize it as Ecclesiastes; the incongruity between the poetry of the original passage and the jarring language of the speakers clash to form the humor. In your writing, you'll need to understand the stylistic conventions of the original: in slang, you import lower-class speech and local lingo; in Hammett's detective style, you drawl the lazy rhythms and overwrought, lowlife imagery of Los Angeles.

In a language-change parody, you alter the original as follows:
- If the original style is plain, exaggerate it, fancy it up, or switch to a different voice or tone.
- If the original style is fancy, understate it, fancy it up even more, or write in a completely different voice or tone.

- If the original style has clearly identifiable characteristics, like Hemingway's, Faulkner's, or Monty Python's, highlight their characteristics by exaggerating them.

Brett Ross anachronistically updates the language in the Bible's creation story to get humor in his parody. Although it transforms God's personality a little, and we're now in the present, the action in the original Genesis basically has been retained.

> Over the next couple of days God *sort of went nuts* creating this and that. And He said to Himself, *"Jehovah, you're on a roll."*

Sometimes changes in language occur through the comments of the narrator, which aren't switches but updated "add on's." This is OK. It doesn't diminish the parody.

> During that time God made animals to live above the water and ones to live below the water. The animals above the water he enabled to fly with wings, lest they just float forever, and called them birds, *after his favorite rock group.*

Look at Brett Ross's manuscript. What connecting clues does Ross give so you know the original source is Genesis? How does he change the original so it becomes a parody? How does he use "anachronisms," references to events from a chronological time later than the period in which the original takes place? Besides being a parody, what's Ross satirizing?

The Creation

BRETT ROSS

In the beginning God created the heavens and the earth. At first the earth was formless and covered with water. Everything was dark and the Spirit of God hovered above the water in the stillness. Boy, were his arms tired.

And God said, "This darkness is nowhere. Let there be light." And it was so. And He said, "Actually, while we're at it, let there be two great lights. One, the sun, shall rule the day. The other, the moon, shall rule the night, but be dimmer, so I can get some sleep. Also let there be flashlights."

The next day God made cocktail and visiting hours. And God said, "This hovering stuff is nowhere, I gotta sit down." And so He separated the waters with great expanses of "land," which was dry, and great for sitting on. God called the expanse above the land "sky," because he liked the word and He was God. God was pleased and tired, so He called it a night, which was good, because it was late. There was an evening, and a morning—a second day.

The next morning God got up late but more than made up for it. He decided to call the waters "seas," and thought that was good. Then God said, "Let this land bring forth vegetation in the form of plants bearing fruit seeds which shall regenerate them."

This wasn't clear, but it didn't matter, because God knew what He meant and there wasn't anybody else around anyway.

And God said, "Let there also be a weed, which shall bring great happiness." It was so, of course, and there was a third day.

Over the next couple of days God sort of went nuts creating this and that. And He said to Himself, "Jehovah, you're on a roll."

During that time God made animals to live above the water and ones to live below the water. The animals above the water he enabled to fly with wings, lest they just float forever, and called them birds, after his favorite rock group. The animals below the water he called fish and they had a smell such that God was glad He lived above the water. The evenings and mornings had become a regular thing, and soon it was the fifth day.

And God said, "This place needs some cows and stuff," and so he created livestock to live on the land. God was happy with what He saw and blew off the rest of the day.

The next day God decided that the livestock and other animals needed tending. And so He created man, in His own image, only much shorter. The man was naked, but not ashamed, for it was no big thing, and he knew no better.

After a while the man got tired of playing with the sheep and so God took one of the man's ribs and made from it woman. She was quite a looker, and the man was psyched.

"Thanks, God!" man exclaimed.

"Getta grip." God replied.

It was now the seventh day and God rested. As He sat in His recliner He spoke unto the man and woman. He said:

"I have given unto you a Garden of Eden. You guys can fool around and eat 'til you're sick, but you shall not partake of the fruit of the Tree of Knowledge, cause if you do, your number's up. I've given you a good life, so don't blow it, okay?"

"Uhuh," said the man.

"Yeah," said the woman.

"Swell," said God.

The two frolicked and played in the Garden for a while until one day when the woman happened upon the serpent, who was really a snake, hanging out on the Tree of Knowledge.

"Hiya kid," said the serpent.

"Hey serpent, what's up?" the woman replied.

"I hear God told you you can't eat the apples."

"He said if we did, we'd die," she said.

"Pish posh," said the snake. "He just knows that if you eat of the fruit you'll get smart. You're not gonna die. Go for it."

"Well," said the woman, "okay."

And she ate of the fruit and her eyes were opened, in the figurative sense, and she saw that she was naked and she blushed. She then gathered the leaves of the fig bush and did make a garment of them. And the woman ran to the man and exclaimed, "The Tree of Knowledge is good! God was wrong!"

And the man said, "What are you wearing those fig leaves for?"

And the woman said, "Cause I was naked, like you are. Here, eat of this fruit."

"But," said the man, "God said . . ."

"Look, am I dead?" the woman asked.

To which the man shrugged and ate of the fruit.

"Mifft shggufn . . ." the man said.

"What?" asked the woman.

"It's good. Holy cow! I'm naked!" the man exclaimed. "Sheesh I'm embarrassed."

"It's no big thing," said the woman, "but I brought you a fig leaf anyway."

And so the man put it on and as he did God appeared in a clap of thunder, as was often His way, and said unto them,

"Hey, what's with the fig leaves?"

And the man said, "The woman ate of the fruit because the snake said it was all right and then she gave me some and then we realized we were naked and so we, ah, covered up."

God was angered. "You mean you're not ignorant anymore?"

And the man said, "Don't get upset, it was only a couple of apples!"

The sky rumbled and God said unto them, "I gave you guys paradise with one lousy drawback. But you had to go eat of the Tree of Knowledge. Grapes, cherries, oranges all over this place and you gotta have apples! I'm really upset with you. You blew it big time."

The man and woman trembled with shame and fear.

"Snake," God said, "you shall slither in the dust for the remainder of your existence." And it was so.

"Woman," God continued, "you shall have great pain in childbirth. And you will be grouchy every so often as a punishment to both of you. And man, you shall have to wear a tie and pay insurance."

The man and woman said, "Awwwwww."

And God said unto them, "Now get outta here before I lose it completely."

And the man said, "Okay, we'll go, but first could you suggest a good tailor."

And God said, "Try Abe Zuckerman in Brooklyn."

With his knowledge of Genesis, Brett Ross imagines a slightly different set of events during those first seven days of creation. During his narrative, how does he tackle the primary question we have about existence: What is God really like? Is he just like you and me, with an everyday kind of personality? What's the philosophical puzzle?

Keep the Language and Style of the Original; Change the Content

As you write, use the same or similar words, sounds, rhythms, or structure as the original, but write on a completely different topic.

In this topic-switch parody, Richard Manfredi spins the "Night Before Christmas" into a gloomy look at society.

Dead Birds Can't Sing

'Twas the week before last
and all through the city,
not a creature was stirring,
the weather was shitty.

All the streetlights were out
from the West to East side,
And the river was smelling
like something had died.

The doors to apartments
were locked very tight
It was obviously going
to be a tough night.

The looters were swarming
all through the streets,

And some of the cops
had deserted their beats.

Windows got broken
and cars got tipped
It seemed just as though
the whole city had flipped.

But Ma had a lighter
and I had a candle
'cause the darkness was getting
to be too much to handle.

When down on the street
there arose such a clatter
I shot up off the couch
to see what was the matter.

Over to the window
I ran in a hurry,
but everything after
was really quite blurry.

I heard a few gun shots
and then someone screamin'
It all went so quickly
I thought I was dreamin'

"On Vinny, On Nicky,
On Louie, On Jack,"
I heard someone yell
from a black Cadillac

"The Mob!" I shrieked
but not very loud
I enjoy living
I'm not overly proud.

The noise from the street

had barely died down
when news of "the hit"
was all over town.

For days after that
I had to lay low
I'd already decided
I was too young to go.

But news hit the papers
the police had a clue
And of course they were looking
for you know who.

I turned myself in
I needed protection
But I wasn't ready
for such a rejection.

"Your info is old
you don't know enough."
When they threatened to leave me
I just made up stuff.

When my info was hitting
the six o'clock news,
I started thinking
of my new cement shoes.

I went into court
and turned state's evidence,
But these guys
had an incredible defense

As we all know, a shotgun
speaks louder than words
So I told them my info
was all for the birds.

It just goes to show you
that everyone's right
You can't make a judgment
on simply your sight.

If anyone asks
If you saw anything
Don't say a word
Dead birds can't sing.

In this parody of NFL football, Scott Giessler retains much of the original style and content of the telecast, but he changes one major element. What's he satirizing? How does the satire overlap with the parody?

Football of the Gods

SCOTT GIESSLER

Ext.—Football Stadium-Blimp Shot

It's nighttime above a football stadium, and it's illuminated with the stadium light. The stadium is packed with spectators cheering wildly. We hear sportscasters Ted Brison and Lank Larraby speaking. Through a pre-game montage sequence, we see two teams, the "Norse Nightmares" and the "Testament Tornadoes," alongside their stats. The Tornadoes are dressed in a combination of robes and football pads. The Nightmares are wearing a cross between Viking clothes and pads.

TED

They came from Israel with nothing but drive and a dream . . .

LANK

They come from the cold lands of Scandinavia, to defend a hard earned title . . .

TED

And tonight, they meet to go head to head, and settle a grudge spawned eons ago.

LANK

Hello, everyone, I'm Lank Larraby.

TED

And I'm Ted Brison. Good evening and welcome to Super Bowl 26, of the NFL Gods and Demigods division.

LANK

Tonight we have a very exciting and long anticipated match up between challengers Testament Tornadoes, and champions, the Norse Nightmares.

TED

The Tornadoes come a long way from the humble origins of Bethlehem, Israel. They've fought a long hard season, led by their coach Jehovah, or as the Tornadoes affectionately call him, "God." Even though they are considered the underdogs, they have the motivation and the ambition that the Nightmares are lacking. If you ask me, Lank, I'd pick the Tornadoes to be the winners.

LANK

Well, Ted, I didn't, and I think you're quite wrong. Unfortunately, the Tornadoes don't have the might or the tactical prowess that the Nightmares have become famous for: Coach Odin's renowned "Conquer and Plunder" strategies, namely the "Denmark Demise," the "Swedish Sack" and "Finland Frisker." Who can forget what happened last time these two met in Valhalla?

TED

Ah, yes, but much of that massacre can be contributed to a home grid advantage. And at the time, they hadn't signed on Superstar, Jesus H. Christ.

LANK

Once again you and I just don't seem to see eye to eye. I think Christ may very well be the Achilles heel of the team. If you look at his stats, he hasn't made a strong showing in close to 2,000 years. Besides, his controversial signing on with the Tornadoes has more than split the team in what could be referred to as a civil war. The offensive line has gone so far as to name themselves after him, while the Jewish defensive line wants nothing to do with him.

TED

But Lank, even with this handicap, I believe that they may still yet prevail. You know the old saying about the meek?

LANK

(Sarcastic) Yes, we've all heard it thank you. But I'm a bit amazed at your confidence. You want to take a look at legendary players, let's look at the Nightmares' star quarterback, Thor. In this season alone Thor has single handedly turned this team around and motivated them to victory.

TED

I'm sorry, Lank, but Thor might make a lot of noise, but when it comes to accomplishments, he just falls short. And I don't think he'll fare well against the Jewish defensive line. We saw their worth just last week when the Tornadoes took on the Islamic Irradiators. The Jews were incredibly outnumbered by the Irradiators' offensive line, but they just couldn't get through.

LANK

Well, Ted, I'm sorry to interrupt you, but the teams have just made their way out on to the playing field and are preparing for the kickoff.

TED

Yes, indeed, Ted, and it appears that the Tornadoes have won the coin toss and have chosen to receive.

LANK

And tonight the national anthem will be sung by Barry Manilow.
(Barry Manilow files out to the microphone. He begins to sing.)

BARRY

Oh-oh, say can you see, by the . . .
(He gets struck by lightning.)

SUGGESTIONS FOR WRITING A PARODY SWITCHING LANGUAGE

Take a well-known fairy tale and update its language. For special effects, dab it with anachronisms, that is, modern-day details that veer the parody wittily out of sync. Try this again for any well-known parable, fable, moral tale, poem, or song. If you can't think of a specific style to use, consider the following "languages":
- pop lyrics, rap words and rhythms
- fancy, formal, upper crust, academic

- bubblegum gush, romance "romantic," sci-fi
- slang, argot, criminal
- occupational (mechanic, computer whiz, advertising executive, scientist)

When you begin your parody, think about the language of the original. What are its sentence structure and syntax like? Long? Short? Clauses within clauses? Is the structure of the original unique in any way? Are there rhyme patterns you could foreground?

Burlesque

Question #1: If a river flows at 600 gallons per second and the wind blows in the opposite direction at 85 miles per hour, how old is my grandmother?

A) 91

B) Sunday

D) Wind blowing at 85 mph, now come on!

E) All of the above

F) None of the above

G) Some of the above

H) Maybe one or two of the above

I) A and B

J) A and C, but sometimes B

Todd Tibbetts

Most of us have been subjected to multiple-choice tests all our lives: in kindergarten we matched wheels with the truck, the fork with the spoon, and the ball with the bat; to get accepted into college, we dutifully filled out multiple-choice questions on numerous questionnaires, like the heart-pounding, bone-trembling, feared SAT. Todd Tibbetts burlesques multiple-choice tests by mimicking their confusing alternatives, and he hints at the Machiavellian intentions of task masters who torture students with impossible choices. Tibbetts's work might be described a parody if it imitates the specific college SAT exam; if, however, we

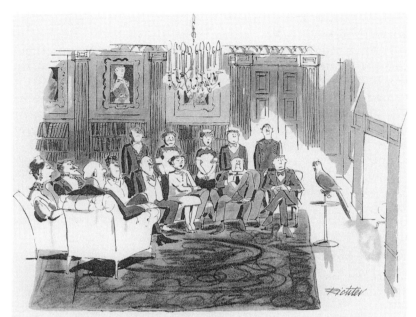

"*The fact that you, Frothingham, claimed you discovered the body at exactly 12:13 P.M. was what first made me suspicious, of course. And then when Billington claimed that he had heard the clock chime the quarter hour just as he and Miss Arbuthnot met for their little assignation in the study, it was clear that you, Merryweather . . .*"

Cartoon 6. © The New Yorker Collection 1981, Mischa Richter from cartoonbank.com. All rights reserved.

see this as a criticism of multiple-choice exams in general, we'd call this a burlesque.

Definition

When we first think of the word "burlesque," we conjure up images of bawdy variety shows of the late nineteenth and early twentieth centuries, with high-stepping kicks of half-dressed women playing to a largely male audience. For writers, however, the literary definition of burlesque, although less colorful, is much more useful.

While parody is a humorous imitation of a specific work, a burlesque is a humorous imitation not associated with a specific work. It's an imitation of a general concept, like a genre, tradition, style, historical period, or artistry. You can burlesque almost anything that is a typical genre or typical behavior.

From the point of view of a writer, the word "burlesque" carries two meanings. First, it's generically interchanged with the word "parody." One casually substitutes for the other, as in "I'm going to burlesque Jerry Seinfeld," although it's more precise to say, "I'm going to parody Jerry Seinfeld," because the imitation refers to a specific person. Second, "burlesque" is used in the more "writerly" way described in this chapter, as an imitation of a general concept (see carton 6, a burlesque of the murder mystery conclusion). You'll want to know these distinctions because they offer creative choices, but at the risk of confusing you a little, you'll see by the end of this chapter that you can mix and match them at will.

History of Burlesque

Burlesque, like parody with which it is interwoven, has a long literary history. The Greek playwright Aristophanes employed burlesque in his plays, as did the Elizabethans in their interludes. One of the most famous burlesques in all literature, Cervantes' *Don Quixote* spoofs the medieval romance as well as other human illusions. In England, the early nineteenth-century writer Jane Austin burlesques sentimental novels in her delightful novel *Northanger Abbey.* Burlesques aren't limited to literature, however; they can appear in sculpture, architecture, music, and dance, like Balanchine's score for circus elephants.

The word comes from the Italian *burlesco,* which means to joke, jest, or caricature; therefore, burlesque is characterized by ridiculous exaggeration, and it's usually broader in tone and manner than parody. You could burlesque, for example, a genre like the detective novel by using all the characteristics that have appeared in numerous detective novels over decades: the hard-boiled detective in a beige, rumpled trench coat; the beautiful secretary; the dirty office; the mysterious client; the lonely, violent city. You could burlesque the media, like television commercials in general, or a style, like the circumloquacious language commonly found in government documents. Historical periods, like the Renaissance or the Victorian age, also give us plenty of material to burlesque. If you were to burlesque the 1960s, for example, you would emphasize its recognizable characteristics: psychedelic paintings; marijuana; long hair; beards; granny glasses; bell-bottoms; flower children; communes; protests.

The possibilities for topics are endless:
- musical genres: opera; country; rock; minimalism
- fiction genres: anti-novel; short-short-short story
- film styles: noir films; musicals; romances; westerns
- poetry genres: lyric; ballad; epic
- politics: politicians; political promises; campaigns; speeches
- language of a particular historical period: the "thee's and thou's" of the Puritan era; the "darling-how-are-you" dialogue of 1930s films

Reasons for Writing Burlesques

- Because you respect the original concept and celebrate its attributes.
- Because you disapprove of the original concept, its folly, flaws, misjudgments. This overlaps with satire.
- Because you want to use this general concept as a vehicle for an original work of your own.

What does Woody Allen burlesque in his "Spring Bulletin"? What's being satirized? Does the nonsense make sense? If yes, why?

Spring Bulletin

WOODY ALLEN

The number of college bulletins and adult-education come-ons that keep turning up in my mailbox convinces me that I must be on a special mailing list for dropouts. Not that I'm complaining; there is something about a list of extension courses that piques my interest with a fascination hitherto reserved for a catalogue of Hong Kong honeymoon accessories, sent to me once by mistake. Each time I read through the latest bulletin of extension courses, I make immediate plans to drop everything and return to school. (I was ejected from college many years ago, the victim of unproved accusations not unlike those once attached to Yellow Kid Weil.) So far, however, I am still an uneducated, unextended adult, and I have fallen into the habit of browsing through an imaginary, handsomely printed course bulletin that is more or less typical of them all:

Summer Session

Economic Theory: A systematic application and critical evaluation of the basic analytic concepts of economic theory, with an emphasis on money and why it's good. Fixed coefficient production functions, cost and supply curves, and nonconvexity comprise the first semester, with the second semester concentrating on spending, making change, and keeping a neat wallet. The

Federal Reserve System is analyzed, and advanced students are coached in the proper method of filling out a deposit slip. Other topics include: Inflation and Depression—how to dress for each. Loans, interest, welching.

History of European Civilization: Ever since the discovery of a fossilized eohippus in the men's washroom at Siddon's Cafeteria in East Rutherford, New Jersey, it has been suspected that at one time Europe and America were connected by a strip of land that later sank or became East Rutherford, New Jersey, or both. This throws a new perspective on the formation of European society and enables historians to conjecture about why it sprang up in an area that would have made a much better Asia. Also studied in the course is the decision to hold the Renaissance in Italy.

Introduction to Psychology: The theory of human behavior. Why some men are called "lovely individuals" and why there are others you just want to punch. Is there a split between mind and body, and, if so, which is better to have? Aggression and rebellion are discussed. (Students particularly interested in these aspects of psychology are advised to take one of these Winter Term courses: Introduction to Hostility; Intermediate Hostility; Advanced Hatred; Theoretical Foundations of Loathing.) Special consideration is given to a study of consciousness as opposed to unconsciousness, with many helpful hints on how to remain conscious.

Psychopathology: Aimed at understanding obsessions and phobias, including the fear of being suddenly captured and stuffed with crabmeat, reluctance to return a volleyball serve, and the inability to say the word "mackinaw" in the presence of women. The compulsion to seek out the company of beavers is analyzed.

Philosophy XXIX-B: Introduction to God. Confrontation with the Creator of the universe through informal lectures and field trips.

SUGGESTIONS FOR WRITING A BURLESQUE

1. Write a scene where your character asks someone for a help in a hospital emergency room. Surround the scene with dialogue from typical television commercials.
2. Your character is involved in a debate at a town meeting about the water supply. Let each person there represent a typical athlete.

High Burlesque

Literary historians divide burlesque into two types: high (mock epic, also called mock heroic) and low (travesty). These further distinctions are helpful to humor writers. Practice a few to get the idea.

High burlesque treats a trivial subject in a mock dignified way. To create high burlesque, use a dignified, formal, pompous style with trivial subject matter. You're pretending respect for the trivial subject, and you burlesque it by calling attention to its pretentiousness through formal language. In addition to the formal language, any formal structure—epic, argument, report, treatise, legal brief, or sermon—can enhance the humor.

If you want to write a mock epic, employ heightened motifs, themes, and characters of the ancient epic form to describe trivial, silly behavior. Alexander Pope's *The Rape of the Lock*, an eighteenth-century mock epic, centers on a battle of revenge for the prankish shearing of Belinda's lock of hair, her most prized and flattering curl. Chaos ensues, in brilliant witty repartee. This is a not-to-be-missed classic. Your purpose for writing in this genre wouldn't be to satirize the epic's poetic conventions but to use its heroic motifs for your own work. Typical characteristics of the epic (*Iliad, Odyssey, Beowulf*) include an invocation, the dress of the warriors, boasting, war preparations, a fierce battle, intrusive gods, and the epic simile.

Jay Schneiderman burlesques both journalism and the "high language" of academia in his reporting of a campus accident:

Science Hall

From 4:15–4:21 P.M. on Tues. March 15th the Science Hall slipped temporarily into the fourth dimension. For the six-minute interim the building could not be seen. Onlookers noted: "It was incredible. You could still smell the formaldehyde but you couldn't see the building."

The strange occurrence was the result of a five-year research project conducted by the college physics department under the direction of Prof. Bert Alenstein. "We were not sure it would work," said Alenstein. "We thought we might make a math error or something." Prof. Alenstein is now working on a method of accelerating his mobile home to the speed of light.

Scott Giessler does a burlesque takeoff from science fiction and slapstick, where the future of mankind battles pie fights and clowns. How many different ways does he touch base with the typical characteristics of science fiction? Of slapstick? Do you see dabs of parody here? Why is it a burlesque?

Excerpt from the novel *The Clown Wars*

Scott Giessler

The year was 2087. The earth was a changed place. Due to the simultaneous economic collapse of the major superpowers on the planet, the human race had spun into chaos. Governments were overthrown, whole cities were leveled by riots, and disco was making yet another comeback. Countries broke down into city-states, and people turned to the entertainment industry to find relief and comfort. But as the situation degenerated, so did funds to create movies and TV shows. The people were subjected day in and day out to reruns of *All My Children, The Dukes of Hazzard,* and the *Mary Tyler Moore Show.*

Finally, the people had enough. Oh, who could forget the great Television Revolt of '71. It started out in a simple neighborhood in a quiet rural town. (Few of these still existed due to great Yuppie massacres of 2060.) Was it a family who had just seen one too many episodes of *Love American Style?* Or was it a deranged old man who suddenly became fed up with being confronted with yet another "to be continued . . ." on *Battlestar Galactica?* History will never be able to answer this question, but what it does know is that on April 17th of that year, people started hurling their TV's out of their windows and into the streets. . . .

By 2087, times were so miserable, so impossible, that the only recourse for the people was to laugh. And the clowns would cause just that. In fact, the clowns were so popular that after a while, all the other acts in show business and on TV became a waste of time and resources. The earth became rampant with roaming clown shows and so many clown shows became available that the competing troops argued over which rubber noses belonged to whom. Then the territorial disputes started again, and these debates grew more and more heated until finally, and inevitably, on the night of April 17th, it happened. "The pie splat heard round the world."

Suggestions for Writing High Burlesque

1. Using the form of a legal brief, write a burlesque on the law. Stay close to fancy legalese.
2. Describe a scene from a well-known film genre. Have your characters act out epic behavior through gestures and language.

Low Burlesque

Low burlesque treats a serious or dignified subject in an undignified way. Low burlesque finds a home in Maggie and Jiggs comic strips where Maggie's social pretensions for opera set the stage (pardon the pun) for Jiggs's put-downs in corned beef and cabbage language. Jiggs tenaciously clings to his "dignity" of lower-class roots while Maggie drags him kicking and screaming into high culture. So, too, in the film *Night at the Opera,* where Groucho Marx foils Margaret Dumont's haughtiness by mocking it in non-sensical puns and white-tie-and-tails slapstick.

Like all burlesque, low burlesque appears throughout history. The Greek *Battle of the Frogs and Mice* (author unknown) is a travesty of Homer; Chaucer burlesques medieval romance in *Sir Thopas* (1383); Cervantes mocks medieval romance in *Don Quixote* (1605); Shakespeare's humor erupts through the low burlesque interludes of his tragedies, *Hamlet* (c. 1599) and *Macbeth* (c. 1603); and Samuel Butler's *Hudibras* (1663) recites the adventures of a Puritan knight in a jingly meter and colloquial idioms. You'll find loads of low burlesque in *Monty Python,* especially in their sketches of British aristocracy.

To create a low burlesque, employ a silly, nonchalant, or irreverent attitude toward a serious subject. (Note that the creative approach for low burlesques overlaps that for stylistic parodies in some instances.) Because you're laughing at an issue that has been taken too seriously, you treat a serious subject with mock respect.

Travesty, a form of low burlesque, mocks a reverent subject in grotesquely extravagant language or in low-class dialect. Gods in a travesty would parse in extremely elevated terms or slur like ruffians.

In the "State of the Union Address" below, what's the "low" style that blends with the "high" subject? What's burlesqued? Why is this sketch satiric?

> I say to you, my fellow Americans, the State of the Union has now reached its pinnacle of moral rectitude. Although we've had a few mishaps—such as when Ms. Erin O'Grady was found backing out of the White House Rose Garden window scantily dressed in a Victoria's Secret bra with curved underwires and Belgian lace panties—we must not adopt that as a metaphor for national moral decrepitude, but merely forgive it as a misjudgment on her part. I can assure you that she was not acting in any official capacity.

SUGGESTIONS FOR WRITING LOW BURLESQUE

1. Write a brief monologue where a normally highly respected persona (god, judge, professor, the president) speaks in low comic language or an out-of-character voice. Have that person talk about his/her ethics. Let that person be excessively serious.
2. Write a sketch between two highfalutin people using a low-level setting: two judges in a men's room; two heads of state scratching themselves; two pompous government officials in jail.

Stirring the Pot

Sometimes a parody or burlesque based on a single source evolves too predictably out of the original, sapping energy and surprise; if you need more spice in your writing, try mixing and matching sources. For example, you might combine "Little Red Ridinghood," "The Three Bears," and "The Three Little Pigs" in one complex fairy tale and maybe squeeze it in a Seinfeld scene. Or you might sketch a Keystone Kops chase scene with three or four different U.S. presidents in the police cars, like Teddy Roosevelt teaming up with Ike Eisenhower. If you're writing a story where your character searches for the meaning of life, maybe she can take on characteristics of both David Letterman and Albert Einstein. Doubling up is a good way to solve the dull one-joke-per-sketch problem.

Feel free to multiply parody and burlesque. Feel free to incorporate parody or burlesque in a satire or comedy. You could also stir a comedy or satire with just a smidgin of parody or burlesque. One caution, however. Be sure this mixing and matching has purpose. Don't let it become confusing or overwrought. Keep your sights on what you're trying to say.

As a model, Mel Brooks's film *Blazing Saddles* offers a cornucopia of parodies and burlesques on the mythology of the American West, with its heroes and villains, law and order, and the film industry. Its grand finale of well over a hundred jokes (maybe two hundred, maybe a thousand) snowballs into the heat of the desert as our two lone cowboys, Sheriff Bart and the Waco Kid (Cleavon Little and Gene Wilder), ride off into the sunset. Yet Mel Brooks stays in full control of his theme—illusion versus reality.

As a taste of what's in this brew, besides the notorious bean-eating-round-the-campfire scene, the last third opens with the myth of "cowboy conquering evil" in a Randolph Scott joke, then immediately entangles parodies and burlesques of evil through "typical" criminals, like those in motorcycle gangs and the KKK who stand orderly on line as they apply for a job with the corrupt Hedly Lamar (Harvey Korman). One criminal gets punished for the crime of chewing gum while the KKK attacks the black sheriff with impunity.

The "great shoot out" includes burlesques of turnpike fees; the ethnic melting of the United States (OK to the Irish); and a town peopled with cardboard figures, an illusionary town in an illusionary movie. During the fight "Marlene Dietrich" (Madeline Kahn) lulls the Nazi contingency into singing sentimental German songs instead of attacking the townspeople; an old frail woman in a bonnet socks a robust villain in the jaw; another villain is foiled by his attacker's bad breath, all burlesques of traditional fight scenes—then we get a long shot and the scene suddenly cartwheels from an illusion of Western film mythology to an illusion of film in general as the camera descends to a movie set where a Busby Berkeley dance routine is being filmed. The cowboy fight storms onto the musical comedy set, and the raucousness continues with parodies and burlesques of Esther Williams, gays, the movie set commissary, tourists, Hitler, and, of course, the great pie fight.

Mel Brooks has even more jokes left, but we'll stop here.

EXAMPLES

In this comic piece, how does Paul Nelson extrapolate the diary genre with hints of old James Cagney movies?

The Sidney Sheldon Papers
(Diary of a Prisoner)

PAUL NELSON

March 3

My first day in prison! I still find it hard to believe that I was convicted of armed robbery. I was nowhere near that bank! Besides, underneath this prisoner's uniform beats the heart of a true wimp. I could never pull off a robbery. I get nervous asking a gas station attendant for a key to the men's room. Well, at least I'm making friends. Today, I met a young Mexican named Carlos. Carlos carries a harmonica constantly but he can only play "Don't Be Cruel" by Elvis Presley.

Hopefully, my stay in prison will not be too long. My girlfriend, Rhoda, assures me that she and my lawyer are working night and day to free me. I can only wait and hope.

March 4

I have been assigned to Carlos' cell. Apparently, his former cellmate had a nervous breakdown after the forty-fifth chorus of "Don't Be Cruel." Carlos and I get along well; in fact, he trusts me so much that he told me of a mass escape being planned. If I want in on it, I am to talk to a man named Harvey in cell block four. I will talk to him tomorrow.

March 5

Today I spoke with Harvey. He is a cook and is supplying the prisoners with spoons with which to dig an escape tunnel. He assured me that I could be part of the escape, which is good because today I also learned that my girlfriend has run off to Rio with my lawyer.

March 8

Today was a quiet day. I got two spoons from Harvey and will start digging tomorrow. Carlos played "Don't Be Cruel" at the prison talent show. The prisoners rioted.

March 9

I can taste freedom! Today I spent seven hours working on the escape tunnel. So far, the digging crew is limited to Harvey, myself and an old man named Saul. Saul is ninety years old, has one leg and two teeth, but he possesses amazing determination when he is awake.

Unfortunately, we are digging our escape tunnel directly under the men's room and every time a toilet is flushed, we are flooded by sewage. But this is a small price to pay for the reward which awaits us. Harvey hopes to have the tunnel completed by April, in spite of the fact that Saul refuses to work on evenings when the Lawrence Welk show is on.

March 14

A minor tragedy today . . . due to heavy activity in the men's room after dinner, Saul was swept off into a storm sewer while working on the tunnel. Fortunately, Carlos has volunteered to take his place.

March 16

A major setback today . . . while digging, we accidentally struck a gas line. Unfortunately, Carlos was smoking at the time. All three of us were catapulted from the tunnel. We managed to escape with minor cuts and bruises, but our tunnel collapsed and we were all given two weeks in solitary confinement. On a more cheerful note, the warden was using the toilet directly above us at the time of the accident.

March 20

Good news! I received word today that Saul is alive and well. He popped up in a men's room in a New Jersey Arco station. Also, my lawyer has returned from Rio and is once again working on freeing me. Evidently, Rhoda, my ex-girlfriend, ran off with a rumba band. Things are looking up!

March 31

Solitary confinement is over! it feels good to be able to move around again. Today, during the exercise period, some prisoners started a riot. Carlos bravely tried to soothe everyone with a few choruses of "Don't Be Cruel," but a guard shot him after the third verse. He is recovering in the infirmary.

April 2

It is a miracle! I am free! My lawyer has just informed me that the man who really robbed the bank I was accused of robbing has been caught. Today, I said goodby to everyone. It was touching scene. Harvey gave me a complete set of metal cookware as a going-away gift and Carlos gave me his much treasured *Elvis' Greatest Hits* album. A tear came to my eye. As I departed from the prison, I could hear in the distance a gentle chorus of "Don't Be Cruel."

David Hearne colors a back-lot portrait of beloved cartoon characters with a darker, more cynical view of their natures. Although the portrait is larger than the sum of its parodic and burlesque parts, Hearne includes enough descriptive details for us to quickly visualize the original cartoon figures and their usual venues. At the same time, these characters transform themselves within Hearne's own rich context. How does Hearne use parody and burlesque in this story? Why might we read the story as a tragicomedy? What do the main characters realize about themselves? What's the theme? I've included a long excerpt here to show its rich literary quality.

Long Days in the Sun

DAVID HEARNE

"As far as I'm concerned, Steven Spielberg and Jerry Katzenberg and Michael Eisner can all get together and kiss my little black ass!"

"They're despicable, right?"

"Shut up!"

Yosemite Sam grinned and took a sip of his home-made whiskey. His friend Daffy had drunk more than a sip of the stuff over the past hour. He knew he was in for hearing a lot of ranting combined with bouts of incredible sentimentality. Those who thought Daffy was entertaining on film should have seen him when he was drunk.

Let him go, thought Yosemite as he looked over the wonderfully wide space of his Nevada ranch. Out here you could go mad and nobody would care. He leaned his chair back, propped up his feet and watched the clouds drift by as Daffy paced about on the porch, waving his hands around, one of which clutched a glass containing a liquid that shot off little sparks.

"Spielberg keeps telling me, 'You and Porky are great together . . .'"

"You are," Sam commented.

"That's beside the point! The point is, I can't stand the little porker!"

Now, this made Sam feel uncomfortable. Everybody thought that Daffy and Bugs were bitter show-biz enemies. Actually, the two were very good friends in real life. It was Porky that gave Daffy trouble.

"I refuse to do a duo act with that fascist!"

"Maybe *he* won't do a duo act with a socialist," said Sam quietly. Daffy's politics had always been pretty leftist. Sam himself was pretty conservative, but he would never let politics bust up a friendship. But, Porky, on the hand . . . he came very close to being a "friendly witness" back in the fifties and he would have undoubtedly named Daffy. It took some strong persuasion from everybody to convince him otherwise.

Besides that, however, Sam had to admit that Porky was an obnoxious pain-in-the-ass. He joined up with the Moral Majority a while back. Ever since then, he had been condescending and superior. He even went as far as saying cartoons should be "cleaned up." Since Sam had made his living by having things explode in his face, he resented this. Porky had not been invited along on this weekend sabbatical at Sam's cabin. So when Daffy shot back with "Don't give me that, Sam. You know what Porky's like," Sam could only shrug.

Sam was grateful when Foghorn came striding in. Of all the Warner Brothers Toons, his real-life persona was closest to his screen image. Which meant that nobody could talk when he was around, drunk or sober.

"Whoo-wee! Sam, that horse of yours can bust harder than Dolly Parton out of a size six bra! Give me a glass of that stuff."

Sam grinned and poured Foghorn a glass. Foghorn gulped down the whiskey in one swallow. Flames spouted from his beak and smoke poured from his ears.

"Ah, now, that's the good stuff!" Foghorn commented.

Son walked in, dressed in his stylish yet tasteful sweater. Son was the boy child of Sylvester. Nobody knew his real name, including Sylvester who had forgotten it a long time ago. (Things like these are common with all toons, especially after a few beers.) So, everybody just called him "Son."

"Afternoon, everybody," he said in his dictioned voice.

"Uh-oh!" declared Foghorn. "The boy genius has arrived! I better skedaddle! Nobody can get a word in edgewise with him around!" And he marched into the house.

"Enjoy your walk, Son?" asked Sam.

"Absolutely. This place is beautiful, Sam!"

"God smiles down upon it, that's for sure."

"By the way, Daffy," said Son, "now that I've got you here . . ."

"If you're going to talk about what I think you're going to talk about," said Daffy, his eyes half-hooded, "then it's a good thing I'm drunk."

Son smiled with a disconcerting confidence. He spread his arms and said, "One word: Hamlet!"

Daffy's bill dropped to the floor, landing with a loud "CLANG!" His eyes protruded outward into two small cones. Sam just fell backwards in his chair. After he was done, Daffy clutched his head.

"Dammit, you made me do a Roger Rabbit! You're out of your mind, Son!"

"Maybe. But think of it, Daffy . . ."

"Only in my worst nightmares."

" . . . an all-toon production of *Hamlet.* With you in the lead!"

"And my ass before the firing squad. They'll make mincemeat out of us!"

"Daffy . . . I know deep down you want to do this."

Daffy looked straight at Son . . . or as straight has his bleary eyes could. He peered down into his half-full glass of whiskey as if he wanted advice from it.

"Who else have you got lined up for this disaster?" he grumbled.

"Dad's going to play the Ghost, Pepe Le Pew is up to play Laertes, Wild E to play Claudius . . ."

"That's crazy!" shouted Daffy. "Sam here would be perfect for Claudius."

Sam shook his head, smiling. "Forget it. I can't take the theater. You know that."

"I'm going to change your mind about that one of these days Sam," said Son, winking.

"That'll be the day I get you on a bronco," Sam said, winking back.

"Anyway, I'm going to offer Polonius to Foghorn. I know he'll jump at it. Dong is going to make a good Horatio. And Elmer is up for the Gravedigger . . ."

"Are you sure he's up to it?" asked Sam. Inside, his mind ran over sad images of Elmer in the sanitarium, mumbling incoherent words. Shit, thought Sam. Elmer was the nicest, sweetest guy on the whole Warner Brothers team, but hard times had worn his psyche down. Why did the world throw its garbage on a saint like Elmer and not on Speedy Gonzales.

"He's in good shape, he's ready for it. Though . . . Droopy has agreed to understudy the role."

"That's all very well," grumbled Daffy. "But, there's one thing you haven't mentioned."

"What?"

"Who the hell is going to play the female roles?"

Leave it to Daffy to open old wounds. Not too many of the original toons were women and none of them were capable of doing *Hamlet*. The tendency of Warner Brothers back then to promote male toons provided considerable embarrassment in the present.

"I'll have you know," said Son a little stiffly, "that the role of Gertrude will be played by a marvelous actress."

"And who may that be?"

"Rebecca from *Tailspin*."

Daffy's beak fell towards the floor, but only halfway this time. He pushed it back up and yelled: "You're going to use a fucking *Disney* toon?"

Another world, there. There was much animosity between the Disney toons and Warner Brothers toons. The former was regarded by the latter as talentless and hammy. (They would admit though that "Donald ain't too bad.") In return, they were regarded as "vulgar." "We believe in family entertainment here," Mickey once said in that voice that made Daffy's fillings throb. "I don't know what they believe over at Warner Brothers." (Mickey was also a born-again and had converted Porky.) "We believe in loud explosions, falling off cliffs and transvestism," Daffy shot back. "Now, that's fucking entertainment."

"Things are different over there," Son said, patiently. "You know that, Daffy."

"Maybe," replied Daffy, sorrily. "But isn't she worried about what Uncle Mickey will say?"

"She is a very brave woman who knows this is important. And she will be marvelous."

"S'marvelous!" a voice crooned. "S'wonderful!"

Out stepped Bugs in a silk dressing gown. He had been indulging the whole morning in a long slumber. This wasn't so bad considering that he got to bed around four. He had spent last night at another ranch with a high percentage of female cowhands. He had been "doing what a rabbit has to do."

"So, my little feline Peter Hall," said Bugs with his patent mixture of sarcasm and sweetness, "got any parts for me in this grand theatrical experience?"

Son swallowed. This had not been the first time he had tried to put toons in "serious theater." The first try had been *Waiting for Godot* with Bugs as Vladimir and Daffy as Estragon. The production was just after *Who Framed Roger Rabbit?* and the toon revival was in full swing. It was the first time that Daffy demonstrated to the world he was more than a great comedian. He was also a great actor, giving his role a comic despair that, as John Simon said, "elicits constant laughter, but an appropriately nervous sort of laughter that has trouble working past our throats."

However, of Bugs, Simon had this to say: "Messr. Bunny is like a professor of theater, giving the audience a complete history of every kind of verbal, body, and facial mugging that's ever been performed." There was no denying Bugs' talent as a comedian. There was no denying that he was the most popular Warner Brothers toon ever, which was why Son had cast him. Yet, as rehearsals went on, Son could only hold his head as Bugs acted as if a pie fight would start the next scene.

SUGGESTIONS FOR WRITING MIXES OF PARODIES AND BURLESQUE

1. Think back to a party you once attended but instead of seeing your usual friends in the room, place at the scene characters from comic strips, cartoons, movies, or television. What happens? What point are you making about parties or friendship? Work for clever wit rather than a drunken brawl.

2. Write a comic memoir:

   a plane trip where your least favorite rock group arrives as unexpected passengers.

   the demise of your "movie star" reputation one night at a local Wendy's.

DO'S AND DON'TS

1. *Select carefully the original work you plan to parody or burlesque.* Obviously, there's a difference between choosing a four-line nursery rhyme and a Shakespearean play. The more

complex the original, the more likely you'll establish a complex foundation for your own work.

2. *Be sure to choose an original source that contains strong, recognizable characteristics.* If you choose some esoteric original that no one recognizes—like an obscure thirteenth-century poem by a cloistered monk in Tuscany—you'll lose the effect. Unless you're writing for a specific audience that can easily recognize the "inside" source, well-known originals work best.

3. *Touch base with the original often enough so we can make a connection.* Sprinkle clues of names, structure, plot, theme, language, rhythms, imagery, or setting. If you don't do this, we won't bridge the two, and we'll miss a major thread of the humor.

4. *Select an original source with a long life.* Avoid parodying a one-time source, like a specific news article from last night's *New York Times.* Even if we've read it, we won't remember it two weeks later. Although current-event originals are valid, their shelf life is short; the best topical sources are those that can be updated, like a parody on presidential incompetence, which can be relevant to both our in-house and any future president. Of course, you could burlesque newspaper columns in general.

5. *Remember that a topic switch from one serious topic to another may fulfill the definition of a parody or burlesque, but it doesn't by itself produce humor.* Unless you paint it with the usual humorous elements like witty language, incongruously playful imagery, or a comic plot, we won't laugh.

6. *Changing both style and content won't establish your work as parody or burlesque.* If you stray too far from the original, the relationship could be lost. Of course, it may be funny, but you just won't have a parody or burlesque. You'll have something else.

7. *Be cautious about parodying a parody.* This may not be effective because two works identical in intention will lack contrasting irony. Also, be careful about parodying a successful parody. You can parody Mel Brooks, but you'll have to be better than he is.

8. *Think twice about parodying works that themselves are in extremely bad taste.* Be wary about parodying violence or sex since exaggeration of these topics produces violence or pornography, not humor.

9. *Think twice about parodying works that contain strokes so broad that exaggerating them has little effect, like tabloid stories or soap operas.* Because a tabloid article is an exaggeration of real life, a parody of it becomes ineffectual since it doesn't have the added dimension of being real. Can we really distinguish this example of "The Daily Blah" from the usual tabloid? Can you see that it's so close to a tabloid that, as funny as it might be, its satiric intent is lost? WOMAN EATS ALLIGATOR . . . THEN MARRIES DEAD BROTHER.

In this example, the writer is trying to exaggerate the dialogue of a soap opera. Does it work?

> Kerry: Hi.
> Sandray: Hi.
> Kerry: How are you.
> Sandray: Fine. How are you.
> Kerry: I'm fine. Are you really fine.
> Sandray: Yes. I am. I said I was fine and I'm really fine.
> Kerry: You don't look fine. Are you sure you're fine?
> Sandray: Yes. I am. Fine. Fine. I said I was fine.
> Kerry: So what do you plan to do today?
> Sandray: Nothing. What do you plan to do today?
> Kerry: Nothing.
> Sandray: Nothing?

(Most people wouldn't be able to take much more of this. We got the point in the first few lines.)

10. *And last, and really important, don't assume that parody for the sake of parody will carry the full weight of the humor. Remember that for punch and vivacity, your writing must be clever and substantive.* Elements of the original can only provide scaffolding; you have to take responsibility for thematic brilliance.

ASK A FRIEND

READER'S WORKSHEET — PARODY OR BURLESQUE

1. Is the work a parody, a burlesque, or a combination of these? Whatever the form, is it developed in a clever way?
2. What clues tap into the original source(s): names? plot? language? structure? imagery? actions? setting? Are there enough common points so that we recognize the original model(s)?

3. List three ways the writer twisted, reversed, exaggerated, or extended the original(s). Are these effective?
4. Does the writer stay so close to the original(s) there isn't much surprise? If so, where would you suggest changes?
5. Locate three places where the humor falls flat, if any. Locate three places where the humor works well.
6. What new, original, brilliant vision does the writer create?

Have You Heard the One about . . . ?

Writing Jokes

Throughout this book, we've used the words "humor" and "joke" interchangeably to mean, in the newer, scholarly sense, a clever clash of two playfully incongruous scripts; now let's look at the word "joke" in its old-fashioned, well-worn vaudevillian sense. *A joke, à la vaudeville, is a brief, single-incident narrative with a clash at the end called the "punch line."* Really short jokes are called "one-liners" because they're one line long.

A one-liner might go as follows: Now that I know what to do, I'm too old to do what I know.

The longer joke anecdote is structured like this:

SETUP: INTRODUCTION TO THE JOKE

> Stumpy McCann walks into a brand new Pittsburgh restaurant, which has just opened next door to his own subway shop and which boasts of having all possible sandwiches. It's named the All-Possible Sandwich Place.

BUILDUP: BACKGROUND DETAILS

> He's sick and tired of all the bragging from his new competition, and he decides to challenge the establishment.
>
> "We don't have menus, sir," says the waiter. "There's nothin' you can name that we don't have. We're the best in Pittsburgh; we're the best in the country; in fact, we're the best sandwich place in the world. We have everything you could want in a sandwich."
>
> "Oh, yeah?" says Stumpy, smirking a little. "Do you have a creamed pheasant sandwich, with horseradish and pimientos?"
>
> "Sure," says the waiter. "'s zat what you want?"
>
> "No," says Stumpy, "let me think. Do you have a Newfoundlander seaweed sandwich with saltfish, capers and yellow peppers?"
>
> "Sure," says the waiter. "'s zat what you want?"

"No," says Stumpy. He thinks for a minute, then sits up in his chair. "What I'm really hankering for is—is—a simple, plain elephant sandwich on rye. You do have elephant, don't you?"

"Oh, sure, oh, sure," says the waiter, slowly. "No problem. No problem."

The waiter goes into the kitchen. Stumpy waits fifteen minutes, then another fifteen minutes, then another fifteen minutes.

"Hey, waiter," he calls out. "What's takin' so long? What's goin' on back there? Where's my sandwich? Don't tell me you don't have any elephant?"

PUNCH LINE: A CLASH OF TWO PLAYFUL INCONGRUOUS ELEMENTS COMING OUT OF THE BACKGROUND

The waiter comes back out of the kitchen, empty-handed. "Oh, sure, oh, sure, we have it all right," he yells. "No problem. But the boss says he ain't cuttin' up a whole elephant for just one sandwich."

BLEND: TRANSITION INTO NEXT JOKE

Of course, the restaurant down the street . . .

These "vaudevillian" jokes boast an ancient heritage in Homer's *Iliad* and *Odyssey*, as well as in ancient Greek, Roman, Indian, and Chinese comic theater. Jokes arise from our need to encapsulate an experience into a common story that offers an emotional and physiological high, and, of course, its subsequent release. Jokes allow us to reason, ease tensions, persuade, learn language—and flirt and seduce.

So what's the bad news? Jokes have a reputation for hurting others, directly or indirectly, as in sexist and ethnic put-downs or in the personal insult. While we shrug off those forbidden feelings with the laughter from a punch line, they mask anger or improper passions. We use jokes to flex muscle when we create in-group or in-law joking. When jokes render characters in simplistic, unoriginal, stereotyped ways, literary critics consider them a lesser art form than satire and comedy, and a joke's artistically limited manner of depicting character assumes a questionable "truth."

And the good news? Jokes can vividly depict a culture's identity and enhance its linguistic tradition. They function to persuade society to behave itself, generally much better than prescriptive lecturing and finger shaking, as witnessed by their pervasive presence in the popular culture of bumper stickers, t-shirt logos, greeting cards, comic strips, and cartoons. No question, good jokes are an integral part of humor, and somebody out there likes them.

Writing Jokes the Hard Way

For some people, spontaneous joking is doin' what comes naturally, and simply repeating jokes circulating around town from years past is next to nothing in effort; but writing jokes on demand is a whole different ball game. Creating never-before-heard original jokes demands hard work—especially when we're writing them the hard way.

The hardest way to write jokes is to begin with a bunch of isolated ideas that center on word play. When you limit your imagination to word play (that is, packaging your ideas in small, isolated units), you distance yourself from larger meanings, and because isolated words don't generate coherence and thematic extension, any writing distanced from meaning becomes hard to do. But still, you might be curious about how this brainstorming works, and if you plan to experiment with single-joke writing, read on. In spite of the rough road in this writing, it does have its purpose. You might create an isolated joke for a cartoon or comic strip, for an insert into more substantive work, or for loose, chain-link joke routines. In any case, try this, just for practice, to see if this way of writing humor suits you.

The Groaning Pun

Hey, if it's good enough for Shakespeare, it's good enough for us.

A pun is a word, phrase, or image that holds two (or more) simultaneous meanings and usually spins on identical or similar sounds. A pun doesn't have to be humorous, especially when acting as a metaphor, as we find in Shakespeare's *Romeo and Juliet*, where Mercutio dies saying: "Ask for me tomorrow, and you shall find me a *grave* man." But most puns are humorous. Besides as words themselves, puns appear as images in art, music, and even fashion, where a person might wear a hat that puns on two different eras, like a tam with an Art Deco geometric cut (1920s) and a parallel geometric ostrich feather (Victorian).

Because most puns are pure word play, which narrows meaning, we thumb our noses at them, tagging them as groaners, the lowest form of humor, and unworthy of great writers. But good puns—those clever, witty, and metaphoric—can create terrific humor. Sometimes you'll deliberately want to jab in a god-awful pun to elicit jeers from the audience, best when audience resistance is low or after it's been warmed up, but you'll get heightened appreciation from your listeners when the pun enriches characterization and meaning.

Go for It

Scribble down some homonyms by checking a synonym-homonym dictionary found in any library or on the Web. (You want homonyms, not synonyms.) Homonyms are words that sound alike but have different meanings and spellings: *air/heir; morning/mourning; guilt/gilt; steal/steel; stair/stare; weight/wait.* Also familiarize yourself with words that sound almost alike: *angel, angle; desert, dessert; medal, metal.* Finally, collect words or phrases that don't change spelling but have different meanings: *light; grave; lay.* It's the mixture of spelling, meaning, and sounds that forms the basis for puns, and all of the above can create them.

Try the following:

1. Play on identical or similar sounds.

    Sign on a Jersey Milk Truck: All I Am I Owe to *Udders* (others).

    When you go into a restaurant, always ask for a table near a *waiter.* (window)

    He caught the ball *clean*, kind of like when you play for the NFL right after you've taken a shower. (easily; not dirty)

2. Mix and match sounds.

    Advertisement on a table mat at Lums Restaurant:

    Apple Danish—an *appletizing* treat (appetizing)

    Cheese Danish—*Scrumpcheese* (scrumptious)

    Did you hear about the Buddhist who refused his dentist's Novocain during root canal work? He wanted to *transcend dental medication.* (transcendental meditation)

    A man entered his local paper's pun contest. He sent in ten different puns, in the hope that at least one of the puns would win. Unfortunately, *no pun in ten did.* (no pun intended)

3. Use a word or words in a literal sense.

    I made a *killing* in the market. I cut up a chicken!

    Man who jumps from tall building jumps to *conclusion.*

    I've never let my *schooling* interfere with my *education.*

4. Play on a word in two different contexts.

    Hurray for *welders:* We're *holding* America together.

Sign on a radiator repair shop: Best place in town to *take a leak.*

IRS: We've *got* what it *takes* to *take* what you've *got.*

Suggestion for Writing

Write three jokes using puns or double meanings about paying a telephone bill. Make at least one of the jokes an anecdote.

Cliché-Wrenching

Clichés are old-fashioned, worn-out expressions like proverbs, epigrams, slogans, mottos, or catchphrases of well-known people. They can be slang or colloquial: "straight from the horse's mouth"; "skating on thin ice"; "hungry as a horse"; "smart as a whip"; "dead as a doornail"; "easy as pie"; "a penny saved is a penny earned"; "It ain't over 'til it's over"; "It ain't over 'til the fat lady sings." You can extend this definition to include any phrase, quote, or expression your audience can quickly recognize. *To wrench a cliché, twist it, vary it, change a word in it, or use it in a different context.* When you wrench a cliché, you parody it through your clever language. Whatever the means, you get the laugh.

To Wrench a Cliché

1. Change a word in the cliché.
   Detergent Co. motto: *Grime* pays.
   Tabloid newspaper motto: *Slime* pays.
   Poverty-stricken poet motto: Crime pays; *rhyme don't.*
2. Change the ending.
   The spirit is willing—*but the flesh needs to renew its spa membership.*
   A penny saved *isn't worth the rescue.*
   To a drunk: You're skating on thin *ice cubes.*
3. Use a cliché as a pun.
   Sign on a plumber's truck: In our business *a flush beats a full house.*
   Gravity: It's not just a good idea, *it's the law.*
   College exam: Easy as *pie . . . in advanced quantum theory, that is.*

Suggestions for Writing

Write three versions of a one-liner, each of which spins on the same cliché. Study the different effects. Can you build tension and character by playing up details?

Similarities

A favorite one-liner of mine comes from a decades-old Art Linkletter show when Linkletter asks a little girl he's interviewing what the girl's leg feels like when it falls asleep. "Oh, that's easy," the little girl says. "When my leg falls asleep—it feels—just like—ginger ale."

Using *similarities (similes and metaphors)* to create jokes makes for lots of good offhand remarks. Similes and metaphors become comic when they're farfetched, extravagant, nonsensical, clichéd, mixed, or illogical; and for wittier jokes, try literary or historical allusions.
1. Mix metaphors.
    Some of the things that policeman said would make *your flesh* (hair) stand on end.—Archie Bunker
    The president should stop blubbering about the deficit. It's unconstapational (unconstitutional).—Archie Bunker
    It's easy to admire a good loser at a strip poker party.—Henny Youngman
2. Use farfetched metaphors that edge toward satire.
    Yeah, I've always wanted to have something in common with a garbage dump. *This $200 perm I just got smells like Times Square after a chug-a-beer political rally.*
    Your prose has about as much flexibility *as a charley horse.*
    Let me explain it to you this way, it's *like the comeback of cherry coke and the Monkees.*—Vicky Puig

Suggestions for Writing

Brainstorm 3–5 jokes using imagery that rib the music industry.

Definitions

You can build jokes or whole monologues around comic definitions.

1. Use imagery.

    Sincerity. You can place all the sincerity in Hollywood *in a flea's navel and still have room for three caraway seeds and the heart of an agent.*—Fred Allen

    You know what the Pentagon is. That's the big building in Washington *that has five sides—on every issue.*
    —Henny Youngman

    A good manager is someone *who keeps the five guys who hate you away from the four who are undecided.*
    —Casey Stengel

2. Split a word into its parts then define the parts literally.

    parable: two male cows

    subdued: male sandwich maker

    descent: what makes a skunk famous

    porcupine: What you get when you cross a pig with an evergreen—Mike Greenzeig

3. Describe the word satirically.

    Ignorance is when you don't know something, and somebody finds it out.—Ambrose Bierce

    A conference is a gathering of important people who singly can do nothing, but together can decide that nothing can be done.—Fred Allen

    When you're driving 55 miles per hour, your biggest problem is trucks—18 wheel trucks. These are vehicles that try to pass you without changing lanes.—Jack Handey

SUGGESTIONS FOR WRITING

Try some one-liners about sport competition, then expand one one-liner into a long anecdote by adding a story introduction and characterization. Which length works better?

Dangling Modifiers

Dangling modifiers cut up the syntax of a sentence so that the modifier describes the wrong word, producing the humor. The syntactical switch jars the logic, and it's especially funny when the mangled syntax hints at a double meaning.

> *After being slaughtered, skinned and quartered,* I felt sorry for the young calf. (The dangling modifier should modify "calf.")

While eating an ice cream cone, the pigeon shat on my head.
(Do pigeons really like ice cream?)
    While still in diapers, mom returned to work.
    Headline: BOY *WITH TWO HEADS* ENTERS CABBAGE
INTO 4-H CONTEST

Suggestions for Writing

Write a conversation between two people riding in a taxi premised on two or three sentences that contain dangling modifiers. Let the dangling modifiers be the center of comic misunderstanding.

Everyday Observations

Will Rogers once said: "I don't make jokes; I just watch the government and report the facts. I never lack material for my humor column when Congress is in session." You might try his way of discovering jokes by observing everyday behavior and asking questions like "why is it so" or "did ya ever think?"

Ever wonder why the Q-tip company can afford a lot of stick but can't afford the cotton?
Did you ever notice that right next to a magazine article on dieting is a recipe for chocolate cake?
Did you ever notice that fashion designers of haute couture themselves dress like unbathed trolls?
How come there's no money in the department budget to give us a raise, but the boss can afford to hire a financial consultant to study department morale?

If jokes show human nature in a rich, comic way or if they twist language in an unusual way, then jokes deserve a place at the humor banquet. Sometimes we love a joke even more when it's awful, kind of like a stranded puppy. And a dumb joke reminds us how smart we are.

Suggestion for Writing

Sit at some public place like a shopping mall or a coffee shop and record what you see. Practice one-liners from what you observe in people's behavior.

Writing Jokes: From Hard to Easy

OK, you're tried your luck on the hard stuff; relax, take a break, then get ready to move on. Let's go from hard to easy, from individually packaged word-play jokes to plain, simple, but very effective, tell-it-as-it-is narrative. *The easy way . . .*

18

So, How All You Guys Doin' Tonight?

The Joke Monologue

The joke monologue is a one-sided conversation delivered dramatically by a single speaker to an audience. It's also called "stand-up comedy" because the speaker traditionally stands as he or she performs.

Background

The joke monologue boasts distinguished ancestors from a long oral tradition: the epic, cautionary tale, journey anecdote, literary monologue, both prose and poetry, and maybe less distinguished but no less loved, the campfire chaw. More recently, it surfaced from English and American vaudeville, those traveling shows of the nineteenth century that brought entertainment to eager small towns and big cities alike. Usually scheduled for a week's engagement with two or more performances daily, the vaudevillians wore many hats to please a critical and often fickle audience. Vaudeville was variety. Singers, dancers, animal acts, and acrobats all vied with comedians, who braved the crowd's scorn for laughs and, more often than not, ducked rotten tomatoes for their grand-finale stage exit.

At first, comedians performed short one-gag skits, often ending in sight gags like sliding on a banana peel or crumbling under a collapsed roof, à la Buster Keaton and Charlie Chaplin. (These could be brilliantly performed, we should add.) But as the circuit blazed sexy red around the 1850s by importing the Parisian can-can of half-clad women fanning their skirts to expose naked ankles and ruffled panties, many comedians followed the fashion of the day. Hence, "burlesque" and its bawdy entertainment moved away from the more pristine "vaudeville," and comic monologues took sides, with the dirty joke drifting into the more disreputable entertainment enjoyed by rowdy, drunken men (and sometimes women), and the clean joke edging toward more well-mannered audiences. Burlesque became risqué; vaudeville stayed clean.

As the twentieth century arrived, joke monologues built on sets of one-liners. The routine would tumble from one joke to the next only loosely connected by topic or theme, like mismatched beads sliding on a thin, tattered string. No comedian bothered to accelerate the topics through characterization or social signif-icance; instead, he went for the laugh with obvious word play. This loose-flowing joke monologue traveled into the 1950s via the Borscht Belt in the Catskill Mountains of New York, named after the beet and cabbage soup served by the area's huge kosher resorts for their New York Jewish guests. The Catskills jump-started the careers of mostly Jewish comedians who performed in the clubs there—Milton Berle, Sid Caesar, Mel Brooks, Jerry Lewis, Mort Sahl, and many others—and as these stage performers moved to television, the vaudevillian monologue continued, with, for ex-ample, Bob Hope and Johnny Carson.

While fancy resort entertainment stayed more or less taste-ful during the early twentieth century, in rough-and-tumble neigh-borhood clubs a male comedian (the rare exception being the African-American female comedian Moms Mabley) continued the monologue's risqué tradition by playing to male audiences with jokes about women and sex, almost always insulting and sexist. For some stand-up comics, however, this joking didn't serve their own artistic integrity and, inevitably, the American stand-up routine drastically changed. Although historical threads are elusive, we might say that the monologue was flipped on its head in the early 1950s by one Lenny Bruce, who grabbed the old joke routine around its neck and threw it—feet up—at the audience. For Bruce, the monologue was satire, and he used it to criticize the puffy, staid, biased nature of postwar U.S. soci-ety, with its prejudices toward Jews, Blacks, gays, and any other group not of its ilk. Bruce's monologues were no longer discon-nected word play but graphic and angry satiric denunciations of human mores, so in addition to the usual parodies, one-liners, and mini-stories, his routines included shocking, angry, physical actions like a raised middle finger and nudity that challenged conformity, performances that did not endear him to the local police.

After Lenny Bruce—and with the prescience of African American satirists like Dick Gregory and Richard Pryor who helped awaken the United States to its racism—the monologue continued on its strange journey in the deconstructive, postmodern vision of the late Andy Kaufmann. Kaufmann demonstrated his bizarre sense of the comic in the early 1980s by breaking down the proscenium wall between performer and audience. He invented the fictional comic persona Tony Clifton, yet adamantly denied that he was Clifton. And the fictional persona Clifton always strongly—and seriously—denied that he was Kaufmann. Kaufman mixed comic and angry signals to such an extent that the audience never quite figured out if he was joking or not. Yet they always came back for more.

Today the stand-up monologue has planted its feet firmly in the likes of Jay Leno, David Letterman, Jerry Seinfeld, and Brett Butler. The biggest change in the way monologues are now written, however, has evolved from the onset of comedy clubs and cable television. With the bursting opportunity of varied audiences, more and more comedians take center stage to say what they want, how they want; thus, the monologue has surged in originality and purpose. Moving beyond a series of "one-liners," although that form still survives, the routines of more creative stand-up comedians now include multi-voices, impressions, sound bites, music, full-fledged stories, patched-in film clips, exchanges with the audience, and long rambling round-the-fire reminiscences. Old and new live side by side, although by the time we get to Garrison Keillor, whose Lake Wobegon stories twist and turn much like a dusty path to a local watering hole, we've returned full circle to the comic as a "teller of tales."

So where's the monologue today? Some critics say it's dying out, but they've been saying that since the seventeenth century when the Puritans closed down the theaters. Most audiences say that theater, grand or not so grand, is embedded in the genes and the monologue will, therefore, last forever. To be sure, we're always up for a good story. And we'll always take a little b.s. No question, whatever zany spirit it assumes, the joke monologue lives on, thriving on television, in nightclubs, and at backyard barbecues.

Talk to Me Baby, Talk to Me

And for the writer of joke monologues?

Begin the way you do any humorous writing by brainstorming topics. Spin on whatever is important to you. Ideas: Do you want to tell a story? Reminisce about your mother, brother, Uncle Henry. Write satire? Maybe rap about something that bothers you: U.S. Congress? Plastic packaging that won't snap open? Airlines that offer frequent flyer miles but only let you cash them one day a year for a place you don't want to go? Maybe you want to teach us something? Who makes the chemical compounds for face masks? Who makes toilet paper and what are their lives like? Or how about analyzing scientific breakthroughs, like the cultural implications of the primordial heliotrope? Or maybe you want to reveal your own personal traumas? Struggles? Heartaches? Frustrations? What scares you? Outrages you? Confuses you? What are you suspicious of?

As usual, get lots of words down fast—then relax for a minute as you think about where you'll go next. Remember, since a monologue is a conversation, you've got to decide on a speaker.

Who's Talkin' Here?

So who's talkin'? What's he or she like? Is that person you or someone different from you? What kind of personality? Have a dialect or a quirk? Young? Old? Physically elastic? Stiff? Casual clothes? Suit and tie? Army fatigues? New Yorker? Texan? College student? What kind of voice? Loud? Soft? Squeaky?

What attitude toward the topic does your comic have? Glad, mad, sad, disgusted, thrilled, or worried? Does your speaker have a problem? A nose like W. C. Fields's? Dandruff? Trouble finding her soul? Spent her childhood living above a pachinko parlor? Seeking ultimate truth in cereal boxes?

You'll come off much more original if you invent your own character but, if you want the practice, you could try writing for an established comic. Not every famous comedian buys outside material, but some do, and even if you can't sell your monologue, it's a good creative experiment. If you write for a specific comic, be sure you understand his or her style. Your material should fit the personality, voice modulation, usual content, usual audience, and usual format. For example, how would you pinpoint Gary Shandling's easygoing but neurotic tone or Lily Tomlin's smacking lips?

Now can we take another monologue about Catholic school? Definitely. Suzanne Smith Jablonski describes a teenager's comic resignation toward her absurd education. In this monologue, the speaker exhibits her satiric voice through the concrete descriptions of middle school nuns. Locate the "internal" jokes. How do they accelerate the movement toward the punch line?

Monologue—Catholic School

SUZANNE SMITH JABLONSKI

Let's see, how many of you went to Catholic school? (Pause.) Ah, I'm glad to see I'm not alone. (Looks around audience.) Then you know all about the bizarre and unusual experience Catholic school provides. The best part about Catholic school is the nuns. I went to St. Margaret of Cortona Elementary School, and we had the best nuns in the business. Sr. Dominic was "nun extraordinaire." I mean, if you looked up nun in your dictionary, there she'd be, glaring at you with her half-smile/half-scowl, just waiting for you to break a rule. (Pause.) I remember the terror I felt when I'd hear her industrial nylon-clad legs (pause), covered with a couple of yards of whatever plaid polyester Jennie's Fabrics had on sale that week. Her sensible shoes would thunder down the hall . . . boom boom boom. (Pause.)

Before the Terminator there she was: (Pause.) Sr. Dominic. (Pause.) She'd walk in the room and we helpless little sheep would have to stand at attention—"Good morning, Sr. Dominic." If we didn't say it like we meant it (which we never did), we'd have to pop up and down in our seats until we got it right. (Pause.) Sr. Dominic had a repertoire of clever little sayings, only *she* seemed to know only the beginnings of them. For example, "neither a lender . . ."—we sheep got up again and added, "or a borrower be." (Pause.) And boy, did she believe that. You had to use a red pen to correct other people's tests, and if you didn't have one, Sister hung out her shop sign and sold it to you. (Pause.) For a woman with a vow of poverty, she sure got jolly when she bled you dry of your lunch money.

Structure

After you have 2–3 pages of writing, check the images, words, and jokes that make you laugh. Which ones fall flat? Block them for further study but focus on the good sections and expand them. Look again for three or four really great lines. Polish again. Maybe you want to dab the routine with asides to the audience or insert visual actions?

Check for overall structure. Do you want a string of jokes or a more integrated narrative? A combination? What's the best order for the sections? What goes first? Why? Chronological? Connected by topic? Least important to most important? Most important to least important? Random? Easygoing conversation? Cut and paste as necessary.

Adam Lantheaume uses a one-trait motif throughout his monologue—pity wars—and each scene gives us a variation on this theme. How does he keep the routine from just repeating itself? Where does it accelerate? What tone do you think he should use in the delivery? Who is his audience?

Monologue—Pity Wars

ADAM LANTHEAUME

C'mon, It's finals week! (Aside: Yo, we love it, don't we?) Gotta stay motivated somehow.

Ahhh, finals week. The time when we all try to make others feel sorry for us. (Looks around.) Yeah you do, you just don't realize that you're doing it. People are having Pity Wars all over campus.

"I have two finals tomorrow."

"Wow, I have one, but it's 7:30 in the morning. When's yours?"

"Not 'till 1:30."

See that evens out. Two vs. one. *But* mine's early. If mine was at 10:30, the person with two would have *juuust* won that round. If mine was at 1:30, and he had two starting at 1:30, then there'd be no contest. I'd have to pity him.

Doesn't *this* final always seem to be a winner though? Yeah, sure it is!

"I have all my finals in one day. From 8:00 'til 10:00 at night I'm in finals back to back."

"Yeah, well, you know the college's dumb exam schedule for my humor exam? I have to do a stand-up joke monologue at 7:30 in the morning."

"Man! You win. That sucks. I pity you."

Yes, we're all fishing for pity. It starts way back when we're little. When it used to be pride . . . and you're one pitiful kid.

Beginnings and Endings . . . and the Stuff in Between

Work for a great beginning, one that opens with wit, a hefty barb, or an observation about the audience that quickly identifies the speaker as unique. *Make sure it's concrete.* Does the speaker introduce himself or herself? Does the speaker acknowledge the audience?

Middle? Don't worry so much about punch lines per se. In narrative structure, the "punch line" hops around in different places rather than always settling at the end of a sentence;

variation surprises us more, although you'll also want punch lines at their regular home, at the end of sentences.

Last line? Have you brought the idea home with a topper? Ending at random can jolt the audience and fizzle in a "loss of control," so end with a spark.

Timing

You learn this by reading your material aloud and concentrating on the meaning you attach to sounds and rhythms. Add any physical signals you think appropriate, like a facial grimace or arm motions. Then try it out on friends and family. If possible, tape your routines so you can listen to yourself and to the audience's laughter. Note where you spoke too fast, too slow, stepped on your own lines, stepped on the laughter. Check the number of places you think you'll get a laugh. Remember that even slow-moving stories can hold buried jokes to keep our interest. Give them time. Expand a joke. (Not sure how to do this? Check the Show and Tell section of chapter 4.) Too slow? Contract it. See what happens. Pencil the places your material was wordy and the punch line lagged a second or so too late. Trim the material to snap the punch line back into place.

How do you know when it's too fast or too slow? Remember that the human brain takes a few seconds to process humor information before it transfers it neurologically into an emotional and physiological response (laughter). That's why comedians need to study timing. Watch the audience for their processing time and adjust accordingly. When you see their bodies tense in anticipation, that signals their time frame for the humor processing and how fast or slow you need to go. Too fast, they haven't had time to process it cognitively. (They didn't yet fully understand the intention of the joke, and you hurried to the punch line.) Too slow results in an anticlimax of laughter. (They got it cognitively, neurologically, and emotionally long before you finished the joke.) Basically, you've got to study body language, and you've got to do this for each audience. After a while, professionals can do this intuitively, but novice comedians need to observe carefully and be cognizant of the unique properties of humor delivery.

Who's out There?

Psych out your audience. Who are they? People in general or a specific group? What political, religious position? Age? Local, regional, or national folk? New Mexico? North Dakota? Will they tolerate blue material? Profanity? Criticism of religion? Remember that a joke monologue is a conversation with the audience. Don't exclude them from the routine. Have fun with them. Use ad-libs to warm them up. Don't insult them, unless you're a Don Rickles. If the audience isn't reacting to your material, try an aside about its apathy or some self-deprecating humor about your failure. (Jokes for hecklers: "And here's another joke you won't like"; "Hey, could I discipline your friend for you?") If necessary, shorten the routine and get off the stage. If you decide to deliver it in full and you get Bronx cheers, use the experience as an experience. Even if you bomb, you learn something.

Steve DiPietro pegs our driving habits in shopping malls. How many ways does he catch us in action? Who's speaking? How does the speaker slide into the topic? This monologue is structured by a series of examples. How many are there? Any thoughts as to performance antics or props if you were directing it?

Malls

STEVE DiPIETRO

I want to talk to you about malls and the whole demented atmosphere that goes along with them. First of all, when you're out in the parking lot and people are searching for parking spots, it's no joke, those shoppers play for keeps. If it comes to death, that's no problem, people will kill for a spot. You know what I'm talking about. You're cruising around like a Great White at feeding time, looking for that person marching towards a car with their keys out. Everyone does the same thing. You get right behind the person and flick on your blinker. It's like some unwritten law, if the blinker's on, he's untouchable. You now own that pedestrian. No one ever violates this. You'll be searching for a spot, you see a person, you say "Yes! There's a sp— . . . aw, shit! That guy's already got 'em." But if you have someone tagged, you just slowly cruise behind them. If they speed up, you speed up. They slow down, you slow down.

Now if they get into their car and out of the space quickly, you're nice and friendly. "Hey catch you 'round, see you later!" You wave to them with a nice big smile. But if they take more than 2 1/2 seconds to get out, you turn into a bastard. "Come on lady! I'm growing old here! Never mind the baby seat, just dump the kid in the trunk for Christ's sake!" As she's driving away, "Yea, thanks for giving me the spot so soon. After all, it is Christmas time, you know, the season of giving!"

The Absolute Cardinal Sin to commit in a parking lot is to steal someone's spot. I don't even think mall security's jurisdiction includes spot theft. CIA handles those cases, because if you steal a spot and you don't get away with it, you're going to need some kind of relocation protection program. If you steal a spot, you'll make even a mild-mannered kindergarten teacher come out of her car with a crowbar. I remember when I was going shopping with my dad when I was around four. I saw this guy just pounding away at a pile of meat with a sledge hammer. I said, "Dad, what's that guy doing? What's that pile of meat he's hitting?" My dad said, "Son, that pile of meat is a motorist. That's what happens when you steal a spot." It scarred me for years.

"Get the f___ out of there, that's my spot. Hey, he has my pedestrian!"

But, as serious a matter as parking spaces are, you can still have some fun with them. I'd be coming out of the mall, going towards my car. Almost instantly I'd have one of those sharks following me to my spot. What I like to do is just walk all over the parking lot for fifteen minutes with a car following me. It's amazing how long they'll follow you for. It's really hard for a driver to break free of a pedestrian once he has already locked on with his blinker. One time I just said screw it. I left my car there and walked all the way home, and the car followed me the whole way! And, as I'm walking into my house, he parks right in my driveway, thinking it's a spot!

The best way to make people flip out is to do this: After leading the car around for about ten to fifteen minutes, finally go to your car. When you're pulling out, stop about half-way. Then pull your car back in, get out, and walk back to the mall. Of course, you should probably run back to the mall, because after that, they'll pretty much mow you down right there, next to the space that's now your cemetery lot.

Where are the jokes in this story monologue by Brett Matthews? At the ends of the lines? Middle of a sentence? All over the place? In what way is a joke topped? How does the effect of this monologue differ from the old-fashioned joke–punch line, joke–punch line structure? What do you think of the topic? If you were delivering this monologue, where would you place the pauses? What voice would you use?

Dog Squares

BRETT C. MATTHEWS

My family is weird. Sure, most people have a crazy Uncle Bob or an Aunt Sue that's a little off her rocker, but my entire family is

coo coo for Cocoa Puffs. I'm not gonna pretend to exclude myself
from this group, although I will put myself closer to sanity than
most of them. You see, my mom is on the forefront. We live in a
suburban town called Liverpool. They call us Liverpudlians, but
I guess you don't really need to know that. Anyway, my mom
has always been a big one on designating chores and when there's
none to designate, she makes them up.

(Pause.)

Like, for example, take my dog Daisy. My mom's into the nature thing, and we have about a million pets named after flowers. We have a cat named Buttercup, a cat named Tigerlilly, a cat
named Posie, another named Pansy, a rabbit named Parsley, and
my dog Daisy. Daisy is a wonderful dog, I mean he really is, and
he takes really, great big wonderful shits. I mean, these mounds
are enormous, and being in suburbia our backyard is tiny and
you can imagine how these mushy mounds appear pretty visible
from the neighbor's view. My mom is the authority figure in the
house, and she's always the one who delegates who's to pick up
Daisy's Mum, as she calls it. She has a chart on the refrigerator
which reads in big boldface lettering: **Poop Duty,** and my name's
always at the top of the list.

(Pause.)

'Course, we don't just throw the poop away like some people, nope, that's wasting valuable fertilizer according to good ol'
mom. She sends us out into the battlefield, shovel in hand, and
tells us to get to work. Who came up with this genius idea, I
don't know, but we're assigned to cut squares into the lawn of
about a foot in width in order to place the poop underneath the
square portion of the lawn. It's all very simple: first you make a
nice neat square in the ground with a shovel, pick up the piece
of grass, place the poop inside, and then place the grass square
on top of the poop, and give it a gentle pat just for good measure.
Voila, Daisy's poop suddenly disappears—sort of.

At the end of the week, depending on Daisy's diet and how
many squirrels he had chomped, he could shit up to forty times
in the backyard, and I'm no math major, but if you have forty
tiny square plots of land that don't exactly fit with the rest of
the lawn, someone is going to notice. Right now, our lawn is
starting to look like a checkerboard.

You can imagine what the neighbors think.

"Uh, honey, why do those Matthews have all those squares
in their back yard?"

"Ahh, forget it. She sends her kids out to bury shit and they
cut the lawn into squares."

"Well, honey, maybe we should bury our shit underneath
lawn squares?"

(Pause.)
Thanks and good night.

SUGGESTIONS FOR WRITING

1. Study three television monologues. Tape them, if possible, so you can rerun them at will.

   What did the comedian talk about? Was it original? Did the comedian develop a personality? What's that person like? List the number of jokes in a set, the timing, the voice intonation. What jokes got the biggest laughs? Sketch the overall structure for each monologue. Is there a pattern to the routine? If so, is it interesting or dull? Does the routine lead to a high point? Does it have a terrific ending or does it fizz?

   If a joke bombed, how did the comic lift herself out of the mess? Did she change the subject? Try a different tone? Use body motion? Change position on the stage?

   Give an overall rating to the monologue. How does it compare with those from other comics?

2. If you can, go to a comedy club. Take notes on the routines, as above.

3. Write a satiric joke monologue on a subject that really bugs you. Include at least three reasons why you're annoyed or angry.

4. Write a "story" joke monologue about a crazy job you had to do.

The Literary Monologue

"The truth can be made up if you know how."
EDITH ANN—A LILY TOMLIN CHARACTER

The Literary Monologue

Like the joke monologue, the humorous literary monologue is a one-sided conversation spoken by a single character to an audience. It's distinguished from the joke monologue in that its primary purpose is to reveal some internal complexity of the speaker and a more conscious theme; humor is secondary. In a joke monologue, the jokes are foregrounded; in a literary monologue, the humor is embedded in the text. Most literary monologues are dramatized as theater or performance pieces, but they also find a home in written literature.

The *speaker* may be alone with her thoughts or may be talking to someone. She reveals information that leads to an uncovering of her personality through her intention, attitude, or conflict. Even when the speaker talks about an impersonal subject, like her hometown, we should get a flavor of how she fits into the scene. The *listener* may be a general audience or specific person(s), present at the scene or "offstage." The listener doesn't converse directly in the monologue but may figure in it through the speaker's references to the listener's presence as the monologue progresses. Sometimes the speaker will ask the listener questions, which the speaker answers herself.

The literary monologue can be constructed several ways. Commonly used as a scene within a play, the *soliloquy* is a monologue where the speaker explores a moral dilemma through introspection. The speaker searches for alternative solutions to a problem, more or less, by talking to herself. The *interior monologue* is a stream-of-consciousness expression of dreams, memories, emotions, or dilemmas where images erupt at random from the subconscious. As a work of art, the randomness of the interior monologue should still make dramatic sense.

Among the most popular literary monologues is the *dramatic monologue,* a one-sided conversation with a specific person or persons. The listener is essential to this monologue because that person defines the intention of the speaker. Usually we know about the listener only through what the speaker tells us, but the listener figures significantly in the motives of the speaker. Perhaps the most common literary monologue is the *narrative.* Though still driven by the personality of the speaker, it distinguishes itself from the others by a more conscious story.

Read the following literary monologue by Kim S. Lazar. Imagine the speaker talking to a stranger she's met in a coffee shop. Or imagine the speaker talking to her psychiatrist. What do you think the actor should emphasize in each instance? Where's the humor?

Maturation in a Blind American Family

Kim S. Lazar

Mom was a writer when I was growing up. I remember watching her on *The Today Show,* listening to her on the radio, and reading about her in newspapers and magazines. Judy Blume was on *The Today Show* with her, talking about talking to God about the first time she bled for six days and didn't die. I could relate. Mom spoke about the just-published second part to her first book, *Moms Make Money at Home, Book Two.* I asked her why she didn't just write one book that contained two parts and save everyone money. She responded by holding out Judy's autograph. One time, my sister and I got to pose for a newspaper photograph with her, each of us gathered under one of her armpits. The negatives forever reprint why my mom wrote the book, to be a mom at home and still get paid through self-employment.

Dad also sometimes worked at home. He spent time teaching his lecture series, "How to Be a Father," and building his private counseling for troubled children. His other job was watching the clock and worrying. Once in eighth grade, I was late for dinner and didn't call. He called my best friend who called the school who called the police to put out a missing child trace. Ten minutes after my weight, height, age and measurements crackled over hundreds of police cars' CB's, I was found necking in the bushes with our seventh-grade computer club president. My dad doesn't worry as much anymore, and now I only neck in private.

My sister Jodi, only one and a half years older than me, was an ally against my parents, a competitor and a playmate during lonely nights. Once boredom struck, when we got fed up with our broken "Operation" game that didn't make a "hah-hah-you-lost-sucker!" noise when one of us failed to properly remove a spleen, we'd be on the loose. When she was fourteen and I was an early budding twelve-year-old, we decided to gather attention by lifting up our shirts as a few speeding cars passed our colonial home. Not only were we no longer bored, we were titillated with the wind that rushed up our underpants, and we spent that night on the porch after our grandfather spotted our breasts instead of the driveway. We've been easier on his heart since then. Now Mom tells us before he comes to visit.

My parents tried their best to celebrate holidays with us as we were growing up. My birthday is only a month away from the December sensationalism, so on my twelfth birthday we tried to combine the two celebrations. Mom baked me a neuter snow person birthday cake with a long licorice nose, gave out yo-yo party favors with snow flakes painted on the string winder, played dreidel games with candy cane prizes and did Menorah lighting with an attempted finale of chestnut roasting. My gifts ranged from a Christmas stocking with blue and white Jewish stars to a new copy of mum's first book, part one. What I really wanted was *Hello God It's Me Margaret* and Ms. Pacman for my Atari set, but I smiled and thanked everyone because my Mom told me if I didn't follow this simple social custom, I couldn't keep anything.

That twelfth year tripped me in my rite of passage. I searched every Seven-Eleven Pepsi aisle, every Levi jean rack, every gas station, short-stop, supermarket and shopping mall for the seed of adulthood. I played basketball, watched political debates, and fought my family, but I felt the same as when I sat on the bench, watched Tom-n-Jerry and beat my Dad at "Donkey Kong." Jodi suddenly became involved with college searching, SATs and talking on the phone about what all of her friends were talking about she was talking about. Mom threw herself into business and Dad found he had to blow dry his bald spot. My friends dispersed into separate clans when we moved into a new high school, and my hamster of ten years died from old age.

I discovered *National Geographic* an hour before I got my braces. Mom dropped me at the orthodontist an hour early, so she could meet publishers for lunch. I had had my last meal of caramel popcorn for four years (when I'd get my braces off) and tried to enjoy my last hour of mouth freedom. Anyway, the man on the cover held a sign that covered "Geo," so the title read

National graphic. I was intrigued. The man held a poster that read: "Initiation, tradition, ceremony . . . Out with the old bring in the NEW!" New? I could not think of our old ones. Next year I would reach Bat Mitzvah, but none of my other friends had one. We didn't get dropped in the woods and have to survive for a week, we didn't have parts of our body severed, sliced, decorated or pierced, we didn't have to catch a lion and bring our family a feast. I was stumped.

To describe his travels in East Asia, Brett Matthews uses journal entries to form this literary monologue. In this excerpt, do the satiric elements criticize the society or the narrator's naivete? What tone does the speaker use? How does it reveal humor?

East Asia Journal

BRETT C. MATTHEWS

We last left the protagonists—Heather being offered a rice souvenir—at the snake temple. I should have known Penang was going to chew moose when our taxi driver who had lived there for twenty-nine years said we could see it in two days. There were some good moments—the Indian guy who made pancakes who called me Nicholas Cage, after he said he saw the movie "The Rock" forty to fifty times. I was thinking after that many times probably everyone would look like Nicholas Cage—but I took that as a compliment, sort of.

We then began our longest trek. As we were descending the trail from the north, Nepal was nearing one of their biggest festivals, so many herders were heading down with their flocks of goats to Pokhara. Which means if you're Hindu, like most of Nepal, goats get the sacrifice, and the holy cows get to roam free. Our guide told us that each plane at the airport will get a sacrificial goat to ensure smooth travel.

On one very steep section we passed, hundreds of feet up on a cliff, one goat got pushed a little too hard and got the bump off the edge by his fellow goatee. We arrived when the goat had already fallen. He was somewhere in the water, and we could hear him scrambling in the bamboo by the Kali Gandaki River, a few hundred feet down out of sight. The herder sold him to some local boys that I think were going to make the effort for rescue—or sacrifice.

We stayed at a place called the Waterfall Lodge where one goat drowned in the river and was afterward sold to the restaurant of the lodge we stayed at. Later going to the bathroom I saw him dissected and his large intestine hooked onto the running faucet for cleaning. You probably won't see that at Denny's on the way to the restroom after ordering the Texas burger, but then again, hopefully this restaurant won't serve goat intestines, among the other pieces of goat usually served, although I've heard even the vegetable curry isn't spared this delicacy.

Besides the goats, we saw little old grannies and grampies with canes, hunched over with heavy loads of wood on their backs, walking in flip flops a lot farther than we were heading. I saw one guy carrying his grandfather on his back in the middle of nowhere. I saw a granny hiking in socks and nothing else. And base camp had heavy-glass big beers available, which means someone was lugging some serious brew hah's up some steep terrain. Given the rocky climb, even our porter blew out his flip flop on the second day, but he fixed it by melting it together with a lighter.

High passes, steep cliffs, landslides, and stairs made my knees hurt and forced upon me many days of aspirin. The whole trek led me to realize that, in general, we Americans are privileged because we don't walk, and we certainly wouldn't think of hiking three days home after our plane flight. Packing my bag every morning at six while the porter waited, after I've hiked an eight-hour day uphill, and I have another eight-hour day uphill after my seventh day of trekking, and all the while, knowing I still have seven more days of this—it made me wonder why I was doing this—and if I was running away from being sacrificed.

How would you classify this excerpted monologue by Mark Matthews: joke, literary, or a little of both? Matthews gives us a new twist on ancient philosophical questions then surrounds the jokes with witty commentary from the narrator. How do the speaker's voice and tone contribute to the humor?

The Plight of Humanity

MARK B. MATTHEWS

I got to thinking again. What if the Messiah came today? I suppose in this time of sin, hedonism and gluttony, He would have a lot to do. The Apocalypse might be His only viable option. In a way, parts of Judgment Day could be fun—sort of like gym class where you count off by ones and twos with all the ones going to the Pearly Gates and all the twos going to somewhere decidedly warmer. Or maybe God could sponsor the biggest game of musical chairs to facilitate the difficult process of sorting through souls. Angels could play harp music from the clouds above the playing ground as the peoples of all nations united in friendly competition for a limited number of seats. They could hand out sun glasses and suntan lotion as consolation prizes to some of the runner up contestants. Of course, the downer to all this frivolity is that most of the people you know won't get into Heaven because they lack the SAT scores. And if you do end up there, not only will you miss a lot of these people, but there's a good chance you won't be very excited about the mandatory harp lessons that last for all eternity.

And what about tattoos? What if somehow they seeped into your soul and followed you into the realm of the afterlife? How do you explain to God that you thought by deliberately scarring the body given to you and filling in self-inflicted wounds with colored ink you thought you were actually enhancing it? How do you explain that you never thought about the relationship between soul and body and what will you say to all the Angels who ask you why you have Walt Disney's Tasmanian devil on your thigh? Now all your new eternal friends have to contend for eternity with what you thought was cool drunk in college. Somehow a "Hey God—lighten up—grab a beer—it looked good at the time" is just not quite going to do it.

As You Write . . .

Think of a literary monologue as having an introduction, background, and a main event, as even very loosely structured monologues have dramatic shape. The monologue should reveal the speaker at a major revelatory moment in his or her life, and the final moments should ascend to a psychological climax.

Let what you want to say determine the kind of monologue you'll write. Ask yourself questions about the speaker and where the conversation is taking place. Is the character doing something in addition to talking? Driving a car? Getting a haircut? What's he telling us? Why? What's his attitude toward the topic? (Definitely give him an attitude.) What psychological crisis is the speaker having? What internal change or understanding occurs in the speaker by the end of the monologue? Who's the listener? Specific or general? Why that person?

SUGGESTIONS FOR WRITING

1. Clean out your pockets. Write about what you (your speaker) carry in them and why. What do the items say about the speaker's internal conflict? What comic action is taking place?
2. Establish a comic or tragicomic persona: a thief; a bartender pushing a grocery cart; a preadolescent about to emit a primordial scream; an older sibling helping a child pull on a boot; a

guy/gal on a road crew; an old man/woman standing in line to get a welfare check. Have him or her talk to us as they go through some physical action. What internal action is driving that physical action? Are both the internal and external action comic? Or is one comic and the other tragic? It can get pretty complex, no?

ASK A FRIEND

READER'S WORKSHEET—MONOLOGUE

1. What's the intention of the writer? Stand-up? Literary? Theatrical performance?
2. Does the speaker exhibit an individual persona? If so, what's the speaker like? If not, any suggestions?
3. How is the monologue structured? Is its structure most effective for its purpose? If not, what change do you suggest?
4. Where are the jokes placed: Ends of sentences? Scattered over the text? How successful is the placement?
5. How original is the subject of the monologue? If clichéd, any suggestions?
6. What's the relationship of the speaker to the audience? Effective or not?

OK, So Who Threw the Tomato?

Psyching Out the Audience

"Wait a minute," you say. "I checked my writing for 'playful incongruity' and all that stuff from the theory chapters of this book and all the revision stuff, and I still didn't get laughs. Why? And what can I do about it?"

True, sometimes even if we have lots of "playful incongruity" and "originality" in our writing, not everyone laughs. Why? Because not everybody laughs at the same things. And there are lots of reasons why.

First, although humor scholars believe that all people in all cultures have the potential to laugh at anything "playfully incongruous" (that is, humor and laugher are universal), individuals and different cultures may not perceive the same things the same way. So humor appreciation gets complicated. Since human beings change constantly, what we laugh at can also change from one instant to the next. Many factors determine those differences. For example, our mood. If your boyfriend just gave you the famous I-Just-Want-To-Be-Friends speech, you're less likely to laugh at a joke than if you've just kissed him with great passion. You make an A on a physics exam, you're happy and you laugh easily; you get an F, you won't.

Age is another factor. And so is level of understanding. What people find funny also varies among historical periods. In fifteenth-century England, the cuckolded husband was a central butt of laughter, since he was too dimwitted to realize his wife was cheating on him. If the lover was a priest, both the husband and the priest were laughed at. Because the church dominated all aspects of behavior at that time, people laughed uproariously at its hypocrisy. In 1950s America, sentimental romantic comedy dominated the airwaves with the plots revolving around silly misunderstandings. This simple humor defined a decade that withdrew from more intense social satire, partly to repress the trauma of World War II.

Different cultures also fail to appreciate each other's humor because they have different interpretations of language and society. One of my friends from Slovakia, visiting the United States for the first time, perceived New York City police who patrol on horseback as being absolutely hysterical. She doubled over in the middle of Times Square because she expected to see horses ridden for sport; she never thought American police used them "for real." On a visit to Japan, I burst out laughing when I discovered that the Japanese have a different concept of the sandwich than Americans do. One restaurant assumed that any food could be placed between two slices of bread, so first on the menu was a vanilla pudding sandwich. I passed on that and instead ordered a fruit cocktail sandwich, dripping with syrup. My Japanese friend ate her noodle sandwich with a straight face.

Unlike the United States, some countries allow men and women to use the same bathrooms openly. On my trip to Asia I encountered over thirty men lined up at a public trough, so to speak, with thirty flowing rainbows. Most American men would be used to this and probably not take much notice. Some American women might be shocked; some, like me, would find it funny.

Because we have to understand the information in a joke, ingroup knowledge also determines who laughs. Jokes at a mathematicians' convention might contain information not understood at a dentists' convention. (Did you hear the one about Pythagoras and the quadratic equation?) And so, too, for the jokes at Hoople High School's 25th class reunion. Unless you graduated from that school, you won't really break up over the joke about Snooky Kermeg's backflip on the football field or Ms. Smedley's military style typing class. The members of that class associate Snooky and Ms. Smedley with numerous pleasant events during high school, and these memories intensify the humor for them. Outsiders hear the joke only within its specific context and, therefore, they laugh less if at all.

Our values and beliefs determine laughter. Someone makes a caustic joke about women in sports, and you're strongly in favor of increasing the funding for women, you might not laugh. This is why some people say feminists don't have a sense of humor, because they don't laugh at jokes about women's oppression. Some people see the corsets women wore at the turn of the century as tragic entrapments of the female body; some find these corsets incredibly sexy; some find them funny.

So all sorts of factors can determine whether an audience

laughs: age, intelligence, individual personality, physical well-being, values and beliefs, cultural conditioning, historical period, or mood. The time, place, and moment in which humor occurs are also major factors. And of special interest to writers, the quality and richness of the material—and its delivery. That matters, too.

"If I take all these factors into account when I write humor I'll never write," you say. "This is too much to think about."

Well, it's easier than you think. Forget the audience for the moment. Go back to square one. Remember that the most important person in your writing is you: write for yourself; then your characters; then your theme or point. At the bottom of the list sits your audience. Audience is important, but who they are and what they laugh at shouldn't be your primary concern in early drafts because if you focus on audience first, you usually end up with packaged, formulaic humor.

"Should I ever put audience first?" you ask.

Sometimes you'll do this if you're writing for humor-on-demand entertainment, like an after-dinner speech for an insurance company's conference or a podiatrists' convention or a routine for your best friend's birthday party. Sometimes your purpose requires that you consider audience right away, for example if you're writing a parody of a business letter and you need to use material current on Wall Street. Since life is never simple, remember that a writer never completely ignores the audience, even when writing great art. You want to think about clarity and effect as you polish your final draft because you hope to be understood. You also want your writing to be enjoyed, and if changing a dab or two gets louder laughs, go for it. But generally, write first, and worry about your audience later.

"Wait a minute," you say. "I still don't get it. I still don't understand the audience. A lot of comics get into trouble with their audience—BIG trouble—and then they're strung up in effigy and burned at the stake. What's going on?"

We said that the audience's variable response to humor is extremely complex; sometimes the comics deserve the bad reviews, and sometimes they're just misunderstood. And sometimes things can get rough, resulting in criminal penalties. Maybe the biggest confusion comes from our belief in artistic freedom. Some comics so urgently insist on their right to free expression that they focus exclusively on themselves and their characters without thinking of the larger implications for their audience.

This devil-may-care attitude can distort the real intention of the writer, and the humor then violates society's norms.

"But can't I say whatever I want to get the laugh?" you ask. Well, yes and no. You've got freedom of speech on the one hand, and a sensitive audience on the other. We can stack up lots of reasons why this clash gets comics in trouble.

Humor, for example, can backfire through miscommunication. A slip of the tongue or a spontaneous gesture can be misread. In 1964 Ed Sullivan, during his live televised variety show, signaled to comedian Jackie Mason that time was short by raising his hand. Mason wiggled his hand in return, saying, "I'm getting lots of fingers tonight." The irate Sullivan believed Mason gave him the finger and subsequently fired him from the show. Mason, ostracized by his profession, didn't really work again for years. Misunderstanding a community's values can outrage its members, and the hapless comic squirms in the hot seat. In 1966 during the Beatles tour of the United States, John Lennon teased the press with mock braggadocio: "We're more popular than Jesus now," he said. A furor over the remark exploded into demonstrations where their records and mementos were burned, and Lennon formally apologized.

Parodies don't necessarily allow the humorist free reign to attack anyone about anything just for the laugh, at least not without consequences. In 1984 the Reverend Jerry Falwell protested a parody of him and his mother in Larry Flynt's magazine, *Hustler.* Described in a forty-five million dollar lawsuit, the charge stated that *Hustler* called Falwell an incestuous drunkard, causing Falwell mental anguish. Many readers found the parody incredibly funny, although the Moral Majority did not. The courts ruled against Falwell, citing freedom of speech, but analysts raised questions of the fairness and validity of the humorous attack.

Insensitivity toward new ideas can also raise objections in an audience. In 1982 one irate reader spun off an angry letter to the editor of a college paper, objecting to this remark made by a local new wave band: "How many test-tube babies we got out there?" The reader deplored the musician's insulting remark and lack of sensibility for children born from in vitro fertilization.

When a comedian distances himself from serious consequences of an event, he might laugh while the victims recoil in anger and horror. When Johnny Carson was arrested for drunken driving in March 1982, he joked about it on his show. "I wish I could explain to all of you that I was doing research for my new special called 'Johnny Goes Home to the Slammer,'" he said. At the end of the program an actor dressed as a police officer ushered him out, to the guffaws of the studio audience. "You don't know how nice that sounds," he told the cheering audience. "Would you like to be my character witnesses?" Carson qualified the joking by speaking seriously about his arrest directly after the opening monologue, telling the audience that "you will never see me do that again." This qualification didn't satisfy Marilyn Beck, president of Mothers Against Drunk Drivers, who objected to the joking as diminishing the crime and discouraging social sanction.

Lacking simple common sense can also pose problems, as many public figures have discovered. In 1983 James Watt, former secretary of the interior, exhibited his insensitivity in a speech to the U.S. Chamber of Commerce when he described the members of his advisory committee for a coal-leasing program as "a black . . . a woman, two Jews and a cripple." Watt apparently tried to show his political correctness, but the joke backfired by the harsh diction. Some political analysts saw the joke as demonstrating Watt's lack of sympathy for affirmative action. Eventually, under pressure from both Republicans and Democrats, Watt resigned.

Sometimes people think they're conspiratorially joking with a nonthreatening in-group and let their defenses down. During Campaign '84, Barbara Bush embarrassingly apologized to Geraldine Ferraro, the Democratic vice-presidential nominee, for her off-the-cuff remark about the candidate. During a plane trip surrounded by press and campaign supporters, Mrs. Bush said that she likes to live "rich," with "no poor boy stuff like that $4 million (referring to Ferraro)—I can't say it, but it rhymes with 'rich.'" Ferraro accepted the apology.

Even people who are supposed to uphold the highest standards of integrity sometimes misjudge their audience. On June 5, 1995, the *New York Times* reported a joke told in Judge Lance Ito's courtroom during the O. J. Simpson murder trial.

> One of Mr. Simpson's lawyers approaches his client. "I have good news and bad news," he says. "Which do you want to hear first?"
> "The bad news," Mr. Simpson says.
> "The bad news is that it is your blood all over the crime scene, that the DNA proves it."

"Well, so what's the good news?" Mr. Simpson asks.
"The good news is that your cholesterol is only 130."

The joke itself is not significant, but it is significant that it was
Judge Ito, wearing his judicial robes, who related it to Mr. Cochran
during a break in testimony.

Sexual-Sexist/Gender Humor

The misunderstanding between comedian and audience can be
especially acute with sexual-sexist humor. Sometimes it's hard
to distinguish between the two, another way that a comic gets in
trouble. "So," you ask, "what's the difference between sexual and
sexist humor?"

*Jokes that illustrate our complex human sexuality are sex-
ual; demeaning put-down jokes that stereotype gender are sexist.*
Given the sexist society we live in, jokes about women, unfortunately, have been more often than not derogatory attacks: the
shrew mother-in-law; the dumb blonde; the domineering wife; old
maids.

Old vaudevillian jokes were very sexist:

Women's physical nature: McDougal prefers a girl who's sexy,
not brainy. He says when he feels intellectual, there's always
the public library.

Hated mother-in-laws: Do you know what mixed emotions are?
It's when you see your mother-in-law drive over a cliff in your
new Cadillac!

Woman's intelligence: If my wife said what she thought, she'd
be speechless.

Women's talkativeness: Women need no eulogy; they speak for
themselves.

A nonsexist joke satirizes society's behavior, not a person's sex.
In the film *Wisecracks*, directed by Gail Singer, one joke goes: A
gasket is $150 but "a gasket, honey," is $250. The wisecrack is
directed toward the sexist behavior of male garage mechanics who
charge extra for service to women they find sexy but uninformed
about cars.

The problems associated with sexist/gendered joking are
widespread in our culture. A *New York Times* report describes
the sexist humor used by a politician running for governor. In

an off-the-cuff remark, a Texas Republican gubernatorial nominee, Clayton Williams, compared the cold, foggy weather that his campaign workers had to endure one day in March to a rape: "If it's inevitable," he said, "just relax and enjoy it." The remark resulted in his withdrawing from the campaign. These difficulties mount with jokes about gays or anyone who does not demonstrate "acceptable" characteristics, accordingly to the dominant unwritten social code. As we all know, negative jokes about gays have reinforced the brutal violence against them, thus irresponsible joking can have enormous consequences. The way to avoid sexist/gendered humor is to think about people as people. If you create rich, complex characters—that is, human beings—you won't stereotype.

"So, what's stereotyping?" you ask.

Stereotypes, Caricatures, and Characters

Stereotypes

Stereotypes are invalid portraits of groups that have been assigned negative traits.

When stereotyping, a writer assigns a negative trait—without sufficient evidence—to a specific group to put down that group. Stereotyping operates under the assumption that only people who make up that group possess the negative trait and that people outside the group are of higher moral caliber since they do not have that trait. Stereotyping is a cruel attack on a specific group, which inflames hatred in the audience. Because the negative traits have never been proven, stereotyping both harms society and ruins rather than enhances the artistic foundation of the writing. The difficulty occurs in humor when the writer mixes up freedom of speech (the maxim that "because it's humor, anything goes") with the integrity of good writing. Unfortunately, stereotypes abound, and when a humorous writer uses them, we have to ask why. Is this art? Is this humor? Or is it something more insidious? Is the comic misusing humor to exorcize his own demons?

Caricatures

"How do caricatures figure in here?" you ask.

Caricatures are cartoon descriptions (visual or verbal) that exaggerate a dominant trait of a person or a group which, arguably, can be proven true.

The exaggerated trait either punctuates an identifiable feature so that we instantly recognize the cartoon figure as a person or symbol, or the exaggeration satirizes. In either case, the caricature has a valid base for humor.

Caricatures are designed for a specific person or group rather than society at large, and the exaggerated trait, usually physical, foregrounds the person as well as his values. Caricatures frequently appear as cartoon drawings, but writers create them in words, too, best known in the novels of Charles Dickens. *The features tweaked in a caricature can be supported with evidence, so the humor jabs at a trait with valid satiric intent.* We caricature lawyers as a group about their high fees and their courthouse antics, and we savor cartoons about fat-bellied congressmen who vote themselves high salaries, because we believe these professionals, who should uphold high values, can be unscrupulous.

Unless we learn the distinction, the thin line between stereotyping and caricature can stretch taut enough to diminish our humorous intentions. Look at cartoon 7. Is it a stereotype or a caricature? Does it tease us about the trials and tribulations of being a librarian? All-in-fun encouragement to enjoy libraries? Or does it stereotype librarians and the elderly?

This cartoon was posted in a college library but some people objected to it because, they said, it depicts librarians as elderly, drab, old-fashioned, and uninteresting. In a letter to the college paper, they also pointed out that it stereotypes the elderly for the same reason, and they noted that the clothing of the figure is extremely out of date. They argued that the cartoonist didn't realize that many elderly people who dress in old-fashioned clothing can't afford a new wardrobe each season and that their worn clothing reflects society's neglect of their financial needs. Older people who can afford it, they said in the letter, dress fashionably.

Characters

Characters are fictional people with multiple and evolving traits that speak to the complexity of human nature. (See chapter 6, Comedy, for a fuller discussion of this.) Still, what if . . .

"If we have freedom of speech in our country," you say, "then we should be able to write anything, including stereotypes. After all, laughter is cathartic. We can't help it. Restraint is unnatural." True?

You'll have to decide for yourself. Misusing humor to vent

Cartoon 7. Artist unknown. *The Cornell Daily Sun,* November 24, 1983, p. 4.

hatred or anger is self-serving, not art. Misusing artistic freedom can lead to numerous problems, such as those that configure the difference between racist and ethnic humor.

Ethnic/Racist Humor

Some *ethnic humor* defines a culture and its struggle for humanity, and this humor is among the best ever created; some ethnic humor stereotypes in the most vicious way, attacking the heart of humanity. Because brutal physical and psychological damage has been done to minorities through bigotry, the consequences of irresponsible humor concern us all. Negative ethnic humor establishes in-group and out-group confrontation, and comics who viciously and without reason diminish a particular group only indulge their own hatred. While those who defend this humor say that expressing taboos allows tensions to dissipate and therefore enhances psychological health, its critics argue that it serves no healthy social purpose and is only used by the comedian as an act of violence. These critics argue that its expressed purpose is to vent malice. Comedians who resort to this, many psychologists state, are extremely insecure about their fears: loss of economic gains; loss of power; loss of identity. Like other insensitive joking, this humor reveals the teller of the joke as uneducated about audience.

As a writer, you'll want to study this debate carefully. For example, what do you think about this ethnic joke told by former president Ronald Reagan on his campaign bus during the 1980 New Hampshire primary? The joke, which Reagan told to Senator Gordon Humphrey and campaign supporters, went this way:

> How do you tell the Polish fellow at a cockfight? He's the one with a duck.
> How do you tell the Italian one? He's the one who bets on the duck.
> How do you know the Mafia is there? The duck wins.

Are you offended by it? An uproar ensued over the ethnic slurs and, nervous that he would hurt his chances for the nomination, Reagan apologized to the nation.

Review your intention in what you've written so far. Do you see any stereotypes? Does your writing depict your characters truthfully? Is there any way the audience might misread your intentions?

Given our discussion in this book, writing humor is a serious undertaking. Your artistic judgment, however, should guide your writing, and if you subscribe to an artistic validity for characterization and purpose, you can avoid insensitive humor.

Humor is also a wondrous undertaking, as its potential for expression is miraculously infinite. It exists to be embraced. Humor can convey the most quotidian moments in life or the most significant, surfacing in both tragedy and comedy, often in the same breath. Elusive and mysterious, yet highly communicative, like all great drama and literature, humor can well serve a writer's imagination. As entertainment, it provides contentment and community; as art, it offers hope and joy.

"Lots to think about," you say.

"True, lots to think about," says the prof.

That's why writing humor offers such a challenge. And such incredible artistic reward. So take your heart in your hand (the writing one), and go for the laughs. And god bless.

Exiting the Stage

So that's it. That's the book. Thanks, everyone, for reading it. We could have said a lot more, but enough is enough and, eventually, even clowns have to go home. We hope we've answered some of your questions and maybe even given you a few laughs. For sure, we hope you're inspired to pick up your pencil or turn on your computer—and write. Cheers and good wishes.

P.S.: Well, there's a little more. Check out the questions, philosophy, glossary, and bibliography. Lots of good stuff there.

Appendix A: A Few More Questions
(Yes, You in the Front Row)

How can I sell my joke monologues?

Walk the beat with your portfolio. Network a lot. Whether you're trying to sell written material or perform stand-up, begin with individual parties, local clubs, local comedians, colleges, hotels, conferences, cruises, radio stations, writing clubs, and arts centers. Check trade papers like *Variety, TV Market List,* and the *Hollywood Reporter.* The American Guild of Variety Artists (AGVA) can provide addresses of performers who accept unsolicited material. If you want to perform as well as write, go prepared with a tape of your work.

Where can I publish humorous short stories or poems?

You can get published in any literary journal or magazine if your work reaches high literary quality. Editors are always interested in good writing. The pay is negligible, however, and usually you're remunerated with a free copy of the magazine. Nevertheless, you'll be inspired to write more when you see your name in print, and it builds a portfolio for a job in the field, since the more you publish, the more convincing your talent becomes to potential publishers. Be sure to familiarize yourself with the journal or magazine to which you're sending your work. See the *International Directory of Little Magazines & Small Presses*, published annually by Dust Books, P.O. Box 100, Paradise, CA 95969; (800) 477–6110. See also the *Directory of Humor Magazines and Humor Organizations* in America and Canada (New York: Wry-Bred Press). They're available in bookstores, in the reference section of your library, and on the Web, as are other similar directories. Directories also contain lists of contests, which offer cash prizes or publication.

How do I send out my writing?

Enclose your work in a large envelope, along with a self-addressed, stamped envelope large enough to hold your manuscript if it's not accepted. Ensuring that your work is returned to you diminishes chance of plagiarism. Include a cover letter but keep it brief, something like:

> Dear (Name of a specific editor. You'll find it in the directories cited above.)
>
> I am enclosing this (story, poem, satire, monologue) for possible publication in your magazine.
>
> (Tell them in two or three sentences a little about your background.)
>
> Thank you very much.

Be sure to include the publisher's full address on the letter, plus the date. You'll need this for your files. Record the name of the work, the publisher's name and address, and date of submission. Keep a hard copy of your cover letter. Recording what went where is essential, because no matter how important your manuscript is to you, you'll forget where you sent it. When you get a response, yea or nay, record that, along with the amount of time the editors took to read your submission. That helps you remember who's speedy and efficient and who's not.

What do I do if my work is rejected?

Nobel Prize winner Isaac Bashevis Singer suggested that you should feel sad for a few hours, then sit down and write. Then send your work out again. Every writer has been rejected at least once, including Singer. If a reviewer has written a comment on your rejected work, feel lucky, since their busy schedules rarely permit any professional responses, and someone thought your work worthy of a few seconds of her time. Don't take rejection so hard. Feel comfortable sending out the rejected work at least a dozen times before you toss in the towel. Some writers have submitted the same work fifty, sixty, seventy times before they've hit the jackpot.

Should I get an agent?

For small works like short stories, poems, and journalistic pieces, no. This work doesn't pay anything and an agent won't take you on if she doesn't expect to earn a percentage from royalties. For a novel, nonfiction book, or script, try to convince an agent to represent you, since they can be more efficient than you at promoting your work. Do not pay an agent to represent you. If she sells your work, she'll take the standard payment of approximately 10–15 percent.

How do I get an agent?

Generally, if you're a newcomer, convincing an agent to represent your work is tough. Be sure to have written enough for a solid portfolio, about one hundred pages. No agent will look at five or ten pages of anything, unless the writer is already well established. Show your work around if you can—to teachers, writers, or friends. Don't expect free favors from them. This is rude. At least offer lunch to anyone who has critiqued your manuscript. *Be sure to send them a thank-you note.* Sometimes your professional friends will recommend you to their agents. Most of us go it alone, so expect lots of footwork.

For more information, write the following:

Writers Guild of America, East, Inc., 555 W. 57 St., New York, NY 10019; Phone: (212) 767–7800; www.wgaeast.org.

Writers Guild of America, West, Inc., 8955 Beverly Blvd., Los Angeles, CA 90048; Phone: (323) 951–4000 in southern California; (800) 548–4532 outside southern California; www.wga.org.

YMCA National Writer's Voice Office, 5 W. 63rd St., New York, NY 10023. Ask for their regional offices. Phone: (213) 875–4261.

Writer's Market, Fiction Writer's Market, Writer's Digest, 9933 Alliance Road, Cincinnati, OH 45242; www.writers markets.com.

Literary Market Place, R. R. Bowker Company, 1180 Avenue of the Americas, New York, NY 10036; www.literary marketplace.com.

The Writer's Handbook, The Writer, Inc., 120 Boylston Street, Boston, MA 02116–4615; www.channell.com/thewriter/thewriter.html.

The Writer's Guide to Book Editors, Publishers, and Literary Agents, Prima Publishing, 3000 Lava Ridge Ct., Roseville, CA 95661; Phone: (916) 787–7000.

CBS, 51 W. 52nd St., New York, NY 10019; www.cbs.com (the Web address will guide you to individual departments and television shows).

NBC, 30 Rockefeller Plaza, New York, NY 10020; www.nbc.
com.
ABC, 1330 Avenue of the Americas, New York, NY 10019;
www.abc.com.
Comedy Central, 1775 Broadway, New York, NY 10019; www.
comedycentral.com.
Associated Writing Programs (AWP), George Mason Univer-
sity, Tallwood House, Mail Stop 1E3, Fairfax, VA 22030;
Phone: (703) 993–4301; www.awpwriter.org.
Poets and Writers, Inc., 72 Spring St., New York, NY 10012;
Phone: (212) 226–3586; www.pw.org.
U.S. Copyright Office; Phone: (202) 707–9100 for the reg-
istration form TX; (202) 707–3000 for other questions.
lcweb.loc.gov/copyright.

What are some sources for those of us who want to perform?

The Clown College of the Ringling Brothers and Barnum & Bailey
Circus offers courses in clowning. See *Comedians: Annual Directory of Comedians and Comedy Clubs*, Creative Concepts, Great
Neck, NY: Annual. Call comedy clubs in your area. For work in
colleges, try the National Association for Campus Activities, 3700
Forest Drive, Suite 200, Columbia, SC 29204. Students are always
up for laughs. For payment, expect minimum wage, a bag of potato
chips, and a soda.

How do I protect my work from being stolen?

Contact the Writer's Guild of America (address above) for ways of
protecting your work from plagiarism. It won't cost you much and
takes little time.

What's another great source of information?

For up-to-date information about humor courses, journals, magazines, and organizations, contact Don L. F. Nilsen, Executive Secretary, International Society of Humor Studies, English Department, Arizona State University, Tempe, AZ 85287–0302. See also
the journal of ISHS, *Humor: International Journal of Humor Research*, for academic articles on the study of humor. See also Web
addresses listed in the bibliography. The ISHS, made up of scholars
from around the world, is a central clearinghouse of information
for those of you interested in all areas of humor. A great resource!

Appendix B: Philosophies of Humor

What Are the Really Great Questions?

Philosophers as far back as the ancient Greeks have speculated on the nature of humor and laughter, puzzling over such questions as: Why do we laugh? What makes us laugh? What's universal about humor? What's the smallest element that defines humor?

Below you'll find summaries of the major theories, formulated through the centuries by philosophers, literary critics, and research scholars. Buyer beware, however. None of the theories encompasses all possible situations; as a result, and perhaps most important, *no single, agreed-upon theory of humor emerges above any other. Each has limitations.* The groupings, for example, are often invalid since some theories fall into more than one category, and parts of others don't really fit any group; nevertheless, although the classifications incite huge debates and academic grumbling, a review of these theories can offer you a valuable historical perspective on the philosophy of humor.

Superiority Theories

The superiority theorists believe that we laugh because we feel superior to a person, idea, or situation and that our disapproving laughter acts as social control for appropriate behavior. They argue that if we laugh at a person for exhibiting improper behavior, that person will be embarrassed enough to reform. Plato, Aristotle, Thomas Hobbes, Henri Bergson, and George Meredith are usually classified under this category. Plato (428–348? B.C.) in *Philebus* defines "comic" as experiencing enjoyment over another's misfortune. Aristotle (384–322 B.C.) in *Poetics* (c. 330 B.C.) sees laughter as disgust over another's improper behavior. In *Leviathan* (1651), Thomas Hobbes proposes that we laugh because we feel superior ("sudden glory") when we compare ourselves or our situation to the misfortunes or infirmities of others. In his essay *From Laughter* (1911), Henri Bergson defines laughter as "something mechanical encrusted on the living." He imagines the comic figure as a person who responds repeatedly in the same way to a problem, no matter how many times he fails. Bergson believes that our laughter comes from our own intelligent and flexible ways of solving problems that differ from the "mechanical fixed behavior" of a foolish person.

Literary critic George Meredith writes in his *Essay on Comedy* (1918) that comedy is a social corrective and that social well-being is related to humor. He, too, sees humor as satire, and, therefore, a writer would feel superior to the satiric object. Take banana-peel laughter, for example. We laugh at someone who slips on a banana peel, superiority theorists would argue, because we feel superior to that person in his clumsiness and because the stupidity makes him a candidate for reform.

These theorists would say this joke employs superiority:

> A priest and rabbi who grew up together in a Brooklyn neighborhood but who have haven't seen each other for years meet on a street.
>
> The priest says, "Ah, Jacob, me boy. It's good to see you."
>
> The rabbi says, "Michael. Yoi, how have you been? It's been such a long time."
>
> The priest looks the rabbi up and down, and decides to puff out his own successful career.
>
> The priest says, "You know, Jacob, me boy, I've just been thinkin' what a hard life you have, choosin' to be a rabbi, when you could 'ov been a priest like me. I mean, now look at what I 've goin' for me. Here I am a priest, but if I do a good job and work hard, someday I could be a bishop. And if I do a good job as bishop and work hard, someday I could be an archbishop. And if I do a good job as archbishop and work hard, well, glory be to god, someday I could even be the Pope!"
>
> He stops to reflect on what he's just said, then looks at Jacob and shakes his head in pity. "Now what do you rabbis have goin' for yourselves? Nothing. Once a rabbi always a rabbi. It's too bad, but as a rabbi, you're always goin' be stuck at the bottom."
>
> The rabbi pauses for a minute, and slowly strokes his beard. "Hmmm . . . maybe so, Michael, . . . hmmm . . . maybe so . . . maybe so . . . ," he says, " . . . but just remember . . . one of our boys made god."

Superiority theorists say we laugh because we identify with the rabbi's put-down of the priest's ethnocentricity and thus feel superior.

The limitation of superiority theory is that it doesn't account for types of humor other than satire, like nonsense, word play, or gentle comedy. The proponents of superiority theory value satire exclusively as the means to strengthen the moral behavior of society.

Biological and Evolution Theories

Proponents of biological and evolutionary theories argue that humor is instinctive, probably evolving as defense mechanisms from our pre-language era. They point out similarities in both defense behavior and laughter, such as loud noises, thrashing of the body, the bearing of teeth, and facial grimaces. Now that we no longer hunt for food, these scholars believe, this instinct is transferred to defending (joking away) our psychological and social inadequacies.

Other researchers contend that laughter is built into our biology because it's good exercise. They argue that laughter strengthens the internal organs, invigorates blood circulation, eases digestion, and relaxes tensions. Some theorists believe humor is a mechanism that wards off depression and possible suicide because laughing encourages our species to live in spite of all odds. A caution here, however, as most of these claims have yet to be scientifically proven.

Herbert Spencer (*Essays on Education*, 1860), Charles Darwin (*The Expression of the Emotions in Man and Animals*, 1872), and Max Eastman (*The Sense of Humor*, 1921) may be classified as major proponents of this position. John Morreall, in his book *The Philosophy of Laughter and Humor* (1987), believes there is some validity to the biological theory. He states that humor encourages us to explore daring and unusual constructs, a necessary survival skill.

Laughing at the following joke may help us cope with the horrors of life as a survival mechanism: In Woody Allen's film *Annie Hall*, Alvy says to Annie: "The world is divided into two types: the horrible (blind cripples) and the miserable (everyone else). You should be glad you're miserable." The limitation of these biological theories is that they restrict themselves to physiology.

Release and Relief Theories

The release and relief theorists believe that laughter occurs when we eject built-up tension from the social inhibitions described in a joke. This release results in excess energy being dispersed in the body, exhibited by laughter.

In *Essays on Education*, Herbert Spencer proposes the theory that we laugh only when we are expecting a large observation but arrive at a small one, and that laughter is the result of overflowing excess energy. According to Sigmund Freud in *Jokes and Their Relation to the Unconscious* (1905), we laugh because we need to rid ourselves of the guilt or embarrassment we carry from our sexual or aggressive inhibitions. Freud calls these jokes "tendentious wit" and contends that when energy in the body is not used because the superego censors it, that energy is released as pleasurable laughter.

Jokes like the following are said to release racial, vulgar, and sexual inhibitions.

> Three Jews who have been sentenced to death are standing in front of the firing squad. The officer asks the first one, "Do you want a blindfold?"
> "Yes," answers the Jew, and he is given one.
> The officer turns to the second: "Do you want a blindfold?"
> "Yes," he answers, and he is given one.
> When the officer addresses the third with the same question, he replies, "No, I don't."
> The second Jew leans over and whispers to him, "Moishe, stop making trouble."

> The dean of women was introducing a visiting politician to her students.
> "I couldn't begin to tell you all of the senator's accomplishments," she said, "but as an indication, you'll be interested to know that he has a nine-inch Who's Who."

Advocates of this theory argue that jokes have a biological purpose in relieving anxieties about taboos and anyone creating this humor challenges society's strictures by breaking the taboo, allowing for psychological freedom. The weakness in this theory, like superiority theory, is that it doesn't include all types of humor. When we write joyous humor, for example, we don't create it to relieve secret anxieties.

Incongruity Theories

Philosophers who advocate incongruity theory believe that laughter and humor derive from a sudden shock, surprise, or the solving of a clever cognitive puzzle. They argue that we laugh when two incompatible things clash, and the point where we fuse the two incongruous planes is the point where the "joke" sparks. Some theorists argue that we only need incongruity for humor to be present; others argue that one needs both incongruity and a resolution of that incongruity. This second version is called configurational theory. Several theorists point out that another element—intelligent perception—must be present since humor is based on intellect and we have to understand the differences between the inconsistencies before we can appreciate the humor.

Incongruity theorists believe we laugh because our line of thought has been surprisingly switched from one context to another. This theory has had many proponents. In 1776 James Beattie suggested in his *Essay on Laughter and Ludicrous Composition* that we laugh when two inconsistent situations come together: "Laughter arises from the view of two or more inconsistent, unsuitable, or incongruous parts or circumstances, considered as united in complex object or assemblage, or as acquiring a sort of mutual relation from the peculiar manner in which the mind takes notice of them." According to Immanuel Kant in *Critique of Judgment* (1790), laughter arises from "the sudden transformation of a strained expectation into nothing." Kant believed that humor consists of a clash of two disparate elements and a resolution, and that surprise was an essential component. In "On Wit and Humour" (1819), William Hazlitt extends Kant's idea, writing that "the essence of the laughable [then] is the incongruous, the disconnecting of one idea from another, or the jostling of one feeling against another." Hazlitt speaks of a disjunction between what is and what ought to be. Restricting the application of Kant's theory to intellectual perception, Arthur Schopenhauer in *The World as Will and Idea* (1860) argues that the incongruities arise from illogical logic.

By the twentieth century, philosophers begin to hone the definition of humor through a complex mapping. Henri Bergson in *From Laughter* (1911) describes a situation as comic "when it belongs simultaneously to two altogether independent series of events and is capable of being interpreted in two entirely different meanings at the same time." In his influential book *The Act of*

Creation (1964), Arthur Koestler writes that a joke is produced by the clash of two incompatible contexts that exist simultaneously. He calls this "bisociation." In humor, he says, both the creation of a joke and the perceiving of a joke involve the mental leap from one plane or associative context to another. In *The Philosophy of Laughter and Humor*, John Morreall adds another element: playfulness. Morreall points out that when we respond aesthetically to a work of art, we enjoy all kinds of incongruity without being amused, like the intellectual, which can produce interest or curiosity, or like the bizarre, fantastic, grotesque, and macabre, which can produce fear, anger, anxiety, repulsion, confusion, or puzzlement. With humor, we experience playful enjoyment. According to Morreall, we do not want the situation changed, as we do when we experience anger or fear, nor do we want our understanding of it changed as we do when we experience puzzlement.

Some examples of incongruity jokes follow, which incongruity theorists would say we enjoy because we experience two playfully different, clashing contexts (scripts).

> I'm not afraid of dying. I just don't want to be around when it happens.
> WOODY ALLEN

In this joke, we "read" it as a logical statement of the speaker's pondering death (script #1) and as an illogical twist that he would prefer not to be present when he dies (script #2).

The same principles hold for these jokes:

> A masochist is a person who likes a cold shower in the morning (script #1) so he takes a hot one (script #2).
> A sadist is a person who is kind to a masochist.

An incongruity theorist would explain the clash of scripts in these jokes as follows: a sadist (script #1: a person who is not kind); masochist (script #2: a person who wants to be hurt).

Although many scholars argue that fully understanding the nature of humor is extremely difficult, if not impossible, because of the fluid variables in any humor context, some scholars believe that incongruity best defines the fundamental element of humor. For its proponents, incongruity forms the foundation for humor theory considered "most universal," one that validates all humor contexts, both perceived and created. The weakness of this theory is that it hasn't yet been sufficiently tested.

This book argues for incongruity theory, as you have seen in the previous chapters.

Linguistic-Semantic Theories of Humor

Linguists analyze language or "text" (usually limited to jokes) using formal, scientific principles to understand how we use words; that is, they study the meaning, intention, and grammar of language. Joining the search for the universal qualities of humor, the linguist tries to determine the difference between a group of words that's funny and a group of words that isn't. Some scholars see linguistic-semantic theories of humor as synonymous with incongruity theory.

In his seminal book *Semantic Mechanisms of Humor* (1985), Victor Raskin has formed a script-based semantic theory of humor, suggesting that the properties of a joke are usually seen as semantic, that is, "language" inherently "means" the joke. Script-based semantic theory combines the meaning of the individual words of a text and all the ways those words interrelate through any extended meanings and/or words coming before or after that sentence, both as part of the actual text and of any language we intuit, including abstract storage of information. Raskin proposes that "the text is a joke if it is compatible, fully or in part, with two distinct scripts." Both Raskin and linguist Salvatore Attardo continue to modify this theory by extending and testing it within the fields of semantics and cognitive science.

Still searching for a definition of "humor," other scholars are exploring larger "comic frames" than the "joke" by analyzing parodies, longer narratives, and theatrical settings, which aren't "jokes" per se but may establish more accurate definitions of humor.

New Research Methodologies

Computer and imaging theorists are studying how we come to understand humor using Magnetic Resonance Imaging (MRI) technologies. Some researchers break down thought processes into the smallest possible steps via the computer in an attempt to duplicate humor responses technologically. Others computer-photograph our physiological reactions to humor by measuring pulse rates, blood pressure, and temperature. Some scholars examine brain waves and patterns via MRIs as a way of charting mental constructs. Because brain and language research is so new, results are still in early stages.

The difficulties with humor theories have to do with the differences in point of view. Some philosophers see humor as an instinctive human process; others view it as a social corrective. Some approaches are cognitive; some emotional; some linguistic. Some theorists study the humorous object; others study the person who perceives the object. Some of the theories are descriptions of humorous situations and some aren't theories at all, just descriptions of how humor functions. Theorists living centuries ago did not have complete information about human physiology or behavior and, therefore, their theories are lacking. Still others mix humor with "comedy," narrowing both to a literary genre. The most promising to date are incongruity theory and MRI imaging; however, few explore the dynamics of the creative act, and even fewer research how we write humor.

All this confusion means that we have to be cautious about making general statements about humor.

Notes

NOTES TO CHAPTER ONE

1. Paul E. McGhee, *Humor: Its Origin and Development* (San Francisco: W. H. Freeman, 1979), 125–67.
2. G. V. N. Dearborn, "The Nature of the Smile and the Laugh," *Science* 11 (June 1, 1900): 851–56.
3. Stanley G. Hall and Arthur Allin, "The Psychology of Tickling, Laughing, and the Comic," *American Journal of Psychology* 9 (1897): 1–41.
4. William Fry, "Physiologic Effects of Humor, Mirth and Laughter," *Journal of the American Medical Association* 267, no. 13 (1992): 1857–58. See also Norman N. Holland, *Laughing: A Psychology of Humor* (Ithaca: Cornell University Press, 1982), 84 passim.
5. Holland, *Laughing,* 76. See also Armand M. Nicholi, Jr., ed., *The Harvard Guide to Modern Psychiatry* (Cambridge, MA: Harvard University Press, 1978).
6. Vincent Zigas, *Laughing Death: The Untold Story of Kuru* (Clifton, NJ: Humana Press, 1990).
7. Joost A. M. Meerloo, "The Biology of Laughter," *Psychoanalytic Review* 53 (1966): 189–208.

NOTES TO CHAPTER TWO

1. I'm especially indebted to Arthur Koestler for his work in bisociation and to John Morreall for his analysis of "incongruity." See Arthur Koestler, *The Act of Creation* (New York: Dell, 1975), John Morreall, *Taking Laughter Seriously* (Albany: State University of New York Press, 1983), and John Morreall, ed., *The Philosophy of Laughter and Humor* (Albany: State University of New York Press, 1987). See also Salvatore Attardo, "The Semantic Foundations of Cognitive Theories of Humor." *Humor Journal* v. 10, no. 4 (1997): 395–420, and Victor Raskin, *Semantic Mechanisms of Humor* (New York: D. Reidel/Kluwer, 1985).

NOTES TO CHAPTER 6

1. Gerald Mast, *The Comic Mind: Comedy and the Movies* (New York: Bobbs-Merrill, 1973), 4–9.
2. Ibid., 12.
3. John Morreall, ed., *The Philosophy of Laughter and Humor* (Albany: State University of New York Press, 1987).

Glossary

absurd. A term used to describe humor that depicts the hopelessness and despair of a meaningless universe.
   See chapter 13, Grotesque, Sick, and Absurd Humor.

absurd, theater of the. Drama that portrays the absurdity and futility of human existence, coined by the American critic Martin Esslin. Eugene Ionesco's *The Bald Soprano* was first described as such in 1950.

American West, humor of (Southwest American humor). Refers to the old Southwest—Georgia, Mississippi, Alabama—and to tall tales of the frontier, like the antics of Davy Crockett who, according to myth, bit rattlesnakes to death. The humor of the slaves included tales about High John, who tricks the greedy white master through wit and intelligence.

anecdote, comic. A short narrative relating a single incident.

antithesis. A phrase or clause that sets up a syntactical balance with opposing words. Ex: Better a witty fool than a foolish wit.—William Shakespeare.

aphorism. A concise statement directing an observation or truth, usually self-evident. It achieves its wit through alliteration, metaphor, or antithesis. Ex: Fish and visitors stink after three days.—Ben Franklin.

archetype. From the Greek, meaning "a pattern from which all others are made." Psychologist Carl G. Jung proposed a theory of a "collective unconscious" where people universally share experiences like birth and death; some humor scholars argue that the high frequency of archetypes in comedy speaks to our subconscious need for repetitive and comforting assurances. Archetypes appear frequently as stock plots, such as yearning for love or conquering impossible odds, and much of our enjoyment comes from fulfilled expectations in the story. Archetypical characters manifest themselves as the young hero, beautiful maiden, braggart, oafish sidekick, and disapproving elders. The love-sex interest in humor suggests our "collective unconscious" wish to be young and procreative. *See chapter 6, Comedy.*

bathos. An overreaching, self-indulgent effort of a writer to achieve a dignified, serious emotion, resulting instead in ridiculous excess. Ex: Not louder shrieks to pitying Heaven are cast / When husbands or when lap dogs breathe their last.—Alexander Pope, *Rape of the Lock.*

Berra, Yogi (Yogi Berraisms). Lawrence Peter Berra, Yankee catcher from 1946 to 1963, known as Yogi Berra, is beloved for his witty paradoxes, as for example, "That place is so crowded nobody goes there anymore." Among our most popular Berraisms is the one shouted by many a sports announcer, "It ain't over till it's over." These phrases generate so much fun that we often attribute to Berra statements he never made. He doesn't claim, "It's déjà vu all over again," but we still ascribe it to him. Also, a derivative as Yogi Bear, a popular Warner Brothers cartoon figure.

black humor. Not to be confused with African American humor, this term refers to the humor of disillusionment, despair, and meaning-lessness in life that first appeared in the l950s as a reaction to World War II. It reveals itself in sick jokes and in the satiric, bitter stand-up comedy of Lenny Bruce, later echoed in Joseph Heller's *Catch-22.* Black humor also describes the absurdist plays of Edward Albee and Eugene Ionesco. Images of violence, scatology, and morbidity trans-mit the existential philosophy. More serious writers use black humor to convey the decay of spiritual values. *See* grotesque, sick jokes. *See chapter 13, Grotesque, Sick, and Absurd Humor.*

blue material. Off-color, sexual jokes. "Blue" actually refers to the pink crevices of sexually erogenous zones. It's possibly derived from the blue pencils censors used to block out risqué material or from the word "bluenoses," which describes the upper classes who issued restrictive theater laws for Sundays.

bombast. Originally the word meant stuffing furniture with horsehair padding. Now it refers to inflated language of the comic braggart. *See* braggart.

braggart (braggadocio). A comic stock figure who struts and boasts about his bravery or accomplishments but who, in truth, is a coward and an incompetent. Although much too complex to be a stock figure, Falstaff, in Shakespeare's *Henry IV* and *V,* is one of the most famous braggarts in literature. *See* bombast.

breakout character. A minor character in a teleplay who smites the au-dience with such charisma that the character is awarded a larger role. Ex: The Fonz in *Happy Days.*

Bulwer-Lytton Fiction Contest. An annual literary event founded by Eng-lish professor Scott Rice and organized by San Jose State University of California. Contestants write the worst possible opening line of a novel, either actual or imagined. The contest is named after Edward George Earle Bulwer-Lytton, whose opening sentence to his notorious 1830 novel epitomizes bad writing: "It was a dark and stormy night."

Charles Schultz's Snoopy struggles with his creativity by varying this line in his novel-in-progress. A past winning entry comes from Sheila Richter of Minneapolis: "The notes blatted skyward as the sun rose over the Canada geese, feathered rumps mooning the day, webbed appendages frantically pedaling unseen bicycles in their search for sustenance, driven by cruel Nature's maxim, 'ya wanna eat, ya gotta work,' and at last I knew Pittsburgh."

burlesque. *See* vaudeville. *See chapters 16, Parody, and 18, The Joke Monologue.*

caricature. An exaggerated portrait, either visual or verbal, that centers on one trait of a character which represents the whole. Though sometimes serious, caricatures usually employ humorous disproportion as a satiric vehicle. The novels of Charles Dickens are famous for their caricatures, like Scrooge's verbal "Bah, humbug" or Mr. Pocket's visual image of lifting himself up by his own hair. Caricatures often ridicule political or social values in their drawn figures, like an exaggerated "Uncle Sam" might symbolize the IRS. *See* stereotyping, stock characters. *See chapter 20, on Audience.*

clerihew. A short, four-line, irregular stanza of two couplets, used to create a humorous biography. It's attributed to Edmund Clerihew Bentley (1875–1956). Ex: Sir Humphrey Davy / Abominated gravy. / He lived in the odium / Of having discovered sodium.

cliché-wrenching. Changing a word or ending to a cliché, motto, or popular phrase to create a joke. *See chapter 17, Jokes.*

clowns. Comic performers representing both comic and tragic elements of human nature through acrobatic antics and slapstick. A poignant yearning for dignity lingers about these figures. Early clowns appear in the work of Aristophanes (5th–4th century B.C.), and in some cultures they act as catharsis for the sins of the community by miming evil. Clowning can take on classical forms, like the archetypical tragic clown who travels the earth making others laugh, an image associated with the much-beloved English performer Joseph Grimaldi (1779–1837). Other famous clowns are Emmett Kelly, loved for his sad face, and Dan Rice, who in the 1840s created the tall, lanky, goateed Yankee now re-created as Uncle Sam.

cock-and-bull story. A tall tale, leading nowhere. Sometimes a story told to disguise the truth about the narrator's misconduct. *See tall tale.*

comedy. *See chapter 6.*

commedia dell'arte. A clowning tradition coming out of the traveling troupes of sixteenth century Italy. The actors performed under the patronage of the guilds, and both men and women assumed comic roles. Improvised from the scantiest scripts, much of the humor was low comedy, like chasing an annoying fly, then catching and eating it. Another popular routine had a character spit cherry pits at another character's face. Audiences quickly identified the stock characters by their distinctive costumes and masks. Among the main characters were the Merchant, recognized by a richly textured cape; Harlequin, identified by colorful chevrons on his loosely fitted suit; and Inamorata, the maiden, noted through the fashionable clothes of the day. Some plots consisted of a love story, interrupted by short slapstick interludes. *See* pantaloon, stock characters, zany.

court jester. Usually a dwarf or a person with physical deformities. This companion of royalty in past centuries was permitted to make outrageous satiric statements about the court and its actions.

dangling modifier humor. Derived from a misplaced clause or phrase so that a sentence's syntax becomes comically illogical. Ex: While giving Dexter a wedgie, the dog tore at my leg. *See chapter 17, Jokes.*

deadpan humor. Conveyed by a straight-faced speaker in a flat ironic tone. Also visual, like the unsmiling face of silent film comedian Buster Keaton.

debat. Common in medieval literature, a verbal exchange between two people over a moral, satiric issue. A judge would then rule the winner. The debat derived from impromptu folk contests and competitions of wit popular in medieval universities. See the eclogues of Theocritus and Virgil. *See* flyting, insult, invective, playing the dozens.

deus ex machina. Literally, "God from the machine." In ancient Greek plays, a mechanical device lowered a god figure onto the stage who pronounced the plot resolved and the play ended. Today the term refers to any artificial, contrived, unexpected, or irrational ending. Though most critics deplore this device, pointing out that resolutions should evolve logically from preceding events, the deus ex machina can enhance the absurdity of plot complications with a totally illogical ending.

In the final scene of the novel *Tom Jones,* seconds before lovable Tom is to be beheaded for his indiscretions, the narrator arbitrarily stops the action with his interjection: "To die for nonsense is the devil, and would be the devil's own nonsense to leave Tom Jones without a rescuer." The author/narrator delightfully ignores the plot requirement that Tom be hanged and, in a flurry of comedic chaos, Tom is cut down from the noose, without a scratch to his youthful body, much to the delight of the ladies.

doggerel. Trivial, crude, sing-song verse. Outrageous or monotonous rhymes and rhythms written to jar our ears. Ex: Here's to the happy bounding flea / You cannot tell the he from she. / Both sexes look alike, you see / But she can tell and so can he.—Retold by Evan Esar.

droll humor. Whimsical or slightly odd, often ironic. Ex: The rider "leaped on his horse and galloped off in all directions."—Stephen Leacock.

dry humor. Understated wit without emotion. Ex: What man was ever content with one crime?—Juvenal, *Satires.*

epigram. A short, witty expression, often satirical. Sometimes a short poem. Ex: A cynic is a man who knows the price of everything and the value of nothing.—Oscar Wilde.

ethnic humor. Associated with a specific ethnic group. Although much of it has stereotyped nationalities, some of it celebrates the uniqueness of those groups. *See* Irish bull, JAP jokes, stereotyping. *See chapter 20, on Audience.*

farce. From the Latin *farcire* (to stuff). Originally referred to interlude scenes within medieval church drama that "stuffed" comedy into the religious moments. Also referred to clown improvisation, which "stuffed" the scripted dialogue. Farce has since evolved into frenzied plots that spin on humorous surprises, misunderstandings, and intrigues, such as lovers hiding in closets from the enraged cuckolded husband or the split-timed switching of dead bodies. The slapstick comes from the balletic ins and outs of the characters. See the Earnest identification scene in Oscar Wilde's *The Importance of Being Earnest*, the trunk scene with the Marx Brothers in their film, *A Night in Casablanca*, and the dead body scene with Bud Abbott and Lou Costello in *Meet the Killer. See chapter 7, Slapstick.*

filler. Improvisation within a monologue in response to the audience. Also an anecdote or joke placed in leftover spaces in a newspaper or magazine.

flyting. A medieval contest of impromptu wit where each contestant verbally insults the other in colorful, metaphoric language. Military boasting was common the night before battle in medieval joists to strengthen courage and camaraderie. See flyting scene in *Henry IV* parts I and II. *See also* debat, insult, invective, playing the dozens.

fool. Old French for simpleton. When he symbolizes negative traits in human nature, the fool is a satiric victim; in twentieth-century comedy, he's sometimes sympathetic. On occasion he speaks with great wisdom in a language full of double meanings. See Shakespeare's fool in *King Lear.*

gag. A one-liner.

gelotology. From the Greek *gelos*, meaning "laughter." The study of laughter.

gig. Slang for a job, referring to stand-up comedy.

Goldwynism. An illogical humorous statement that's almost logical. Named after Sam Goldwyn, the Hollywood producer famous for verbal paradoxes, Goldwyn disliked having his name associated with them. Now refers to any witty paradox. Ex: We're overpaying him, but he's worth it. If I want your opinion, I'll tell it to you. A verbal contract isn't worth the paper it's written on.

grotesque. Humor plus horror. *See* black humor, sick jokes. *See chapter 13, Grotesque, Sick, and Absurd Humor.*

Horatian satire. Offered in a gentle tone and mildly corrective. Named after the Roman poet and satirist Horace (65–8 B.C.). *See* Juvenalian satire (its opposite). *See chapter 11, Satire.*

humor. Commonly refers to any person, object, action, situation, stimulus, physiological response, or language that elicits laughter. Also loosely refers to anything comic, whimsical, nonsensical, or satiric and to any humorous genre like plays, teleplays, stories, satires, or monologues. Its definition, in fact, so lacks precision that some dictionaries define it circularly—humor is anything that is amusing. Humor scholars have been working for decades to refine its meaning for a common understanding. In this book we define it as follows: Humor is playful incongruity that contains a tension between two levels of meaning followed by a clash of sufficient complexity that surprises and delights and that leads to a resolution of that meaning. The playful incongruity must be understood and appreciated by the intellect, and it must be accepted by the social, cultural, psychological, individual, and momentary contexts. *See chapter 2, Humor, and Appendix B, Philosophies of Humor.*

humorist. Generally refers to a storyteller or a social commentator as distinguished from a comedy writer or a stand-up comedian. A teller of tales rather than of jokes.

hyperbole. From the Greek, meaning "excess." A figure of speech that magnifies a word picture. Extreme exaggeration. Ex: It's so hot even my hat's sunburned. *See* meiosis, understatement (its opposites).

incongruity. A clash of opposites imbedding a tension. *See chapter 2, Humor.*

insult. Comic put-downs of one character by another. Sometimes given in friendship as mock insults; sometimes projected as satire. Many sitcoms use insults as the primary foundation for joking. See *Designing Women, Golden Girls, Murphy Brown. See* debat, flyting, invective, lampoon, playing the dozens, roast.

invective. Derogatory name-calling sometimes disguised as humor. Intended to confuse an audience; usually isn't humorous. This tone can alienate an audience through its accusatory attack, although invective for comic or satiric purposes may be perceived as funny. See the work of stand-up comedians Andy Kaufman, Don Rickles, and Sam Kennison. *See* debat, flyting, insult, lampoon, playing the dozens.

Irish bull. Paradoxical quips. Identified with the Irish through its particular linguistic phrasing. Some sociologists hypothesize that the Irish are skilled at these double meanings because of their country's historical oppression by the British, which forced the Irish to camouflage language. In Irish bull, the naive speaker doesn't realize he's created a paradox. Ex: I didn't get as much for my pig as I thought I'd get, but then I didn't expect that I would. No matter who was last, Murphy was always behind him. See ethnic humor, paradox.

irony. A tension between cause and effect or between what's said and what's meant. "Sure, this diet is great. So what if I never eat another cookie." *See chapter 12, Irony and Wit.*

JAP jokes. Jokes about Jewish women, called Jewish-American princesses (JAPs), which deride their materialism, gaudy dress, sexual inhibitions, and exploitation of husbands and fathers. Highly stereotypical. Ex: How do you get a JAP to stop having sex? Marry her. *See* ethnic humor. *See chapter 20, on Audience.*

jingle. A humorous poem that employs bouncy rhymes and sing-song rhythms to achieve its effect. Usually silly. Often refers to nursery rhymes.

joke. Commonly, a brief anecdote with description or narration ending in a punch line, so called because it surprises by clashing a double meaning then resolving it. Used by scholars to refer to the humor process *See also* humor, punch line. *See chapters 2, Humor, and 17, Jokes.*

joke monologue. *See chapter 18.*

Juvenalian satire. Satire whose tone is sharp, angry, or contemptuous. Named after the Roman poet and satirist Juvenal (c. 65–c. 135 A.D.). *See* Horatian satire (its opposite). *See chapter 11, Satire.*

knock-knock jokes. Invented by Dorothy Parker for the Algonquin Round Table in the 1920s, perhaps from the secret knocking and passwords of speakeasies during Prohibition, these question-answer exchanges play on outrageous or obvious puns. Popular among preadolescent children. Ex: Person #1: Knock knock. Person #2: Who's there? Person #1: Stupid. Person #2: Stupid who? Person #1: Stupendous.

lampoon. Commonly used to mean "making fun of someone" or "mocking someone." More narrowly, refers to a biting, verbal attack on a specific person with satiric intent. In this narrow sense, a lampoon is always directed at a single person, not society at large. Alexander Pope wrote several famous lampoons. Now restricted due to libel laws. *See* invective, insult, roast.

laughing machine. Invented by Charley Douglass in 1952. Produces sounds of human laughter from pre-recorded laughs. Working like a small organ, it consists of horizontal and vertical keys and a foot pedal. By playing out different combinations of sounds, the operator can reproduce hundreds of different laughs to run the gamut of a full audience.

laughingstock. The butt of satiric laughter, usually caused by shameful or foolish behavior. A pathetic figure who has earned the scorn of society.

light opera (operetta.) Differing from grand opera, its main theme is sentimental, lighthearted love. See Gilbert and Sullivan's *Pirates of Penzance.*

light verse. Playful poetry characterized by bouncing rhythms, clever rhymes, and trivial subjects. Often urban and sophisticated, it can employ several words in a single rhyme to effect witty conciseness. Cole Porter's lyrics are excellent examples of light verse in music. Ex: "I get no kick from champagne / I'm sure if I took even one sip / It would bore me terrifically too / but I get a kick out of you." Light verse includes nonsense, satire, limericks, jingles, and nursery rhymes. It has been used by such great writers as Shakespeare, John Milton, and T. S. Eliot.

limerick. A comic five-line poem of specific conventions for rhythm and rhyme. *See chapter 15, Light Verse.*

litotes. Understatement that employs a witty double negative. Usually ironic. Ex: He was not uninhibited when he untold the truth. *See* understatement.

macabre wit. Uses images of death and destruction. *See chapter 13, Grotesque, Sick, and Absurd Humor.*

magician. An illusionist who performs sleights of hand. Elicits amazement and often humor.

malaprops. Named after the character Mrs. Malaprop who appears in Richard Sheridan's play *The Rivals* (1775). Refers to amusing misuses of vocabulary. Pretentiously substituting polysyllabic words for ones that sound similar, Mrs. Malaprop crunches half puns, both amusing and ironic, unaware of her affectation. Ex: "I would have her instructed in geometry that she might know something of the boundaries of *contagious* (contiguous) countries." Popular to this day, they have reappeared in the character Archie Bunker, exemplifying his bigotry and ignorance. "What do you mean by that insinuendo?" he asks (innuendo and insinuation). *See* spoonerism.

mass repetition compulsion. The rapid transmitting across large areas, even a whole country, of a joke or a series of jokes, usually grotesque or sick, in reaction to a national tragedy (for example, Chernobyl jokes). Ex: What's the weather report from Kiev? Overcast and 10,000 degrees. What do you call a man exiled to Siberia two weeks ago? Lucky.

meiosis. From the Greek, meaning "to make smaller." Understatement. Ex: (cartoon) Everyone in the boss's office is fighting furiously with each other. Caption reads: "Shall we assume this meeting has adjourned?" *See* hyperbole (its opposite), understatement.

melodrama. Drama filled with sentimental emotions, coincidences, and an arbitrary ending. Some melodramas develop Gothic elements like violence and threatening settings, but the happier ones are characterized by their self-righteous and self-pitying characters. Characters are types, and facial expressions are overwrought and contorted. Virtue always wins. Melodrama gets laughs from modern audiences, even if the writer's intention is serious, because it's so obviously a call for unearned emotions. Critics devalue melodrama as less literary than comedy because of its moral overtones. Parodies of melodrama abound in silent films, as in the classic scene where the heroine is tied to train tracks and the train rapidly approaches. *See* Buster Keaton silents, *Rocky and Bullwinkle Horror Show. See* sentimental comedy.

mimicry. A dramatic imitation of a recognizable person aped so well that we laugh because we recognize both the person and the exaggerated caricature.

minstrel show. An American vaudevillian show popular in the nineteenth century that used white men in blackface to elicit a folk quality to the humor. Highly stereotyped African-American characterization. In addition to songs about Southern plantation life, accompanied by a banjo, fiddle, and other folk instruments, a central characteristic of this entertainment was a skit by two blackfaced men and the white master of ceremonies, who bantered with each other in a light satiric exchange. The men in blackface would win this verbal battle, to the cheers of the audience. *See* ethnic humor. *See chapter 20, on Audience.*

mockery. Ridicule, scorn, satire. Not always humorous.

monologues. *See* joke monologue. *See chapters 18 and 19.*

Museum of Humor. International Resource for Humor founded in Montreal in the early 1990s with Pasquale L. Iacobacci as its first director. "As the world's first humor museum, we are serious about humor," Iacobacci said. "The museum will not only ennoble a field that has been seen as a secondary art, or even vulgar expression," he added, "but also give creators and scholars a chance to work with the complexity of documents that are available in humor." The concept grew out of Montreal's annual Just for Laughs Festival, founded by Gilbert Rozon, a rock-and-roll promoter, to preserve documents and artifacts. It also housed a library. As of this writing the museum has closed due to lack of funds.

nonsense. *See chapter 14.*

nonsequitur. Latin for "it does not follow." Illogical cause and effect, resulting in humor. Most effective when the break in logic contains underlying sense. Ex.: "Sometimes his blue eyes remind me of hamsters or my Aunt Emma's pot roast. But this is really a Marxist observation." *See chapter 14, Nonsense.*

pantaloon. Character in commedia dell'arte. A greedy, gullible old man. *See* commedia dell'arte.

pantomime (mime). Drama without words. Using costumes, masks, music, and especially gestures to narrate the story, the actor creates comic and witty illusions. Coming out of fifth-century Italian itinerant shows, the pantomime reached levels of high art in the performances of Charlie Chaplin, Jacques Tati, and Marcel Marceau.

paradox. A self-contradictory statement with some underlying truth. Ex: When two politicians accuse each other of lying, both of them are telling the truth. *See* Irish bull. *See chapter 14, Nonsense.*

parody. *See chapter 16.*

picaresque comedy. *See* rogue comedy.

pink script and white script. A written teleplay, so named for the color of its paper to indicate its version. For pink, the draft before the final draft. For white, the final draft, although it, too, can be revised during taping.

pitching. Term used by joke-writing teams when they brainstorm ideas together. Tossing an idea or a joke out to the group for their comments or follow-up. Collaborative writing.

playing the dozens. Verbal debates. One-upmanship. A game of verbal agility improvisationally played in urban areas, with each player taking a turn. A test of imagination and wit. Ex: #1—Your dad has so many double chins he needs a bookmark to find his collar. #2—Yeah, well, your dad has so many chins Nobel Prize physicists measure them for chaos theory. *See* debat, flyting, insult, retort.

practical joke. Based on outwitting, teasing, embarrassing, or hurting the butt of the joke. Sometimes physical, like pulling a chair out from under someone; sometimes intellectual, like sending witty, mysterious messages. The intentions of the practical joker range from genial gestures of friendship to dangerous insults.

proverb. Concise phrase of advice or wisdom. Ex: If vinegar is free, it's sweeter than honey.

punch line. The precise instant the two scripts of a joke clash, revealing the logical (however illogical) connection in the narrative. Also refers to the last line of a joke that delivers its "kick." *See* humor, jokes. *See chapters 2, Humor, and 17, Jokes.*

puns. Words with identical or similar sounds that can be twisted into humorous double meanings. *See chapter 17, jokes.*

quip. Brief jesting remark.

reductio ad absurdum. Latin for "reduction to absurdity." Taking any element and whittling it down to its smallest component. Ex: Richard Armour's "Looking over the Overlooked Elbow." *See chapter 14, Nonsense.*

repartee. A form of wit where two people rapidly exchange satiric comments of one-upmanship. Less caustic than the retort. Ex: Oscar Wilde's *The Importance of Being Earnest*, Act II: (Jack and Algernon banter about the proper dress for someone in mourning.)
Jack: Well, will you go if I change my clothes?
Algernon: Yes, if you are not too long. I never saw anybody take so long to dress, and with such little result.
Jack: Well, at any rate, that is better than being always over-dressed as you are.
Algernon: If I am occasionally a little over-dressed, I make up for it by being always immensely over-educated.
   See playing the dozens, retort.

retort. A snappy response to a put-down; a topper to an insult from the person who "supposedly" was insulted. Sir Winston Churchill's reputed retort to Lady Nancy Astor: "Winston, if you were my husband, I'd put poison in your coffee!" "Nancy, if you were my wife, I'd drink it." *See* repartee, playing the dozens, wisecrack.

revue. A vaudevillian extravaganza containing a variety of performances in succession like dances, songs, or mime. Very popular in the late nineteenth and early twentieth centuries, the most famous being the Ziegfeld Follies.

ridiculous. Foolish, extreme, or absurd humor.

ritual clown. *See* scapegoat.

roast. A party or banquet for an honored guest who is playfully insulted with satiric joking that describes his character. Done out of respect, each round of insults is followed by a toast. Common in festivities such as weddings, where the newly married couple is teased, usually by the best man. Also refers to the joke itself. *See* insult, toast.

rogue comedy. Also known as picaresque comedy. Comic behavior where the protagonist outwits opponents in a rapidly accelerating series of unlawful and outrageous actions: escaping from jails, absconding with money, seducing women. See *Tom Jones* (novel and film).

running gag. Visual or verbal motif, introduced early in a humorous work and then repeated periodically, either identical to the original or varied and accelerated, getting its laughs from the audience's memory of the earlier gag. Ex: Characters Tom, Gerry, and Janet slip on a banana peel. Jay enters. Everyone thinks he'll slip too, but instead he unknowingly averts the danger by sheer luck. We think the gag is over, but it's topped when eventually Jay slips, not on the banana peel, but on cow manure.

sado stand-up. Hard-core, super-macho monologues. Highly offensive to many.

sarcasm. Derived from the Greek, meaning "to tear flesh." Used with an angry and bitter tone, it's more often intended to hurt, insult, and humiliate than reform. Ex: (Passenger sneers to driver of a car who has misjudged a turn on the road): "Shit, you really know how to read a map." *See chapter 12, Irony and Wit.*

satire. Humorous criticism of society for the purpose of reform. *See* Horatian satire, Juvenalian satire. *See chapter 11, Satire.*

scapegoat. A ritual clown who receives the punishment someone else deserves. One who sacrifices for the sins of others. A stock figure in many comedies; rooted in ancient cultural ceremonies whose purpose brought forth a ritual catharsis by the scapegoat. The scapegoat would absorb the community's sins through a ritual punishment and banishment and, as the intermediary, save the community from damnation. Some cultures, in mocking laughter, have pummelled or urinated on this ritual clown as they symbolically banished him from the town. *See* ritual clown.

scatology. From the Greek, meaning "the study of dung." Refers to obscene humor, particularly references to body functions like defecation and urination.

sentimental comedy. Drama that exploits effusive, superficial emotion, virtue over vice, exaggerated facial expressions, and contrived endings. Characters are either all good or all bad. Ex: The hero cries when the villain cries for forgiveness. Comedians known for parodying sentimental comedy include Sid Caesar and Carol Burnett. *See* melodrama.

shaggy dog story. A long-winded, rambling narrative leading nowhere. The humor lies in the trick of the meandering plot and the anticlimactic end. The ending, neither witty nor clever, fizzes into a non-ending. That's the joke—the audience anticipates an ending and it never happens. In these stories, the value of humor lies in colorful language and whimsical characters.

sick jokes. Exploitation of the darker side of human nature by making light of our deepest fears like death, destruction, and illness. The characters in these jokes take special delight in the existence of pain. Some psychologists say this humor cleanses our anxieties; some critics argue that they are enjoyed by people with distorted values. *See chapter 13, Grotesque, Sick, and Absurd Humor.*

situation comedy (sitcom). A lighthearted drama produced for television, one-half hour in length (minus commercials), with the same characters reappearing weekly to confront a new comically complicated but nonthreatening situation. The humor can be subtle or broad, frivolous or satiric. Although characters can change and develop, like the submissive Edith Bunker who evolves into a confident, strong individual, or Murphy Brown, who confronts serious medical problems, generally characters are stock figures who react the same way to each new conflict. Although characters coalesce the series, sitcoms are plot dominated and the comedy rests in how each new situation untangles. Sitcoms have rarely introduced moral quandaries or character growth, with *All in the Family, M*A*S*H,* and *Ellen* as exceptions. *See chapter 10, Script Writing.*

sketch. A brief performance developed around one character or one incident. Could be a problem-solving narrative, like Ernie Kovacs' famous logic routine where he puzzles out why his carton of milk spills at an forty-five-degree angle. Also refers to an interlude within a play or one of several routines in a variety show or vaudeville performance. A skit.

skit. *See* sketch.

slapstick. Derived from a wooden paddle composed of two slats that smack loudly when slapped painlessly against the comic butt. Now refers to any highly physical, acrobatic action like getting a pie in the face, sliding on the ice, or a drunken brawl. *See chapter 7.*

spoof. A hoax of an event or a hoax-parody of a person, like Bob Hope's *Hope for President.*

spoonerism. Named for Dr. W. A. Spooner (1844–1930) from Oxford University, "spoonerism" is a label given to a play on language where initial letters of a phrase are exchanged in a humorous way, like "well-boiled icicle" for "well-oiled bicycle." *See* malaprops.

stereotyping. Applying a negative characteristic to a specific group, without proof of its validity, and limiting that negative characteristic to that specific group. Though one can generalize in a positive way, this term refers to a negative label. Humorous writers can confuse caricatures or stock characters with stereotypes, particularly when they want to satirize behavior. A Jewish mother or an Italian restauranteur as a stock figure would be depicted as more complex, with some positive traits, than a stereotype of these characters. *See* caricature, JAP jokes, stock characters. *See chapter 20, on Audience.*

stock characters. Appear repeatedly in numerous literary works throughout history and among cultures: the hypocrite, boaster, buffoon, clown, bumbling sidekick, drunkard, straight man, young lovers, their servants, disapproving parents, lecherous old man, shrewd aunt, villain. Their distinguishing characteristics are broad and generalized. See the *Rocky and Bullwinkle Show* and its villain, Snidely Whiplash, with his lacquered curled mustache, sneering facial expressions, low-brimmed hat, and black cape. Falstaff in Shakespeare's *Henry IV* parts I and II is a variation of the stock braggart soldier from Roman comedy. *See* caricature, commedia dell'arte, stereotyping.

subtle humor. Joking that requires complex cognition to create or understand the joke. The joke distinguishes among narrow levels of meaning (incongruity) or elusive social verities about a highly sophisticated or esoteric topic.

tale. A narrative that emphasizes events rather than characterization. Often imbued with local color of a particular setting, place, and time. Dialect is foregrounded. Common in peasant and frontier narratives. Also appears frequently in children's literature. See tales of Uncle Remus. *See* tall tale, yarn.

tall tale. An exaggerated narrative of superhuman exploits or impossible events, sprinkled with colorful characters and setting. Many tall tales employ language confined to a specific locale. See tall tales in the stories of Mark Twain. *See* tale, yarn.

time lag. The gap between the end of a joke and the understanding of it by the audience. Performers need to be sensitive to this cognitive phenomenon so that the distance between jokes allows for neurological time processing by the audience.

toast. From the Latin *torrere*, "to dry out." A request to drink to the honor of someone or some event. In "roasts," a toast is always playfully insulting. *See* roast.

tongue twister. Verbal play of alliterative language used primarily by children for playful humor. Ex: Sally Seaman sells seashells by the seashore.

topper. A second, third, or fourth punch line to a joke or comic action. *See chapter 3, Techniques for Writing Humor.*

tragicomedy. Coined by the Roman dramatic poet Plautus (c. 254–184 B.C.). A literary work or play that has both serious and comic elements. *See chapter 6, Comedy.*

trickster. A comic figure who outwits the villain by his keen intelligence.

understatement. Restraint; ironically stating that something is less important than it really is. Using a trivial tone or trivial imagery to describe something serious. Ex: Swift: "Last week I saw a woman flayed, and you will hardly believe how much it altered her person for the worse." *See* litotes, meiosis, hyperbole. *See chapter 3, Techniques for Writing Humor.*

unintentional humor. Unplanned, accidental, spontaneous humor. Slips of the tongue; clumsy but playful actions; unforeseen but clever wit. Ex: Accidentally squirting whipped cream on someone in a restaurant. Saying "sexual intercourse" when you meant to say "verbal discourse."

variety show. A variation on vaudeville. Includes a welcoming monologue, guest performances, and comic skits. The host often joins weekly guests in skits. The show ends with everyone participating in a grande finale. Popular both on stage and early television. See the variety shows of Milton Berle, Bob Hope, the Smothers Brothers, Flip Wilson, and Carol Burnett.

vaudeville. Derived from the satiric songs of the Vire Valley in Normandy, France, these variety shows appealed to unsophisticated audiences in the nineteenth and early twentieth centuries. Made up of brief successive acts such as jugglers, trained animals, comic skits, dancers, magicians, and stand-up comedians, vaudeville distinguishes its "clean" reputation from burlesque, which was bawdy. First appearing in the United States about 1865, vaudevillian entertainment was so popular by 1883 that B. F. Keith was able to establish a permanent theater in Boston. The most famous theater was the Palace in New York. You hadn't made it until you played the Palace.

vice. A comic symbol of evil-as-buffoon, which appeared in sixteenth-century morality plays riding on the devil's back.

whimsy. Fanciful, quaint, or fantastic humor. Writing that's capricious, odd, or eccentric. Appears often in children's literature. See Lewis Carroll's *Alice in Wonderland.*

wisecrack. A sarcastic or cynical remark that insults. Ex: Father to his rebellious, leather-jacketed son: "You got a head too big for your brain." *See* retort.

wistful. Sadly ironic, tinged with humor. This differs by degree from the sharp irony in satire. Ex: One kindergarten kid to another: Are you sure these are the best years of our lives?

wit. A condensed phrase with satiric intent that derives its humor from an intellectual play on language. Ex:

Jack: I have lost both my parents.

Lacy Bracknell: To lose one parent, Mr. Worthing, may be regarded as a misfortune; to lose both looks like carelessness.—Act I, *The Importance of Being Earnest, Oscar Wilde. See chapter 12, Irony and Wit.*

yarn. From nautical slang, referring to spin. A story that slides from one exaggerated adventure to another, told by a narrator whose colorful details strain belief. *See* tale, tall tale.

zany. A character in old Italian drama. A clown would mimic the serious characters, and the zany mimicked the clown. In commedia dell'arte, the clown's assistant. Now refers to any clown. *See* commedia dell'arte.

zeugma. From the Greek, meaning "to yoke." A sentence structured so that the verb refers to two or more nouns, one literally and one figuratively. Ex: The pitcher threw a fast ball—and a loud obscenity.

Bibliography

Websites with Bibliographies in Humor Research

Don L. F. Nilsen

http://www.oryxpress.com/scripts/book.idc?acro=HUMOR
http://www.uni-duesseldorf.de/WWW/MathNat/Ruch/
SecretaryPage.html
http://info.greenwood.com/books/0313294/0313294240.html

Art Gliner Center for Humor Studies, University of Maryland

http://www.otal.umd.edu/amst/humorcenter/

Jason Rutter

http://les.man.ac.uk/cric/Jason_Rutter/HumourResearch/Search.htm

Mark Twain

http://marktwain.miningco.com/

Other

Writer's Write: http://www.writerswrite.com
Writing Resources: http://www.inkspot.com
WordSmith's WebBook: http://alfalfapress.com/ws/wswb.html
The Write Page: http://www.writepage.com/index.html
The Internet Movie Database: http://www.us.imdb.com/
Time Warner's Pathfinder Network (CNN and various magazines and
news services) http://www.pathfinder.com/welcome/
Screenwriters and Playwrights Home Page: http://www.teleport.com/-
cdeemer/scrwriter.html

Theoretical (Scholarly References)

Agee, James. "Comedy's Greatest Era." In *Humor in America*. Ed. Enid
Vernon, 281–96. NY: Harcourt, 1976.
Apte, Mahadev L. *Humor and Laughter: An Anthropological Approach.*
Ithaca: Cornell University Press, 1985.

Attardo, Salvatore. "The Analysis of Humorous Narratives." *Humor Journal* 11, no. 3 (1998): 231–60.

———. "The Semantic Foundations of Cognitive Theories of Humor." *Humor Journal* 10, no.4 (1997): 395–420.

Barreca, Regina. *Last Laughs: Perspectives on Women and Comedy.* Newark: Gordon and Breach, 1989.

———. *New Perspectives on Women and Comedy.* Newark: Gordon and Breach, 1992.

Beattie, James. "An Essay on Laughter and Ludicrous Composition." In *Essays,* 3d ed. London, 1779.

Bergson, H. *Laughter: An Essay on the Meaning of the Comic.* New York: Macmillan, 1911.

Boskin, Joseph. *Humor and Social Change in Twentieth Century America.* Boston: Public Library of the City of Boston, 1979.

Chapman, Anthony, and Hugh Foot, eds. *It's a Funny Thing, Humour.* Oxford, NY: Pergamon, 1977.

Charney, Maurice. *Comedy High and Low.* New York: Oxford University Press, 1978.

Cohen, Sarah Blacher, ed. *Comic Relief: Humor in Contemporary American Literature.* Detroit: Wayne State University Press, 1992.

———. *Jewish Wry: Essays on Jewish Humor.* Detroit: Wayne State University Press, 1991.

Corrigan, Robert W., ed. *Comedy: A Critical Anthology.* New York: Houghton Mifflin, 1971.

———. *Comedy: Meaning and Form.* 2d ed. New York: Harper and Row, 1981.

Davies, Christie. *Ethnic Humor around the World: A Comparative Analysis.* Bloomington: Indiana University Press, 1990.

Dearborn, G. V. N. "The Nature of the Smile and the Laugh." *Science* 11 (June 1, 1900): 851–56.

Eastman, Max. *The Enjoyment of Laughter.* New York: Simon and Schuster, 1936.

———. *The Sense of Humor.* New York: Scribners, 1921.

Enck, John J., Elizabeth T. Forter, and Alvin Whitley, eds. *The Comic in Theory & Practice.* Englewood Cliffs, NJ: Prentice-Hall, 1960.

Esar, Evan. *The Comic Encyclopedia.* New York: Doubleday, 1978.

Felheim, Marvin. *Comedy: Plays, Theory & Criticism.* New York: Harcourt Brace Jovanovich, 1962.

Freud, Sigmund. *Jokes and Their Relation to the Unconscious.* Trans. James Strachey. 1905. Reprint, New York: Norton, 1960.

Friedman, Bruce Jay, ed. *Black Humor.* New York: Bantam, 1965.

Fry, William F. "Physiologic Effects of Humor, Mirth and Laughter." *Journal of the American Medical Association* 267, no. 13 (1992): 1857–58.

———. *Sweet Madness.* Palo Alto: Pacific, 1963.

Frye, Northrop. *Anatomy of Criticism.* Princeton: Princeton University Press, 1973.

Goldstein, Jeffrey H., and Paul E. McGhee, eds. *The Psychology of Humor.* New York: Academic Press, 1972.

Grieg, J. Y. T. *The Psychology of Laughter and Comedy.* New York: Dodd and Mead, 1925.

Gruner, Charles R. *The Game of Humor: A Comprehensive Theory of Why We Laugh.* New Brunswick, NJ: Transaction, 1997.

———. *Understanding Laughter: The Workings of Wit and Humor.* Chicago: Nelson-Hall, 1978.

Hall, Stanley G., and Arthur Allin. "The Psychology of Tickling, Laughing, and the Comic." *American Journal of Psychology* 9 (1897): 1–41.

Hengen, Shannon, ed. *Performing Gender: Theories, Texts and Contexts.* Canada and the Netherlands: Gordon and Breach, 1998.

Holland, Norman. *Laughing: A Psychology of Humor.* Ithaca: Cornell University Press, 1982.

Keith-Spiegel, Patricia. "Early Concepts of Humor: Varieties and Issues." In *The Psychology of Humor.* Ed. Jeffrey Goldstein and Paul McGhee, 3–39. New York: Academic Press, 1972.

Koestler, Arthur. *The Act of Creation.* New York: Dell, 1975.

Lewis, Paul. *Comic Effects: Interdisciplinary Approaches to Humor in Literature.* Albany: State University of New York Press, 1989.

Lipman, Steve. *Laughter in Hell.* Northvale, NJ: Jason Aronson, 1991.

Marc, David. *Comic Visions: Television Comedy and American Culture.* London: Blackwell, 1989.

Mast, Gerald. *The Comic Mind: Comedy and the Movies.* New York: Bobbs-Merrill, 1973.

McGhee, Paul E. *Humor: Its Origin and Development.* San Francisco: Freeman, 1979.

Meerloo, Joost A. M. "The Biology of Laughter." *Psychoanalytic Review* 53 (1966): 189–208.

Mindess, Harvey. *Laughter and Liberation.* Los Angeles: Nash, 1971.

Mintz, Lawrence E., ed. *Humor in America: A Research Guide to Genres and Topics.* Westport, CT: Greenwood, 1988.

Monro, D. H. *Argument of Laughter.* Melbourne: Melbourne University Press, 1951.

Morreall, John. *Taking Laughter Seriously.* Albany: State University of New York Press, 1983.

———, ed. *The Philosophy of Laughter and Humor.* Albany: State University of New York Press, 1987.

Nicholi, Armand M., Jr., ed. *The Harvard Guide to Modern Psychiatry.* Cambridge, MA: Harvard University Press, 1978.

Nilsen, Alleen Pace. *Living Language: Reading, Thinking, and Writing.* Needham Heights, MA: Allyn and Bacon, 1999.

Nilsen, Alleen Pace, and Don L. F. Nilsen. *Encyclopedia of 20th-Century American Humor.* Phoenix: Oryx Press, 2000.

———. *Encyclopedia of Humor and Comedy.* Phoenix: Oryx Press, 1999.

Nilsen, Don L. F. *Humor in American Literature.* New York: Garland, 1992.

———. *Humor Scholarship: A Research Bibliography.* Westport, CT: Greenwood, 1993.

Nilsen, Don L. F., and Alleen Pace Nilsen, eds. *The Language of Humor: The Humor of Language.* Tempe: Arizona State University Press, 1983.

———. *Language Play: An Introduction to Linguistics.* Rowley, MA: Newbury House, 1978.

Norrick, Neal R. "Intertextuality in Humor." *Humor Journal* 2, no. 2 (1989): 117–39.

Oring, Elliott. *Jokes and Their Relations.* Lexington: University Press of Kentucky, 1992.

Palmer, Jerry. *Taking Humour Seriously.* New York: Routledge, 1993.

———. "Theory of Comic Narrative: Semantic and Pragmatic Elements." *Humor Journal* 1, no. 2 (1988): 111–26.

Paton, George, Chris Powell, and Steve Wagg, eds. *The Social Faces of Humour.* Brookfield, VT: Arena, 1996.

Provine, Robert R. *Laughter: A Scientific Investigation.* New York: Viking, 2000.

Radcliffe-Brown, A. R. "A Further Note on Joking Relationships." *Africa* 19 (1949): 133–40.

———. "On Joking Relationships." *Africa* 13 (1940): 195–210.

Raskin, Victor. *Semantic Mechanisms of Humor.* New York: D. Reidel/ Kluwer, 1985.

Rourke, C. *American Humor: A Study of National Character.* New York: Harcourt, 1931.

Ruch, Willibald. *The Sense of Humor.* New York: Mouton de Gruyter, 1998.

Safer, Elaine B. *The Contemporary American Comic Epic: The Novels of Barth, Pynchon, Gaddis, and Kesey.* Detroit: Wayne State University Press, 1991.

Schaeffer, Neil. *The Art of Laughter.* New York: Columbia University Press, 1981.

Stearns, Frederic. *Laughing, Physiology, Pathophysiology, Psychology, Pathopsychology, and Development.* Springfield, IL: Charles C. Thomas, 1972.

Stein, Charles W., ed. *American Vaudeville.* New York: Knopf, 1985.

Sully, James. *An Essay on Laughter.* London: Longmans, Green, 1902.

Sypher, Wylie, ed. *Comedy: An Essay on Comedy.* Baltimore: Johns Hopkins University Press, 1990.

Veatch, Thomas C. "A Theory of Humor." *Humor Journal* 11, no. 2 (1998): 161–215.

Walker, Nancy. *What's So Funny? Humor in American Culture.* Wilmington, DE: Scholarly Resources, 1998.

Watkins, Mel. *On the Real Side: Laughing, Lying and Signifying—the Underground Tradition of African-American Humor That Transformed American Culture, from Slavery to Richard Pryor.* New York: Simon and Schuster, 1994.

Zigas, Vincent. *Laughing Death: The Untold Story of Kuru.* Clifton, NJ: Humana Press, 1990.

Ziv, Avner. *Personality and Sense of Humor.* New York: Springer, 1984.

GENERAL (EASYGOIN' STUFF)

Allen, Woody. *Getting Even.* New York: Warner Books, 1972.

———. *Side Effects.* New York: Ballantine, 1981.

———. *Without Feathers.* New York: Random House, 1975.

Asimov, Isaac, and John Ciardi. *Limericks: Too Gross.* New York: W. W. Norton, 1978.

Auden, W. H. *The Oxford Book of Light Verse.* New York: Oxford University Press, 1973.

Baker, Russell. *All Things Considered.* Westport, CT: Greenwood, 1981.

Barry, Dave. *Dave Barry Slept Here: A Sort of History of the United States.* New York: Random House, 1989.

Bombeck, Erma. *The Grass Is Always Greener over the Septic Tank.* New York: Fawcett, 1979.

Britt, Suzanne. *Skinny People Are Dull and Crunchy Like Carrots.* New York: Tower, 1982.

Bruce, Lenny. *How to Talk Dirty and Influence People.* Chicago: Playboy Press, 1966.

Buchwald, Art. "Brother, Can You Spare a John?" *Newsweek,* February 4, 1980, p. 15.

———. *Down the Seine and Up the Potomac.* New York: Fawcett, 1977.

Cleese, John, Terry Gilliam, Eric Idle, Terry Jones, Michael Palin, and Graham Chapman. Scripts from 45 episodes. From Monty Python series, BBC, 1969–74. *The Complete Monty Python's Flying Circus.* Vols. 1 and 2. Barnes and Noble.

Cosby, Bill. *Fat Albert's Survival Kit.* New York: Dutton, 1975.

De Vries, Peter. *Sauce for the Goose.* Boston: Little, Brown, 1981.

Gregory, Dick. *From the Back of the Bus.* Ed. Bob Orben. New York: Dutton, 1962.

Johnson, Kim "Howard,"ed. *The First 200 Years of Monty Python.* New York: St Martin's, 1989.

Nash, Ogden. *The Selected Verse of Ogden Nash.* New York: The Modern Library, 1945.

HISTORICAL SURVEYS AND COLLECTIONS

Barreca, Regina, ed. *The Penguin Book of Women's Humor.* New York: Penguin, 1966.

Blair, Walter, and Hamlin Hill. *America's Humor: From Poor Richard to Doonesbury.* New York: Oxford University Press, 1978.

Kiley, Frederick, and J. M. Shuttleworth, eds. *Satire from Aesop to Buchwald.* New York: Odyssey, 1971.

Rosen, Michael J., ed. *Mirth of a Nation.* New York: Perennial, 2000.

Walker, Nancy, and Zita Dressner, eds. *Redressing the Balance: American Women's Literary Humor from Colonial Times to the 1980s.* Oxford: University of Mississippi Press, 1996.

White, E. B., and Katharine S. White, eds. *A Subtreasury of American Humor.* New York: Coward-McCann, 1941.

CLASSICAL AND MODERN LITERATURE

Aleichem, Sholem. *Tevye the Dairyman and the Railroad Stories.* New York: Random House, 1990.

Aristophanes. *The Complete Plays of Aristophanes.* Ed. Moses Hadas. New York: Bantam, 1984.

Austen, Jane. *Pride and Prejudice.* New York: Viking Penguin, 1997.

Carroll, Lewis. *Alice's Adventures in Wonderland and Through the Looking Glass.* New York: Grosset and Dunlap, 1946.

Cervantes, Miguel de. *Don Quixote.* New York: W. W. Norton, 1981.

Chaucer, Geoffrey. *The Canterbury Tales.* New York: Knopf, 1992.

Chekhov, Anton. *Chekhov: The Comic Stories.* Chicago: Ivan R. Dee, 1999.

———. *Chekhov: The Complete Plays.* Trans. Paul Schmidt. New York: HarperCollins, 1997.

———. *Seven Short Novels.* New York: Norton, 1971.

Congreve, William. *The Way of the World.* New York: Dover, 1993.

Dickens, Charles. *The Pickwick Papers.* New York: Viking Penguin, 1973.

Faulkner, William. *As I Lay Dying.* New York: Random, 1991.

Fielding, Henry. *The History of Tom Jones.* New York: Random House, 1994.

Gogol, Nikolai. *Dead Souls.* New York: Random House, 1997.

Heller, Joseph. *Catch-22.* New York: Simon and Schuster, 1996.

Henry, O. *Selected Stories.* Ed. Guy Davenport. New York: Viking Penguin, 1993.

Holley, Marietta. *Samantha Rattles the Woman Question (1836–1926).* Ed. Jane Curry. Champaign: University of Illinois Press, 1986.

Hughes, Langston. *Langston Hughes and the Chicago Defender: Essays on Race, Politics, and Culture (1942–62).* Ed. Christopher C. DeSantis. Champaign: University of Illinois Press, 1995.

Ionesco, Eugene. *Rhinoceros, and Other Plays.* New York: Grove, 1960.
Jonson, Ben. *Volpone.* New York: Dover, 1994.
Keillor, Garrison. *Lake Wobegon Days.* New York: Penguin, 1988.
Kingston, Maxine Hong. *Tripmaster Monkey.* New York: Vintage, 1990.
Lardner, Ring. *Haircut and Other Stories.* New York: Macmillan, 1991.
Lurie, Alison. *Foreign Affairs.* New York: Random House, 1984.
Malamud, Bernard. *The Magic Barrel.* New York: Farrar, Straus and Cudahy, 1958.
McCarthy, Mary. *The Groves of Academe.* New York: Harbrace, 1992.
Melville, Herman. "Bartleby the Scrivener." In *The Piazza Tales and Other Prose Pieces,* 13–45. Evanston and Chicago: Northwestern University Press and Newberry Library, 1987.
Mitford, Jessica. "Embalming Mr. Jones." *The Compact Reader.* Ed. Jane E. Aaron, 110–19. New York: St. Martin's, 1984.
Molière, Jean-Baptiste. *Eight Plays by Molière.* Trans. Morris Bishop. New York: Modern Library, 1957.
O'Connor, Flannery. *Everything That Rises Must Converge.* New York: Farrar, Straus and Giroux, 1967.
Plautus. *Three Comedies.* Trans. Erich Segal. New York: Bantam, 1985.
Pope, Alexander. "The Rape of the Lock." In *Selected Poetry & Prose.* Ed. William K. Wimsatt, Jr., 85–110. New York: Holt, 1965.
Rabelais, François. *Gargantua and Pantagruel.* New York: W. W. Norton, 1991.
Roth, Philip. *Portnoy's Complaint.* New York: Random House, 1969.
Salinger, J. D. *Catcher in the Rye.* Boston: Little Brown, 1991.
Shakespeare, William. *Four Great Comedies.* New York: Viking Penguin, 1982.
———. *Henry IV Part One, Part Two.* New York: Bantam, 1988.
Shaw, George Bernard. *Major Barbara.* New York: Viking Penguin, 1989.
Singer, Isaac B. *Gimpel the Fool and Other Stories.* Trans. Saul Bellow. New York: Farrar, Straus and Giroux, 1988.
Smiley, Jane. *Moo.* New York: Fawcett, 1995.
Sterne, Laurence. *The Life and Adventures of Tristram Shandy, Gentleman.* Garden City, NY: Doubleday, 1960.
Swift, Jonathan. *A Modest Proposal and Other Satire.* Buffalo: Prometheus, 1994.
Thurber, James. *My Life and Hard Times.* New York: Harper, 1973.
———. *Thurber Carnival.* New York: Harper and Row, 1975.
Twain, Mark. *Adventures of Huckleberry Finn.* New York: W. W. Norton, 1977.
———. *The Complete Humorous Sketches and Tales of Mark Twain.* Ed. Charles Neider. New York: Doubleday, 1961.
Updike, John. *Pigeon Feathers and Other Stories.* New York: Knopf, 1962.
Waugh, Evelyn. *The Loved One.* Boston: Little Brown, 1977.
Welty, Eudora. *The Collected Stories.* New York: Harcourt Brace, 1980.
Wilde, Oscar. *The Importance of Being Earnest.* New York: Avon, 1965.

Classic Films

Abbott and Costello Meet Frankenstein
Annie Hall
Apartment, The
Arsenic and Old Lace
Blazing Saddles
Butch Cassidy and the Sundance Kid
Cabaret
Closely Watched Trains
Crimes and Misdemeanors
Dr. Strangelove; or, How I Learned to Stop Worrying and Love the Bomb
Duck Soup
8 1/2
Fiddler on the Roof
The Front Page
Funny Thing Happened on the Way to the Forum
General, The
Gold Rush, The
Graduate, The
Great Dictator
Hail the Conquering Hero
Harold and Maude
M*A*S*H
Miracle of Morgan's Creek
Modern Times
Monty Python's Life of Brian
Murder by Death
Music Box, The
My Life as a Dog
Night at the Opera
Ninotchka
Odd Couple, The
One Flew over the Cuckoo's Nest
Paper Moon
Philadelphia Story, The
Producers, The
Slapshot
Some Like It Hot
Tin Men
Tom Jones
Torch Song Trilogy
Wizard of Oz
World of Comedy, Harold Lloyd's
Young Frankenstein

RADIO

Canned Laughter. Tapes. Burns & Allen, Will Rogers, Groucho Marx, Jack Benny, Jonathan Winters.
Radio's Greatest Comedies. Tapes. Jack Benny, Groucho Marx, Burns & Allen, Fibber McGee & Molly, and W. C. Fields.
Wireless, Minnesota Public Radio, P.O. Box 70870, St. Paul, MN 55170–0252.

TELEVISION

Classic Shows
All in the Family
The Bill Cosby Show
Burns and Allen
Cheers
Designing Women
Ellen
Frank's Place
Golden Girls
Jack Benny Show
Jackie Gleason Show
The Honeymooners
I Love Lucy
The Mary Tyler Moore Show
*M*A*S*H*
Monty Python
Seinfeld
Taxi

SECONDARY SOURCES

Grote, David. *The End of Comedy: The Sitcom and the Comedic Tradition.* Hamden, CT: Anchor Books, 1983.
O'Connor, John E. *American History of American Television.* New York: Frederick Ungar, 1983.
Reynolds, Gene, Don Reo, Allan Katz, and Jay Folb. *M*A*S*H.* "Movie Tonight." Script. December 15, 1976.

BOOKS ON WRITING HUMOR

Allen, Steve, with Jane Wollman. *How to Be Funny: Discovering the Comic in You.* New York: McGraw-Hill, 1987.
Arizona English Bulletin. "Humor and Satire in the English Classroom." Arizona English Teachers Association. Vol 16, No. 1, Oct. 1973.

Armour, Richard. *Writing Light Verse and Prose Humor.* Boston: The Writer, 1971.

Bassindale, Bob. *How Speakers Make People Laugh.* West Nyack, NY: Parker Publishing, 1976.

Behrens, Laurence, and Leonard J. Rosen. "Varieties of Humor." In *Writing and Reading across the Curriculum,* 301–79. 3d ed. Glenview, IL: Scott, Foresman, 1988.

Berger, Arthur Asa. *The Art of Comedy Writing.* New Brunswick, NJ: Transaction, 1997.

———. *Scripts: Writing for Radio and Television.* Newbury Park, CA: Sage, 1990.

Berk, Ron. *Professors Are from Mars; Students Are from Snickers: How to Write and Deliver Humor in the Classroom and in Professional Presentations.* Madison, WI: Mendota Press, 1998.

Birk, Newman P., and Genevieve B. Birk. *Understanding and Using English.* 4th ed. New York: Odyssey Press, 1965.

Bloom, Lynn Z. "Humorous Writing." In *The Lexington Reader,* 493–570. Lexington, MA: D. C. Heath, 1987.

———. "Writing Humor." In *Fact and Artifact: Writing Nonfiction,* 191–226. New York: Harcourt Brace Jovanovich, 1985.

Blum, Richard A. *Television Writing: From Concept to Contract.* New York: Hastings House, 1980.

Brady, Ben. *The Keys to Writing for Television and Film.* 3d ed. Dubuque, IA: Kendall/Hunt Publishing Co., 1978.

Burack, A. S., ed. *Writing and Selling Fillers and Short Humor.* Boston: The Writer, 1963.

Carver, Ron. *How to Write Comedy and Humor.* Hollywood: The Hollywood School of Comedy Writing, 1964.

Corbin, Martin. *Humorous Dramatic Interpretation.* Creative Speaking Series. National Textbook Co., 1980.

Cousin, Michelle. *Writing a Television Play.* Boston: The Writer, 1975.

Dancyger, Ken, and Jeff Russ. *Alternative Scriptwriting.* 2d ed. Boston: Focal, 1995.

Dickson, Paul. "How to Tell a Joke." In *Dimensions of Language.* Ed. Boyce H. Davis, 235–43. New York: Macmillan, 1993.

Dietrich, Julia, and Marjorie M. Kaiser. "Experiencing the Process." In *Writing: Self-Expression and Communication,* 3–31. New York: Harcourt, 1986.

Fry, William F., and Melanie Allen. *Life Studies of Comedy Writers.* New Brunswick, NJ: Transaction, 1997.

———. *Make 'em Laugh.* Palo Alto: Science and Behavior Books, 1975.

Helitzer, Melvin. *Comedy Techniques for Writers and Performers.* Athens, OH: Lawhead Press, 1984.

———. *Comedy Writing Secrets.* Cincinnati: Writer's Digest Books, 1987.

Herman, Lewis. *A Practical Manual of Screen Playwriting for Theater and Television Films.* New York: Meridian/New American Library, l952.

Horton, Andrew. *Laughing Out Loud: Writing the Comedy-Centered Screenplay.* Berkeley: University of California Press, 2000.

Josefsberg, Milt. *Comedy Writing for Television and Hollywood.* New York: Harper and Row, 1987.

Kiniry, Malcolm, and Mike Rose. "What's Funny? Investigating the Comic." In *Critical Strategies for Academic Writing,* 664–725. Boston: St. Martin, 1990.

Lunsford, Andrea A., and John J. Ruszkiewicz. "Humor and Argument." In *Everything's an Argument,* 199–217. New York: St. Martin's, 1999.

McGhee, Paul E. *Punchline: How to Think Like a Humorist If You're Humor Impaired.* Dubuque, IA: Kendall/Hunt, l993.

McManus, Ed, and Bill Nicholas. *We're Roasting Harry Tuesday Night: How to Plan, Write and Conduct the Business/Social Roast.* Englewood Cliffs, NJ: Prentice-Hall, l984.

Miller, William. *Screenwriting for Narrative Film and Television.* New York: Hastings House, l980.

Morressy, John. "Approximately Seven Pillars of Humorous Fiction." *Writer's Digest,* June l989, pp. 32–35.

Perret, Gene. *Comedy Writing Workbook.* New York: Sterling, 1990.

———. *How to Write and Sell Your Sense of Humor.* Cincinnati: Writer's Digest Books, l986.

———. *Successful Stand-up Comedy.* Hollywood: Samuel French, 1994.

Rorabacher, Louise R., and Georgia Dunbar. "Satire." In *Assignments in Exposition,* 276–87. 6th ed. New York: Harper and Row, l979.

Saks, Sol. *The Craft of Comedy Writing.* Cincinnati: Writer's Digest Books, 1985.

Settel, Irving. *Writing TV Comedy.* Boston: The Writer, l958.

Sommers, Jeffrey. "The Humorous Voice." In *Model Voices,* 15–112. New York: McGraw-Hill, l989.

Swain, Dwight V. *Film Scriptwriting.* New York: Hastings House, l976.

Vorhaus, John. *The Comic Toolbox: How to Be funny Even If You're Not.* Los Angeles: Silman-James, 1994.

Wilde, Larry. *The Great Comedians Talk about Comedy.* Secaucus, NJ: Citadel, l968.

———. *How the Great Comedy Writers Create Laughter.* Chicago: Nelson-Hall, l976.

Willson, Robert F., Jr. "Humor." In *Writing: Analysis and Application,* 168–81. New York: Macmillan, l980.

Wilson, Christopher. *Jokes, Form, Content, Use and Function.* London: Academic Press, l979.

Wright, Milton. *What's Funny—and Why.* New York: McGraw-Hill, l939.

Contributors

WOODY ALLEN, a major figure in American film history, has written and starred in many comic films, including *Sleeper* (1973), *Love and Death* (1975), *Annie Hall* (1977), *Manhattan* (1979), *Stardust Memories* (1980), *Hannah and Her Sisters* (1986), *Radio Days* (1987), *Crimes and Misdemeanors* (1989), *Manhattan Murder Mystery* (1993), *Bullets over Broadway* (1994), and *Mighty Aphrodite* (1995). He has also written stories and sketches, which have been published in the *New Yorker* and later anthologized in his books, *Getting Even* (1971) and *Without Feathers* (1975).

DAN AMRICH is a senior editor at *GamePro Magazine,* where he reviews video games (yes, for a living). Writing under the nom de 'toon of Dan Elektro, he has found a way to remain perpetually thirteen years old. He is no longer wanted in eight states; in fact, he was asked to leave several of them.

RICHARD W. ANDERSON lives and teaches in Ithaca, New York.

RICHARD ARMOUR was a popular writer of whimsical sketches and verse. Among his many books are *It All Started with Columbus* and *It All Started with Stones and Clubs*. A highly respected authority on Chaucer and the English Romantic poets, he taught at Scripps College in Claremont from 1945 to 1966.

SUSAN ARONSON has been producing movies for television since graduating from Ithaca College. (She took a few years off to reproduce three children.) She also took a stab at television writing—a sitcom pilot for Nickelodeon that was never produced, despite her skills as a producer. Her CBS movie *A Matter of Conscience*, starring Eli Wallach, won an Emmy for Outstanding Children's Program. She is currently developing a Showtime family movie.

313

Ken Ayoub works for Innovative USA, a book publisher, where he makes toys and games and writes really cool books for kids. He lives in Connecticut with his wife Lynn and their two cats, Tiger and Trouble.

Suzanne Britt is best known for her social satire. Her essays examine people and their foibles, and while her tone is gentle, her tongue-in-cheek commentary zeroes in on complex social interactions. She has published widely in various magazines, and the essay included here was first published in *Newsweek* then later expanded in her book *Skinny People Are Dull and Crunchy Like Carrots*.

Art Buchwald, an internationally respected and loved satirist, writes a syndicated column that appears in over five hundred newspapers. He has published dozens and dozens of books.

Julie Switzer Caplan lives happily ever after with her husband, Craig, in Falls Church, Virginia. She is a manager at a marketing company. These days, the only fiction she writes is for performance reviews.

Chris Capozzi is an infantry captain in the U.S. Army. While his mother still enjoys his sense of humor, his superiors definitely do not.

Philip Cormier is a freelance cinematographer based in Falmouth, Maine, where he lives happily with his wife, Annie, and son, Ray. Ten years ago he began work on a documentary about potatoes. He has no real intentions of finishing it. It's just a cool thing to do.

Christine Decker works in advertising in New York City and recently bought her own apartment. Feel free to send any donations you'd like, as her bank account now stands at $2.34.

Anne Marie Dinardo now calls Washington, D.C., her home after completing an internship at the White House. Her alter ego is the "Community Manager" for C-SPAN's online community, where she heads up the network's forum for political discussion on the Internet. She recently earned an M.A. from Georgetown University's communications, culture, and technology graduate program.

Steve DiPietro works by day for the FOX Broadcasting Company in Los Angeles. By night, he flies over the city keeping an eye on crime and helping out where he can. He's half an inch shy of six feet, but still growing.

Peter Dranoff lives unobtrusively in New York.

JOHN DUFF works at North Shore Community College in Massachusetts and is currently studying for a masters degree in critical and creative thinking. He spends his free time either outdoors or writing (or writing outdoors). He and his wife are currently planning on walking from Mexico to Canada or as far as their knees hold up. Look for a book to follow. (With, it is hoped, more humorous writing, but if tragedy is more marketable, the trip will be changed accordingly.)

PAUL DUNSCOMB majored in TV/Radio at Ithaca College and worked in television for five years before realizing he'd picked the wrong major. After receiving an M.A. from SUNY-Albany, he traveled to Japan for two years as a Fulbright scholar. If all goes well, he will receive his Ph.D. in modern Japanese history from the University of Kansas in 2001. He hopes to pay off his student loans about the same time he draws his first social security check.

BOB ELLIOTT and RAY GOULDING made up one of the funniest comedy teams on radio and television for over four decades. In 1946 they quickly established radio as their home, and they performed together up until the time of Ray Goulding's death in 1990. For their shows, they produced, wrote, and delivered a parade of improbable characters including Mary McGoon, a cooking authority, and Wally Ballou, the bumbling interviewer of subjects famous and obscure. Unlike some comedy teams, Bob and Ray were close friends and trusting business partners throughout their lives.

SCOTT GIESSLER lives in Los Angeles with his wife, Phoebe, where he works in a public relations firm. He continues to write both scripts and short stories, although not nearly as much as his imaginary fans would like. Currently, he's laboring to start a web site company, because as puts it, "There just aren't enough of them."

LISEL M. GORELL is a professional actor living in southern California. She teaches at the La Jolla Playhouse/San Diego County School District Arts Academy. She has appeared in the La Jolla Playhouse's "Outreach" show and in several regional commercials in San Diego and the Midwest. She recently played the lead in the independent feature film, *An Intimate Friendship.*

MICHAEL GREENZEIG is a director of sales for a computer software company. In his remaining waking moments, he is a husband to his wife, Stacy, and a father to his twin children, Cassidy and Clayton.

ALAN HAFT spent many years making feature films, television, and cable movies for Universal, Time Warner, HBO, and other companies.

While he is still actively involved in the entertainment business, he is also serving as vice president of a publicly traded Internet technology company and continues to write whenever he gets the chance.

STEVEN HARTMAN received an M.F.A. in creative writing from the American University in 1992. He has received a Fulbright to Sweden, two Pushcart nominations, and the FOLIO Fiction Prize. His work has appeared in *Grand Street, Georgia Review*, and *Southern Review*, among others. In addition to directing the creative writing program in English at Stockholm University, he is completing a Ph.D. in English at SUNY-Albany.

DAVID HEARNE is currently running a used bookstore in Middlebury, Vermont.

JOSEPH HELLER (1923–99) drew on his experiences as a bombardier in Italy during World War II for his satiric novel *Catch-22*. The novel established the ironies and tragedies of war for the later Vietnam generation.

SUZANNE SMITH JABLONSKI (Ithaca College '92) is getting her Master of Public Administration in Nonprofit Management at Seton Hall University and is working as a fund-raising consultant. Following graduation, she worked in development for the New York Botanical Garden and the Hudson River Museum. Although she writes everyday, none of it is funny (that is, unless you count that paper extolling the virtues of statistical analysis, which is still getting laughs in the hallowed halls of academe.) She and her husband, Bill Jablonski ('93), live in Montclair, New Jersey.

LAURA KLINK has recently graduated from Ithaca College. She is working on two film scripts and plans to move to Los Angeles.

ADAM LANTHEAUME is currently running from the Chimpanzee Brothers, the notorious leaders of the chimpanzee mob, for calling one of them "a tall drink of water." So, if you see him around Boston with his wife, Diane, please don't tell anyone under four feet tall his whereabouts.

KIM S. LAZAR, while still looking for the meaning of normalcy, is teaching kindergarten in California.

SCOTT LEVY is a lighting designer (also known as "gaffer") for film and television. He founded Eastern Effects, Inc., a lighting and grip equipment rental house based in Brooklyn that caters to the industry.

TOM LONGO spent ten years flying helicopters in the Marine Corps. He was named Writer of the Year in 1990 by *Approach Magazine.* He lives with his wife and two children near Philadelphia where he flies an emergency medical helicopter for the Hospital University of Pennsylvania. He can't do any creative writing until after he finishes his masters degree in English.

KATHARYN HOWD MACHAN is a widely anthologized, award-winning poet who has published over seventeen books of poetry. An associate professor in the Department of Writing at Ithaca College, she teaches poetry writing as well as a course on writing children's literature. A strong voice for encouraging young poets, both tragic and comic, she braved the teaching of Ithaca College's course titled "Humorous Writing." She is also a professional belly dancer who has performed internationally, most recently in Greece.

RICH MANFREDI stage-manages *One Life to Live* for ABC-TV with his wife, actress Marcy DeGonge-Manfredi. They live in New Jersey with their two sons, Nicholas and Lucas.

BRETT MATTHEWS lives in San Francisco but is finishing up a six-month stint in Southeast Asia via bus, jeep, and camel. Upon his return to the United States, he plans to reapply for his former high school job as the mouse at Chuck E. Cheese in Syracuse, New York.

MARK B. MATTHEWS has aided prominent veterinarians by ultrasounding animals; he has shoveled through frozen dirt under the critical gaze of burly foremen; and with utmost bravery he has sailed to Europe and Central America—and lived to tell about it. Currently among the legions of mouse clickers going blind from the Internet, when not sleeping or practicing yoga, he is an editor at a website.

ALAN S. MILLER teaches high school English in Binghamton, New York. He is also a poet and singer/songwriter, but is quite lazy about all this stuff. Nevertheless, occasionally good things happen. Mostly, he spends lots of time with his family and hopes to work for his wife's aromatherapy business.

JENNIFER LYNNE MILLER has worked and traveled widely, particularly in Indonesia. She has recently moved back to Ithaca, New York, and is employed by Tompkins County as a community development planner. Perhaps her preponderant use of the letter "p" in the prose previously presented predestined her to pursue a profession that would provide plenty of opportunities to participate in the development of public policies and procedures.

MICHAEL ALAN MILLER is currently waging an attack on people's senses via the Internet as creative director and vice president of SetNow.com, a Web-based multimedia design company. He and his wife, Sarah, live in Ewing, New Jersey.

OGDEN NASH (1902–71) was born and raised in Rye, New York, and Savannah, Georgia. While working in advertising after a brief stint at Harvard, he began writing children's books and light verse. Beloved for generations for his wit and clever turns of phrase, he published nineteen books of poetry. In 1950 he was elected to the National Institute of Arts and Letters.

PAUL NELSON lives in central Pennsylvania with his wife, Cynthia, and son, Michael, where he is completing his M.L.A. degree in music. He also teaches music in the local school district, where his students seem to find him quite humorous.

CATHERINE E. CARCHIA PHILLIPS, after some rock-and-roll years in radio, married firefighter Steve Phillips. Currently, they are enjoying their children: Becky, Casey, and Danny. Cathy also spends time volunteering with a teen leadership and wellness program, the Teen Institute of the Garden State.

VICKY I. PUIG lives in Brooklyn, New York, top floor.

CHRIS REGAN has written for *Saturday Night Live*'s "Weekend Update" segment, and he now writes for *The Daily Show with Jon Stewart* on Comedy Central.

GENE REYNOLDS, DON REO, ALLAN KATZ, and JAY FOLB have accumulated numerous script-writing credits. They call California home.

BRETT ROSS lives in Glens Falls, New York.

RUDY RUIZ, a pseudonym, lives alone in a basement. His shower is currently backed up and unusable. He hopes to take his showers at the gym. He was recently mugged.

JOHN SANGIMINO, JR., is currently at large in the city of Chicago, posing as an information architect with Lante Corporation (an e-market

consulting firm). When he's not battling the evil forces of cyber
space, or trying to find a parking place, he enjoys documenting his
Windy City adventures in the hope that . . . some day . . . they can
be used to answer the inevitable question: "What happened?"

JAY SCHNEIDERMAN is (for now) supervisor of a small resort town on
eastern Long Island. He also recently taught science, math, and
African drumming to teenagers and adults. He lives in Montauk
with his wife, Jen, and their daughter, Magda, where he dreams of
retiring from small-town politics and taking up sculpting.

CHARLES SCHULTZ is one of the most beloved cartoonists in the world.
His cartoon, *Charlie Brown*, featuring the characters Charlie, Lucy,
Schroeder, Pigpen, and the wonderful Snoopy, has been translated
in almost every language. When he died in 2000, his work was
celebrated by cartoonists worldwide in cartoon tributes.

MICHAEL SIMONOFF spent some time living the life of a freelance writer,
turning in grossly underpaid work for *Billboard Magazine*, *Guitar
School*, and the *Wall Street Journal* (ah, maybe not the *Journal*).
When his NYC rent got too high, he sold his soul to the public
relations profession. After stints at two PR agencies, he's now doc-
toring spin in Internet space as director for public relations at Im-
mersant, Inc., an Internet consulting and development company.
He also moved to a Brooklyn brownstone with much, MUCH more
reasonable rent.

STEVE SIMONS is a literary agent in Los Angeles working with writers in
television.

GREGORY TEBBANO is currently seeking the self in upstate New York
through the mediums of song, poetry, and fiction.

JAMES THURBER (1894–1961), internationally known for his witty
sketches, stories, and cartoons, published much of his work in
the *New Yorker*. Born in Columbus, Ohio, he began his career as
a journalist, writing briefly for the *Columbus Dispatch*, then the
Paris edition of the *Chicago Tribune*. Hired at the *New Yorker* as
a manager, he stated shortly after his arrival that he managed to
"work himself down to a more comfortable position." Dorothy
Parker once described his famous line-drawn cartoons as "unbaked
cookies." His collected works encompass over twenty volumes,
including the best-known *My Life and Hard Times* (1933).

TODD TIBBETTS resides in Seattle, Washington. He draws cartoons.

DAVE VERGANO lives with his wife, Terri, in Miami Beach, Florida. He works as a website developer and continues to write, although now his humor has taken on the form of computer bugs, which are enjoyed by an audience of Internet users all over the world.

Index

Books in the Humor in Life and Letters Series

The Contemporary American Comic Epic: The Novels of Barth, Pynchon, Gaddis, and Kesey, by Elaine B. Safer, 1988

The Mocking of the President: A History of Campaign Humor from Ike to Ronnie, by Gerald Gardner, 1988

Circus of the Mind in Motion: Postmodernism and the Comic Vision, by Lance Olsen, 1990

Jewish Wry: Essays on Jewish Humor, edited by Sarah Blacher Cohen, 1991 (reprint)

Horsing Around: Contemporary Cowboy Humor, edited by Lawrence Clayton and Kenneth Davis, 1991

Women's Comic Visions, edited by June Sochen, 1991

Never Try to Teach a Pig to Sing: Still More Urban Folklore from the Paperwork Empire, by Alan Dundes and Carl R. Pagter, 1991

Comic Relief: Humor in Contemporary American Literature, edited by Sarah Blacher Cohen, 1992 (reprint)

Untamed and Unabashed: Essays on Women and Humor in British Literature, by Regina Barreca, 1993

Campaign Comedy: Political Humor from Clinton to Kennedy, by Gerald Gardner, 1994

The Ironic Temper and the Comic Imagination, by Morton Gurewitch, 1994

The Comedian as Confidence Man: Studies in Irony Fatigue, by Will Kaufman, 1997

Tilting at Mortality: Narrative Strategies in Joseph Heller's Fiction, by David M. Craig, 1997

The Humor Prism in 20th-Century America, edited by Joseph Boskin, 1997

Laughing Feminism: Subversive Comedy in Frances Burney, Maria Edgeworth, and Jane Austen, by Audrey Bilger, 1998

Taking Penguins to the Movies: Ethnic Humor in Russia, by Emil A. Draitser, 1998

Humor in Borges, by René de Costa, 2000

Writing Humor: Creativity and the Comic Mind, by Mary Ann Rishel, 2002

Dec 20/07